The Portable Poetry W

CW00544847

The Portable Poetry Workshop

Edited by

Nigel McLoughlin

 palgrave

Editorial matter and his own chapters © Nigel McLoughlin 2017
Chapters © individual authors 2017

All rights reserved. No reproduction, copy or transmission of this
publication may be made without written permission.

No portion of this publication may be reproduced, copied or transmitted
save with written permission or in accordance with the provisions of the
Copyright, Designs and Patents Act 1988, or under the terms of any licence
permitting limited copying issued by the Copyright Licensing Agency,
Saffron House, 6–10 Kirby Street, London EC1N 8TS.

Any person who does any unauthorised act in relation to this publication
may be liable to criminal prosecution and civil claims for damages.

The author has asserted his right to be identified as the author of this
work in accordance with the Copyright, Designs and Patents Act 1988.

First published 2017 by
PALGRAVE

Palgrave in the UK is an imprint of Macmillan Publishers Limited,
registered in England, company number 785998, of 4 Crinan Street,
London, N1 9XW.

Palgrave® and Macmillan® are registered trademarks in the United States,
the United Kingdom, Europe and other countries.

ISBN 978–1–137–60703–4 hardback
ISBN 978–0–230–52230–5 paperback

This book is printed on paper suitable for recycling and made from fully
managed and sustained forest sources. Logging, pulping and manufacturing
processes are expected to conform to the environmental regulations of the
country of origin.

A catalogue record for this book is available from the British Library.

A catalog record for this book is available from the Library of Congress.

Contents

Notes on Contributors

Ros Barber PhD a lecturer at Goldsmiths, University of London, is the author of blank verse novel *The Marlowe Papers* (2012), winner of the Desmond Elliott Prize and long-listed for the Bailey's Prize; *Devotion* (2015), shortlisted for the Encore Award; and three collections of poetry including *Material* (2008), a Poetry Book Society Recommendation. Her research on Shakespeare and Marlowe has been published in journals including *Rethinking History, Critical Survey and the Journal of Early Modern Studies*. www.rosbarber.com.

Siobhan Campbell PhD is the author of five works of poetry, most recently *Cross-Talk* (Seren) and *Heat Signatures* due 2017, and writes criticism for *Poetry London*, the *ILS* and *Poetry Ireland Review*. She is on faculty at the Department of English, the Open University, having been Associate Professor of English Literature and Creative Writing at Kingston University London. Pedagogic contributions include *Beyond the Workshop: Creative Writing, Theory and Practice* (2012) and *The Expressive Life Writing Handbook* (2016). Widely anthologized and with many awards including the Oxford Brookes International in 2016, Campbell is also the recipient of an Arts Council award and the Templar Poetry Prize.

Claire Crowther PhD has published three poetry collections. The first, *Stretch of Closures*, was shortlisted for the Aldeburgh Best First Collection prize. Her work has appeared in many journals, including the *London Review of Books, New Statesman, PN Review, Poetry Review, Poetry Wales* and the *Times Literary Supplement*. Her pamphlet *Bare George*, resulting from a year-long residency at the Royal Mint Museum, was published in June 2016.

Susan Millar DuMars has published four collections with Salmon Poetry. The most recent, *Bone Fire*, appeared in 2016. She is the author of one book of short stories, *Lights in the Distance* (2010) and is at work on a second collection. Her work has appeared in publications in the United States and Europe and in several anthologies. She lives in Galway, Ireland, where she and her husband have run the Over the Edge readings series since 2003. Susan is the editor of the anthology *Over the Edge: The First Ten Years* (2013).

Ann Drysdale is a poet, author and journalist. She has taught creative writing at Cardiff University and the University of the West of England, where she also spent time as Visiting Writer. A past winner in the National Poetry Competition, she has published six full poetry collections as well as several non-fiction books and is currently joint editor of Angle Journal of Poetry in English.

Carrie Etter, originally from Normal, Illinois, has lived in England since 2001 and has taught at Bath Spa University since 2004, where she is a Reader in Creative Writing. She has published three collections of poetry: *The Tethers* (2009), winner of the London New Poetry Prize, *Divining for Starters* (2011) and *Imagined Sons* (2014), shortlisted for the Ted Hughes Award for New Work in Poetry. Additionally, she edited the anthology *Infinite Difference: Other Poetries by UK Women Poets* (2010) and Linda Lamus's posthumous collection, *A Crater the Size of Calcutta* (2015). She also publishes short stories, reviews and the occasional essay.

Martin Figura is a writer, performer and photographer living in Norwich. His poetry collection and multi-media Spoken Word show *Whistle* (Arrowhead Press, 2010) was shortlisted for the Ted Hughes Award and won the 2013 Saboteur Award for 'Best Spoken Word Show' and the Poetry Society's 2010 Hamish Canham Prize. He performed the show, to excellent reviews, over 60 times between 2010 and 2015, including a week at the London Roundhouse, a British Council tour of India and a full run at the Edinburgh Festival Fringe. Two further collections, *Dr Zeeman's Catastrophe Machine* (Cinnamon Press) and *Shed* (Gatehouse Press) where both published in 2016. His spoken work show, *Dr Zeeman's Catastrophe Machine* is showcasing at the London Roundhouse and regional venues in 2016. www.martinfigura.co.uk.

Angela France has had poems published in many of the leading journals and has been anthologised a number of times. Her publications include *Occupation* (2009), *Lessons in Mallemaroking* (2011) and *Hide* (2013). She has an MA in Creative and Critical Writing and a PhD from the University of Gloucestershire. Angela teaches creative writing at the University of Gloucestershire and in various community settings as well as working for a local charity. She runs a reading series in Cheltenham, 'Buzzwords'.

Paul Hardwick is Professor of English at Leeds Trinity University, where he is Programme Leader for Creative Writing. As Oz Hardwick, he has published five collections of poetry, most recently *The Ringmaster's Apprentice* (2014), and has appeared in many anthologies and journals. He has also published extensively on medieval art and literature, with particular focus upon misericords and animal iconography, including the monograph, *English Misericords: The Margins of Meaning* (2011). His interests are most closely intertwined in *An Eschatological Bestiary* (2013).

Kevin Higgins is co-organiser of Over The Edge literary events in Galway, Ireland. He has published five collections of poems: *The Boy With No Face* (2005), *Time Gentlemen, Please* (2008), *Frightening New Furniture* (2010), *The Ghost In The Lobby* (2014), & *2016 – The Selected Satires of Kevin Higgins*. His poems feature in *Identity Parade – New British and Irish Poets* (2010) and in *The Hundred Years' War: Modern War Poems* (2014). Kevin is satirist-in-residence with the alternative literature website The Bogman's Cannon (https://bogmanscannon.com). *Stinging Fly* magazine recently described Kevin as 'likely the most widely read living poet in Ireland'.

Andrea Holland is a Lecturer in Creative Writing at the University of East Anglia. Her collection of poems, *Broadcasting* (Gatehouse Press, 2013) was the winner of the 2012 Norfolk Commission for Poetry. Her first collection *Borrowed*, was published by Smith/Doorstop in 2007. She has poems in *MsLexia*, *The Rialto*, *The North* and other literary journals as well as online. She has also collaborated with visual artists on a number of commissioned projects. Andrea resides in Norwich with her family, after studying and teaching in the USA for a number of years. www.andreacholland.co.uk

Helen Ivory is a poet and visual artist. Her fourth Bloodaxe Books collection is the semi-autobiographical *Waiting for Bluebeard* (2013). She has co-edited with George Szirtes *In Their Own Words: Contemporary Poets on their Poetry* (Salt 2012). *Fool's World* – a collaborative Tarot with the artist Tom de Freston was published by Gatehouse Press in 2015. In 2016 Knives Forks and Spoons Press published a book of her mixed media collage poems *Hear What the Moon Told Me*. She edits the webzine Ink Sweat and Tears and is tutor and Course Director for the UEA/WCN online creative writing programme.

Ashley Lister is a freelance writer, author and occasional performance poet from the north-west of England. He lectures in creative writing.

Nigel McLoughlin is a Northern Irish poet with five collections published, the latest of which is *Chora: New and Selected Poems* (2009). His work has been widely published and recordings of his work can be found on *The Poetry Archive*. He is Professor of Creativity and Poetics at the University of Gloucestershire.

Kate North writes poetry and fiction. Her novel, *Eva Shell*, was published in 2008, and her poetry collection, *Bistro,* in 2012. She teaches creative writing at Cardiff Metropolitan University.

Paul Perry is the author of five collections of poetry, most recently Gunpowder Valentine, (Dedalus Press, 2014.) He is Writer Fellow at University College Dublin.

Mario Petrucci is an innovator, educator and award-winning poet. His major poetry residencies include the Imperial War Museum and BBC Radio 3. *Heavy Water: a poem for Chernobyl* (2004) secured the *Daily Telegraph* Arvon Prize and 'inflicts … the finest sort of shock, not just to the senses, but to the conscience, to the soul' (*Poetry London*). *i tulips* (2010) takes its name from his 1111-strong Anglo-American sequence, of which *crib* (2014) and *anima* (2013) are also part. These 'modernist marvels' (*Poetry*

Book Society) exemplify Petrucci's distinctive combination of innovation and humanity. www.mariopetrucci.com.

Robert Sheppard is a poet-critic and his books include *History or Sleep*, *Selected Poems* (2015), his autobiographical *Words Out of Time* (2015) and his critical study *The Meaning of Form in Contemporary Innovative Poetry* (2016). He is Professor of Poetry and Poetics at Edge Hill University, where he is Programme Leader of the MA in Creative Writing. He lives in Liverpool, where he co-runs Storm and Golden Sky Readings. He blogs at robertsheppard.blogpot.com.

Barbara Smith lives and works in Ireland as a creative writing tutor and adult educator. She is a passionate supporter of the transformative power of adult education, being a late bloomer. She has two collections of poetry published by Doghouse Book, Kerry: *Kairos*, 2007 and *The Angels' Share*, 2012. When not writing she loves travelling in Europe. When not doing this she enjoys using social media to make rich connections in the cultural world. In the summertime she may be found performing in a tent near you with the Poetry Divas collective, an ensemble that promotes poetry to a diverse audience.

Todd Swift is currently an independent scholar, with a PhD in creative and critical writing from the University of East Anglia and over ten years' teaching experience at UK universities, including at London Met, Kingston, Glasgow and Worcester, where he was a Senior Lecturer. He has published nine full poetry collections, many more pamphlets and edited or co-edited numerous international anthologies. His poetry has appeared in many anthologies, and his other publications include *Language Acts* (a collection of essays on Anglo-Quebec Poetry 1976–2006), co-edited with Jason Camlot and *Modern Canadian Poetry: An Anthology* (co-edited with Evan Jones). He is Director of Eyewear Publishing.

Angela Topping is a widely published poet and author. She has had eight full collections of poetry and five chapbooks out. Her most recent collection is *The Five Petals of Elderflower,* from Red Squirrel Press. She has written three monographs for Greenwich Exchange; the most recent is on the poetry of John Clare. A former teacher, she now works freelance, leading workshops, giving readings and lectures and mentoring. She completed two degrees at the University of Liverpool and took a Masters at the University of Chester. She has co-authored three books for Oxford University Press, and contributed chapters to NAWE's Handbook of Creative Writing.

J.T. Welsch has published six chapbooks of poetry, including *Orchids* (2010), *Waterloo* (2012) and *Hell Creek Anthology* (2015). His published research focuses on modernist writers, especially William Carlos Williams, T.S. Eliot, and James Joyce, and later twentieth-century American poets, including Elizabeth Bishop, John Berryman and Delmore Schwartz. He also speaks and writes regularly on contemporary UK poetry culture. He lives in York, UK, where he is Lecturer in English and Creative Industries at the University of York.

Tony Williams is Senior Lecturer in Creative Writing at Northumbria University where his research interests include poetry and landscape, writing practice and everyday life, and contemporary borrowings of medieval writing practices. His poetry publications include *The Corner of Arundel Lane and Charles Street* (2009; shortlisted for the Aldeburgh, Portico and Michael Murphy Memorial Prizes), *All the Rooms of Uncle's Head* (2012, a Poetry Book Society pamphlet choice) and *The Midlands* (2014).

Introduction

Welcome to *The Portable Poetry Workshop*. This book is written from a practice-based rather than academic perspective and is aimed primarily at those readers aiming to improve their practice in writing poetry whether they are students of creative writing in universities or poets practising their art outside the academy. It will also be of use to those who want to think more deeply about poetry, how it is made, what other poets have thought about their writing and where poetry may go next.

Apprentice poets in the early stages of their development will find this book of benefit to them in learning about structure and form, and about the use of trope and device to make their work more sophisticated. It may also be of use to English students who are studying poetry, because it teaches the art from the inside out and will help students with their critical awareness of what is happening in a poem, through understanding how poems are made and what their constituent parts do.

The book is split into three main parts, which focus on form and structure; trope and device; and poetics and practice, respectively. These sections contain bite-sized chapters written by practising poets who are also teachers of poetry. Many of the contributors have made careers teaching the writing of poetry as well as its critical study in universities and elsewhere. The book begins with the basic structures of poetry, builds to making poems more sophisticated and adding additional levels to the work, and culminates in thinking about what poetry is meant to do and how it might achieve its aims.

In Part I, each short bite-sized chapter tackles one of the set poetic forms. There is some discussion of the history of each form, and a description of the way the form is normally made by focusing on worked examples of the main features using well-known classic poems and/or the work of modern exponents. Coupled to these short chapters will often be creative trigger exercises geared towards getting the student writing, and providing hints for avoiding common pitfalls and for effective rewriting and revision. Even where there is no overt exercise suggested, sufficient examples are provided for the student to make their own attempt at the form.

Part II concentrates on the major tropes and structural devices used by poets in the construction of poems. As before, in each short bite-sized chapter the trope is explained and shown in action. Again, learning is reinforced with creative trigger exercises designed to allow the student to use what they have learned, provide useful advice on avoiding common problems, and help students rewrite and revise effectively.

Part III focuses on various approaches poets have developed and used in their work. This section will look at and explain each in turn, often using the original writings of the poet as a base, and look at examples of work which help show the theory in action. In this section, also, there are creative trigger exercises designed to allow the student to use what they have learned, and which provide useful advice on avoiding common problems and helping students rewrite and revise effectively.

All three parts include examples that the reader can seek out for themselves to deepen their understanding, some suggestions for other poems and poets to look at more generally, and ideas and exercises that will be of practical use to the reader. I'm sure those who engage with this book will reap the benefit of the years of writing and teaching experience contained within it.

Nigel McLoughlin

PART I:
FORM & STRUCTURE

1
Varieties of the Sonnet

Nigel McLoughlin

What is a sonnet?

Traditionally, the sonnet is thought of as a poem of 14 lines which exists in two main variant forms: the Petrarchan sonnet and the Shakespearean sonnet. These two main forms take their names from Francesco Petrarca and William Shakespeare, but the sonnet evolved gradually. It is thought to have originated in Provence although the location is disputed. Originally, the Italian word *sonetto* meant 'a little song' or 'short refrain' and was recited to musical accompaniment, and it became fashionable in English poetry after it was imported from Italy around the start of the 1500s.

In the sixteenth century, Sir Thomas Wyatt and Henry Howard, Earl of Surrey, brought the sonnet form to England mainly through translations of Continental poets. Howard modified the form and began a process of evolution. He used a variant that became the Shakespearean sonnet. Later, Sir Philip Sidney used Petrarch as a model, but with some variation, when he composed his sonnet sequence *Astrophel and Stella*. These various early acts of translation, modification and modelling offered flexibility and hybrid vigour, and resulted in a strong tradition of sonnets in English.

The form has continued to evolve, and different parts of its structure became more or less important. As it developed, there emerged unrhymed sonnets; tailed sonnets (15–20 lines); such as those by Milton, and curtal (or curtailed) sonnets (10–13 lines); perhaps most famously by Gerard Manley Hopkins. The various sonnet types have been put to good use by every major movement within poetry, from Donne and other metaphysical poets through to the eras of the Romantics and the Victorians. A strong sonnet tradition persists today, and poets continue to innovate, as can be seen, for example, in the work of Geraldine Monk, Keith Jebb and Robert Sheppard; however, poets such as Rose Kelleher and Seamus Heaney have also continued to use the form in more classic mode.

How does a Petrarchan sonnet work?

The Petrarchan variety of the sonnet generally consists of 14 lines, which are usually split into an octave (8 lines) and a sestet (6 lines), though the actual poem may appear as a 14-line unit. There will usually be a *volta*, or a classic turn, and this will usually be found between the octave and sestet, though there may be some variation in its exact position. Classically, the Petrarchan sonnet is metrically regular (usually in iambic pentameter) with a formal rhyme scheme, though these constraints are more honoured in the breach than the observance these days.

On His Being Arrived to the Age of Twenty-Three

How **soon** hath **Time**, the **subt**le **thief** of **youth**,	A
Stolen on his **wing** my **three** and **twen**tieth **year**!	B
My **hasting days** fly **on** with **full** career,	B
But my late spring no bud or blossom shew'th.	A
Perhaps my semblance might deceive the truth,	A
That I to manhood am arrived so near,	B
And inward ripeness doth much less appear,	B
That some more timely-happy spirits indu'th.	A
Yet be it less or more, or soon or slow,	C
It shall be still in strictest measure even	D
To that same lot, however mean or high,	E
Toward which Time leads me, and the will of Heaven,	D
All is, if I have grace to use it so,	C
As ever in my great Task-master's eye.	E

John Milton

Although John Milton's poem above is presented as a single unit, when we analyse the structure one can see immediately that the poem is split into an octave (ABBAABBA) and a sestet (CDEDCE) by the regular rhyme scheme. This is further reinforced by the fact that a counterargument begins to be developed at the start of line 8: 'Yet be it less or more ...' This is what is meant by the *volta*. The poem shifts perspective in some way. This may be a movement from external description to a meditation on what that means, or it may be a change of viewpoint. Metrically it is quite regular, and the basic rhythm, as set up by the first line, is iambic pentameter. The second line is more naturally scanned with a metrical substitution of a trochee instead of an iamb in the first foot and with 'stolen' pronounced as one syllable:

Stolen on \ his **wing** \ my **three** \ and **twen** \ tieth **year**!
Trochee   \ Iamb   \ Iamb   \ Iamb   \ Iamb

Line 3 restores the regular iambic rhythm. Although one could argue that the stress more naturally falls on 'fly' as well as 'on'. This depends on how it is read and a reading as below with a spondaic substitution is quite acceptable:

My **hasting days fly on** with **full** ca**reer**

On balance the poem can be said to be in iambic pentameter (an unstressed syllable followed by a stressed one, repeated five times) with some substitution of feet. This is normal, however. It is not usual that poems are completely metrically regular since that tends to lead to a very mechanical sound. That said, while reciting, some people will attempt to stress a poem as if it were composed in a completely regular measure and this usually results in words like 'of' and 'to' receiving stress when they really should not. This distorts the sound of the poem.

Consider the following sonnet by Elizabeth Barrett Browning:

XLIV

(From *Sonnets from the Portuguese*)

Beloved, **thou** hast **brought** me **many flowers**	A
Plucked in the **gar**den, **all** the **summer through**	B
And **win**ter, **and** it **seemed** as **if** they **grew**	B
In **this** close **room**, nor **missed** the **sun** and **show**ers.	A
So, in the like name of that love of ours,	A
Take back these thoughts which here unfolded too,	B
And which on warm and cold days I withdrew	B
From my heart's ground. Indeed, those beds and bowers	A
Be overgrown with bitter weeds and rue,	B
And wait thy weeding; yet here's eglantine,	C
Here's ivy!—take them, as I used to do	B
Thy flowers, and keep them where they shall not pine	C
Instruct thine eyes to keep their colours true,	B
And tell thy soul their roots are left in mine.	C

Elizabeth Barrett Browning

As can be seen, this example is based on three rhyming sounds, which are here shown as A, B and C, and the *volta* is not as clearly marked in this poem. It occurs halfway along line 8. This means that there is not quite the traditional 8/6 split – it's more 7½/6½. The rhyme scheme changes from ABBAABBA to BCBCBC in the second part of the poem, which is a traditional sonnet scheme. The continuation of the B-rhyme across the whole sonnet acts as a binding device which links the sestet to the octave more closely and reinforces the more obscure *volta* in allowing a much more unified feel to the poem than the more strict Petrarchan style.

The meter is basically iambic pentameter, but there are several substitutions of feet, notably a trochee (a stressed syllable followed by an unstressed one) at the start of line 2, which, because it follows a weak final syllable in line 1, has the effect of compensation and so sounds like a trochee followed by a pyrrhic foot (two unstressed syllables), while the caesura after 'garden' helps restore the iambic rhythm. The general effect when reading the poem is that the verse is metrically very regular, yet it has a conversational flow that does not sound mechanical.

How does a Shakespearean sonnet work?

The Shakespearean variety of the sonnet also usually has 14 lines, which are normally split into three verses of four lines (also called quatrains), and it usually finishes with a two-line couplet. The poem may appear as a single unit on the page or it may be physically split in a variety of ways. The couplet tends to form an epigrammatic close which provides a 'summing up' of the main theme of the poem. It generally has a regular rhyme scheme and regular meter (classically iambic pentameter). Again, sometimes not all of the above features are included.

Sonnet 130

My **mistress' eyes** are **nothing like** the **sun**;	A
Coral is **far** more **red** than **her** lips' **red**;	B
If **snow** be **white**, why **then** her **breasts** are **dun**;	A
If **hairs** be **wires**, **black** wires **grow** on her **head**.	B
I have seen roses damask'd, red and white,	C
But no such roses see I in her cheeks;	D
And in some perfumes is there more delight	C
Than in the breath that from my mistress reeks.	D
I love to hear her speak, yet well I know	E
That music hath a far more pleasing sound;	F
I grant I never saw a goddess go;	E
My mistress, when she walks, treads on the ground:	F
And yet, by heaven, I think my love as rare	G
As any she belied with false compare.	G

William Shakespeare

Although the poem is not physically broken up into three quatrains and a couplet, in terms of its structure it will easily divide along those lines.

The rhyme scheme can be broken into units of ABAB, CDCD, EFEF, GG, and there are full stops at line 4 and line 8 and a colon at line 12, which break it into sense units based on a 4/4/4/2 structure. The basic meter is iambic pentameter with some substitution. Note that the final couplet forms an 'epigrammatic close', a memorable summing up of what the poem demonstrates, rather than what it actually says and thereby does not merely summarize and repeat but also adds to the poem.

Notably, the sonnet goes against the classic 'courtly love' poem by failing to compare the beloved as exceeding all the usual clichéd measures: snow-white breast, eyes like the sun and so on. Yet because of that the lover of the poem is more real, and more 'really' loved as the assertion of the final couplet demonstrates.

The Spenserian sonnet

This variety of the sonnet form usually has three quatrains and a couplet, though not an epigrammatic couplet. Usually, it has an interlocking rhyme scheme (as can be seen in the example below). In the classic Spenserian form the rhyme and meter are usually regular, but again, experimentally, many of these constraints may be bent or broken. It does not usually have a *volta*, and it may be thought of as closer to the Shakespearean form than the Petrarchan, but also as an intermediary form between the two on the evolutionary path of the sonnet.

Sonnet 70
(from *Amoretti*)

Fresh **Spring**, the **her**ald of **loves migh**ty **king**,	A
In **whose cote arm**our **rich**ly are **display**d	B
All **sorts** of **flowres** the **which** on **earth** do **spring**	A
In **good**ly **col**ours **glor**iously arrayd:	B
Goe to my Love, where she is carelesse layd,	B
Yet in her winters bowre not well awake:	C
Tell her the ioyous time wil not be staid	B
Unlesse she doe him by the forelock take.	C
Bid her therefore her selfe soone ready make,	C
To wayt on Love amongst his lovely crew,	D
Where every one that misseth then her make	C
Shall be by him amearst with penance dew.	D
Make haste therefore sweet Love, while it is prime,	E
For none can call againe the passed time.	E

Edmund Spenser

The first thing to note is that, again, although the poem is physically one unit, the rhyme scheme suggests subunits as follows: ABAB, BCBC, CDCD, EE. This demonstrates the interlocking nature of the rhyme scheme, which musically binds each stanza to the one that succeeds it and allows the final couplet a certain musical separation.

The basic meter is again iambic pentameter but with a little variation, notably a pyrrhic foot in line 4 which gives a four-stress line instead of five and makes it feel metrically different, accentuates the break in sense at line 4, and disrupts the music of the first line of the couplet at lines 4 and 5. Something similar occurs also at lines 8 and 9, where the metrical rhythm of the second line of the couplet is disrupted – this time with the use of trochaic meter towards the start of line 9.

Variants in the sonnet form: the double sonnet

Dulce et Decorum Est

Bent double, like old beggars under sacks,	A
Knock-kneed, coughing like hags, we cursed through sludge,	B
Till on the haunting flares we turned our backs,	A
And towards our distant rest began to trudge.	B
Men marched asleep. Many had lost their boots,	C
But limped on, blood-shod. All went lame, all blind;	D
Drunk with fatigue; deaf even to the hoots	C
Of tired, outstripped Five-Nines that dropped behind.	D
Gas! GAS! Quick, boys! – An ecstasy of fumbling,	E
Fitting the clumsy helmets just in time,	F
But someone still was yelling out and stumbling	E
And floundering like a man in fire or lime...	F
Dim, through the misty panes and thick green light,	G
As under a green sea, I saw him drowning.	H
In all my dreams, before my helpless sight,	G
He plunges at me, guttering, choking, drowning.	H
If in some smothering dreams you too could pace	I
Behind the wagon that we flung him in,	J
And watch the white eyes writhing in his face,	I
His hanging face, like a devil's sick of sin;	J
If you could hear, at every jolt, the blood	K
Come gargling from the froth-corrupted lungs,	L
Obscene as cancer, bitter as the cud	K
Of vile, incurable sores on innocent tongues, –	L

My friend, you would not tell with such high zest	M
To children ardent for some desperate glory,	N
The old Lie: Dulce et decorum est	M
Pro patria mori.	N

Wilfred Owen

Wilfred Owen's famous double sonnet above is an interesting use of the form for several reasons. First, it combines both Petrarchan and Shakespearean aspects of the form. The first 14 lines are shown with a clear division on the page into an octave and a sestet. This is reinforced by the rhyme scheme, which is ABABCDCD, EFEFGH, and a clear break in the sense of the poem beginning with the exclamations in line 9. Both parts of the first sonnet are in the past tense, but the second part has a much more immediate feel, set up by lines 9–11, which use a past progressive form of the verbs ('fumbling', 'fitting', 'was yelling'), to indicate that the past action was in progress, and the adverb 'still' to place the reader more immediately in the event. This is in contrast to the octave of the first sonnet, where the narrative is told in either the simple past ('we cursed', 'we turned', 'limped', 'went lame') or the perfect ('had lost'), indicating completed action. This move from completed action to actions more immediately described creates the *volta* of the first sonnet, as Owen moves to realize the central incident of the poem.

The second *volta* occurs before the two isolated lines, lines 15 and 16, in which the speaker of the poem describes, in simple present and progressive forms of the verb, that he still sees the soldier 'guttering, choking, drowning' as 'he plunges' towards him. Again, this move to the psychological effects on the witness presents a different aspect of the traumatic experience told in the first stanza. A third *volta*, where the speaker of the poem returns to the details of the aftermath of the gas attack in the past, leads us into the final section of 12 lines that concludes the poem. Formally, this looks like a reversed Shakespearean sonnet, with the isolated two lines structurally mirroring the closing lines of a Shakespearean sonnet, while the section of 12 lines that follows them is split into three rhymed sections of four lines (GH – IJIJKLKLMNMN). It is noteworthy that the rhymes that connect the two sonnets interlock, so that the last two lines of the sestet of the Petrarchan sonnet and the first two lines of the Shakespearean sonnet rhyme GHGH, where the H rhyme is identical – 'drowning-drowning'. This acts to bind the two sonnets together into a single poetic unit at the sonic level. The narrative sense and its movements also create a unity in the poem through its focus on an incident and its direct and later aftermath.

The body of the Shakespearean sonnet is couched in the conditional – 'if ... you too could pace', 'could hear' – and the implied conditional – '[could] watch' – which create the conditions for the 'you would not tell' towards the end of the poem. The poem also mirrors the epigrammatic close of the Shakespearean sonnet, ending as it does with the ironic Latin epigraph, which translated means: 'It is sweet and fitting to die for one's country.' The entire poem belies this, of course, through its graphic descriptions of the death of the soldier in the gas attack and the subsequent treatment of the body. It is certainly neither a sweet death nor a fitting treatment of the dead and dying.

Two other main sonnet variants exist: curtailed sonnets, which have less than 14 lines; and caudate or tailed sonnets, which have more than 14 lines. Good examples of these are to be found in Milton's tailed sonnet 'On the New Forcers of Conscience Under the Long Parliament', which extends the basic Petrarchan form by a further 6 lines, and Hopkins' 'Pied Beauty', which offers a shortened sonnet but in the correct ratio. A normal Petrarchan is 8/6. Hopkins uses 6/4½, which is the normal octave reduced by a quarter (¾ × 8 = 6) and likewise the sestet is also reduced by a quarter (¾ × 6 = 4½). As well as these, sonnet sequences have also been popular. A corona of sonnets and a crown of sonnets are set forms, which have a sequence of 7 or 14 sonnets linked by using the last line of one sonnet as the starting line of the next, and so on. There is also a form known as the heroic crown which adds a fifteenth sonnet made up of the first lines of all the others in order. Sonnet sequences such as these may be found in John Donne's *Corona*; Lady Mary Wroth's *A Crown of Sonnets Dedicated to Love*; and Marilyn Nelson's *A Wreath for Emmett Till*.

What is the sonnet used for?

The sonnet is one of the most flexible forms of poetry. Robert Frost is supposed to have advised 'if you want to say something for eight lines and take it back for six then write a sonnet'. While that advice may well have been a little tongue in cheek, the Petrarchan form offers the chance to do just that, of course. Yet it can also be used to support different perspectives on a subject – an immediate description for example, followed by a short meditation on its meaning or consequence. The Shakespearean version can afford more scope for narrative, with a short closing 'summing up' or change of perspective, which offers the reader some new way of seeing the preceding narrative. The form is very flexible, and may be fruitfully extended by sequences for longer narratives or combined with other forms as Frost does in 'Acquainted with the Night' – a sonnet that is also a terza rima, formed of four three-line stanzas and a couplet.

Exercise

Try to find examples of modern poems that have experimented with the sonnet form. Which features tend to be changed, and which features tend to be kept? What do you think makes a sonnet a sonnet? Try to write three sonnets, dispensing with rhyme and meter in one, dispensing with the *volta* in another and experimenting with structure in the other. Finally, here is one of mine. Is it a sonnet at all? If so, why? If not, why not?

Aubade

                    the night balances
at quarter to three
                    and the boat rolls
                                        my arm outstretched
        my younger son   turns into me
            his brother
                            and his mother
sleep in the other
            bed
                    head to head
                                    and breathe in unison
        everyone sleeps except me
                            in the car
in the still-dark
            I pass the lonely hour
                        composing this
        I turn and turn
                        the verses over in my head
    in the dawn
                there is the dust of frost
                        it ungreens and thickens
to a covering of snow
                the further south we go
                            and the morning is white
from head to toe
            England is asleep
                        this morning's mine
this morning is all rime

Bibliography

Fuller, John (ed.) (2000) *The Oxford Book of Sonnets* (Oxford: Oxford University Press)

Hilson, Jeff (ed.) (2008) *The Reality Street Book of Sonnets* (Hastings: Reality Street Editions)

2
Terza Rima

Martin Figura

What is it?

A *terza rima* is a linked rhyming lyric and/or narrative poem made up of three-line stanzas (tercets); it translates from Italian as 'third rhyme'. Iambic pentameter is often used in English, but it is not a specific requirement. The rhyme scheme runs a-b-a, b-c-b, c-d-c and so on until the end – there's no fixed length to a terza rima. The structure of the final stanza can be varied to a single line – for example, d-e-d, e – or a couplet – for example, d-e-d, e-e. The rhyme scheme has been described as 'two steps forward, one step back' giving it a rolling momentum and waltz-like rhythm, with the middle lines as backward glances.

The *capitolo* is a fifteenth-century Italian form that shares the same meter, rhyme and structure as a terza rima. It came into being when terza rimas became more didactic. By the nineteenth century it evolved to be a term used for light or satirical terza rimas. A later variation invented by Edward Lowbury (1913–2007) is the *piccola*, which restricts lines to six syllables.

History

Dante Alighieri introduced the terza rima in his *Divine Comedy* (ca. 1308–1321). It is thought he may have been influenced by *sirventès*, a lyric form used by the troubadours. Geoffrey Chaucer's (1343–1400) *Complaint to His Lady* is the first known example in English. Sir Thomas Wyatt brought the terza rima wider attention in the sixteenth century. Poets have continued to use it since, from Milton (1608–1674) to the Romantics and on into the twentieth century and beyond, with poets including Sylvia Plath, Robert Frost, W. H. Auden and the Hungarian-born poet George Szirtes whose poem *Noir* we look at later in the chapter.

Shelley's *Ode to The West Wind* (1819) is made up of five cantos: each of four tercets and a final couplet, they have been described as 'terza rima sonnets'. The terza rima rhyme scheme is closest to the Spenserian sonnet with its interlocking rhyme scheme and conclusive final couplet. Robert Frost's *Acquainted with the Night* is a later example of this variation.

How does it work?

This is the third canto from *Ode to The West Wind*:

III

Thou who didst waken from his summer dreams	A
The blue Mediterranean, where he lay,	B
Lulled by the coil of his crystalline streams,	A
Beside a pumice isle in Baiae's bay,	B
And saw in sleep old palaces and towers	C
Quivering within the wave's intenser day,	B
All overgrown with azure moss and flowers	C
So sweet, the sense faints picturing them! Thou	D
For whose path the Atlantic's level powers	C
Cleave themselves into chasms, while far below	D
The sea-blooms and the oozy woods which wear	E
The sapless foliage of the ocean, know	D
Thy voice, and suddenly grow grey with fear,	E
And tremble and despoil themselves: O hear!	E

In comparison with Italian, English has limited rhyming possibilities. Because of this a certain amount of leeway in rhyme is generally considered to be acceptable. In the example above, Shelley has, in places, used 'half/slant rhyme': Thou/below/know and 'sight rhyme': wear/fear/hear. Without this licence it's easy for end-rhyming to become clumsy and obvious in English.

It is possible to have unrhymed sonnets, but with terza rima we are indisputably dealing with rhyme. The rhyme limitations of English present particular difficulties in translation. In translating Dante's *Inferno*, Pinsky wanted to capture the spirit of Dante's work and present it in a readable contemporary idiom. He wanted to avoid archaic or stilted language and argued momentum was key, rather than adherence to a strict rhyme scheme. He employed consonantal and slant rhyme to achieve his aim, stating: 'This system of like sounds happens to respond to some preference of my own ear, a personal taste: for me such rhymes as, say, "swans/stones" or "gibe/club" or "south/both" often sound more beautiful and interesting than such hard-rhyme combinations as "bones/stones", "rub/club", or "south/mouth"' (see http://bigthink.com/ideas/1679).

In his *New York Times* review of Pinsky's translation, John Ahern writes: 'He shapes sinewy lines whose edges you can actually hear. This is true verse, not the typographical arrangement of poetic prose. Rejecting both blank verse and a clanging triple rhyme that would have reproduced the scheme of the original, he translates into an effective half-strength terza rima. Unlike some translators, he does not match every Italian line with a line in English. Without missing a jot or a tittle, he makes cantos as much as 20 lines shorter than the originals and so attains a truly Dantean velocity. Epic similes come out clean, not clunky.'

Here is the beginning of *Canto I* in Pinsky's translation, which you should read aloud to hear the effect.

> Midway on our life's journey, I found myself
> In dark woods, the right road lost. To tell
> About those woods is hard—so tangled and rough
>
> And savage that thinking of it now, I feel
> The old fear stirring: death is hardly more bitter.
> And yet, to treat the good I found there as well
>
> I'll tell what I saw, though how I came to enter
> I cannot well say, being so full of sleep
> Whatever moment it was I began to blunder
>
> Off the true path. But when I came to stop
> Below a hill that marked one end of the valley
> That had pierced my heart with terror, I looked up
>
> Toward the crest and saw its shoulders already
> Mantled in rays of that bright planet that shows
> The road to everyone, whatever our journey.

It is also worth noting that the use of enjambment helps to keep the momentum. This is particularly true where harder end-rhymes, which can arrest momentum, are employed, for example bitter/enter/blunder.

How can I use it?

I think we can safely say that if relaxing the strict rhyme scheme is good enough for Shelley and Pinsky, then it's good enough for us. Only the self-appointed 'defenders' of English poetry are likely to take you to task and if your poem annoys them, then it's achieved something already. So, what is the point of writing in form, only to then play fast and loose with its constraints? In order to answer this question, we must ask why we set out to write within a rhyme scheme in the first place – what does it give us?

Rhyme in general will be dealt with in Chapter 14, so I will only touch on it briefly here. The corollary to English's limited scope for rhymes is that it is difficult to do well. So why would we limit our creative process; what is to be gained? On a surface level, rhyme creates something that is always recognizably a poem. Form provides you with a framework: the terza rima's 'two steps forward and one step back' gives work both momentum and a reflection in its ongoing backward glance. In terms of imagination, we head off the predicted path of what we already know and plan to say. Out in the wild undergrowth, in search of rhyme and meter, who knows what we'll find to surprise and delight our readers and us. There's also the pleasure to be had in a well-made object – we can admire a poem for its craftsmanship, elegance and proportions. The terza rima with its three-rhyme sets is less 'rhyme' demanding than most other forms.

I have discovered an additional benefit, and I should probably not be telling you this! I often start to write poems as terza rima and persist for some time, but often the demands of the form defeat it. It can become forced, lose its inner logic or have clumsy line ends in meeting the rhyme scheme. I don't give up easily, but when I do I find that all the effort has not been wasted; I can break up the terza rima for spares. When other superfluous words are removed, some end-rhymes are moved to the middle of lines where they relax and can be more natural. You can even add more rhymes if you wish or re-order the poem. The effect is to populate a poem with assonances rolling through it, giving it a musicality and momentum. I won't dwell on this as it goes against the intention of the chapter, but here's an example of one of my 'broken' terza rimas.

Victor
'True Stories of Men at War'

As fathers stroll home from work
there is no birdsong and the November light
is all but gone.

Small boys run amok in avenues,
take cover behind privet hedges –
the smell of cordite, heavy in the air.

Over the traffic, the sound of battle:
grenades whistling overhead, the sporadic
rattle of toy guns from doorways.

At tea time, those whose turn it is
break cover, make a zigzagging run for it
shouting – ACHTUNG ACHTUNG.

They go down in a hail of bullets,
competing for the most dramatic death.
The pavement is so littered with Germans

the men must pick a way through
to reach their gates and take their sons
down paths into quiet houses.

So we can see some still recognizable survivors from the form: work/amok/
sporadic/dramatic/pick – light/cordite/it/quiet – birdsong/zigzagging/
achtung – battle/rattle. We can see that I extended the first run of half-
rhymes to, I hope, good effect.

We should now look at a proper terza rima by a contemporary master of the
form, George Szirtes. You can hear him read it on the Poetry Archive website at:
www.poetryarchive.org/poetryarchive/singlePoem.do?poemId=228.

Noir

With a firm hand, she dabs at two pink pancakes
and smooths herself right out. The man next door
crushes his cigarette in the ashtray and makes

a call. A car draws up below. There are more
cars by the curbside, waiting with lights on.
Everything is ready. Lights on the floor

above snap off. Whatever business was being done
is done. It's time for bed. Boys stir in sleep
to the sounds of drumming that might be a handgun.

The plot is too complex and runs too deep
for neat solutions. There are only cars
and endless cruising. There are secrets you keep

and secrets you don't yet know. There are scars
below scars and, eventually, daylight over the hill
to wipe the windscreens by the all-night bars

but shadows remain on the lung and the grille
of the sedan parked by the gate. What troubles you?
Why so anxious? Why do you stand so still?

from *Reel* (Bloodaxe, 2004), © George Szirtes 2004, used by
permission of the author and Bloodaxe Books.

In his introduction to the Poetry Archive reading of *Noir*, discussing the terza rima form, Szirtes states: 'each verse leads you on to the next and the whole thing unrolls or unspools like a reel of film'. He adds that 'again it's related to memory in my mind'. The poem follows two lengthy terza rima sequences in the opening section of his T. S. Eliot prize-winning collection *Reel*, the title opening sequence of which follows a film crew shooting Budapest as Berlin.

Szirtes has written about the genre of film noir in general on his (highly recommended) blog http://georgeszirtes.blogspot.co.uk/2009/10/noir-note.html. In this, he states: 'The narrative is nearly always complex, often unclear. Some evil has been done, is being done, or is about to be done.' I don't intend to unpick the meaning in the poem too much here, but to get on with the practicalities. Yet it is necessary to some extent, in order to demonstrate how Szirtes has married style and form with the subject matter.

In the aforementioned blog, Szirtes writes:

> The language of film noir is pretty formal. Its devices are rhythmical and expected, like meter and rhyme: staircase, wall, lamppost, hand, drifting light, vertigo, swing of hair, great pool of shadow, glimpse, a look away, the broad shoulder with the jacket thrown over it, swing of hip, the half-open door, desk, back of chair, desklight, cigarette, a hulking back, a craggy face, car fin and car door. These images and others like them form the stanza, the rhyme scheme, the chorus.

Noir is a meditation on mood that Szirtes captures by matching the subject and content to the recurring devices of film noir: the relationship of film to memory and its echo in the rhyme and backward glance of terza rima; and the rolling momentum of terza rima and the film reel. *Noir* picks up some of the motifs of the previous sequences (both of which have the atmosphere of film noir) in the collection. Film noir provides the signifiers that facilitate the examination of the subject matter – cars, the leitmotif that runs through the first three poems/sequences in *Reel*, literally become the vehicles in which to transport sinister Cold War cargo.

Szirtes has no qualms about using slant rhymes in his terza rimas, but *Noir* is a relatively short poem and Szirtes' rhymes are full – only on/done/handgun having the subtlest of slants. The language of the rhymes is straightforward and un-showy; Szirtes is not trying to dazzle us with unusual rhymes here. In fact, to do so, would distract us from the poem's intent. The rhymes, although full, manage not to be forced, nor do they clunk heavily into place. The poem's momentum is not built around them, so their presence is discrete.

Szirtes achieved this, mainly through enjambment, so the poem runs past the rhymes. Only two rhymes finish sentences: the line-5 rhyme, 'on', falls in the middle of a run of short bursts, so doesn't seem any more emphatic than what precedes and follows it – 'There are more/cars by the curbside, waiting with lights on./everything is ready. Lights on the floor//above snap off.' The other, ending line 9 – 'to the sounds of drumming that might be a handgun.' – is dead centre, ending the first half of the poem. The rhyme acts as a definitive pause, being at the end of a sentence, the end of a line and the end of a stanza. The firm rhyme has a clear purpose in the shape of the poem as it shifts from description to observation; in this respect *Noir* has something of the sonnet about it.

Caesura follows from enjambment and Szirtes makes skilful use of both to create drama and suspense within the poem, which adds to the atmosphere created by the stock 'noir' characters and motifs. We don't actually witness the characters meeting or anything bad happening – that is left to the imagination. Often the sentences are short, so even though they are full stops, the sense of urgency and anxiety is maintained.

The pace and suspense is also sustained by quick repetition: 'A car draws up below. There are more/cars by the curbside, waiting with lights on./ Everything is ready. Lights on the floor'. And: 'There are only cars/'. Then: 'scars/below scars'. The repetition reinforces the following rhyme of 'bars', so the pace is maintained despite the caesuras.

In terms of meter, the stresses are sometimes ambiguous and difficult to discern. 'Two pink pancakes' could be read as 'Two pink pancakes' or 'Two pink pancakes', or even 'Two pink pancakes'. There are clear iambic runs in the poem – 'a call. A car draws up below. There are more/cars' – but they are not sustained for long and, in this example, are disrupted by caesura, so the rhythm doesn't lapse into the jaunty te-TUM, te-TUM, te-TUM, te-TUM, te-TUM of iambic pentameter, which would undermine the mood of the poem.

As stated, *Noir* follows on from two lengthy terza rima sequences *Reel* and *Meeting Austerlitz* in that first section, which is completed with another terza rima – *Sheringham*. This opening section is followed by *Flesh: An Early Family History*, which consists of five sequences of five terza rimas, each with a single line final stanza, and each sequence ending with an *Eclogue*. Szirtes is a master of the form and you could do no better than to look at these poems closely and to read his *Terza Rima – A Defence of Rhyme* on his blog at: http://georgeszirtes.blogspot.co.uk/2010/02/terza-rima-defence-of-rhyme. html.

In summary, take on board Pinsky's philosophy of inhabiting the spirit of the form and don't be tempted into being a slave to the rhyme – to misquote Grace Jones. Make friends with enjambment, caesura and repetition; let them guide you around the pitfalls to the qualities of terza rima. Be ambitious enough to get form and content to work together.

Exercise – *punctum*

As a poet and a photographer I have found that the two have much in common. Critical essays about one can almost certainly be applied to the other. A poem and photograph exist in a frame, both physical and in time. Photographs have their own rhymes through shape and colours.

More importantly, we look to photographs as fixed signposts back through our blurred and fractured memory. We keep them in albums, on Facebook, we text them by phone – by and large we hate to lose them. Here are two quotes from *Camera Lucida*, but you really should read the whole book:

'I was interested in Photography only for "sentimental" reasons; I wanted to explore it not as a question (a theme) but as a wound: I see, I feel, hence I notice, I observe, and I think.'

'A photograph's *punctum* is that accident which pricks me (but also bruises me, is poignant to me).'

Roland Barthes, *Camera Lucida* (Vintage Classics, 1980)

1. Choose six of your personal photographs that you have on display in some way – in a wallet, a frame, on your phone.
2. Lay them out on the desk in front of you in no particular order.
3. Look at each one in turn and identify the *punctum* – the emotional connection to it – and write it down.
4. Write two tercets on each picture, linking them together to make a 12-stanza terza rima.
5. Make the *punctum* of each image your starting point, but resist making the writing 'over-wrought' – leave metaphor and sub-text to do their work.
6. Hand over responsibility of narrative order to rhyme.
7. Make use of the devices such as repetition, enjambment and caesura where they serve your purpose.
8. Feel free to use slant/half-rhymes.

Bibliography

Barthes, Roland (1980) *Camera Lucida* (London: Vintage Classics)
Szirtes, George (2004) *Reel* (Tarset: Bloodaxe Books)

3
The Villanelle

Siobhan Campbell

What is it?

The villanelle is a poem of 19 lines made up of five 3-line stanzas and a 4-line stanza (quatrain) at the end. It has two repeated refrain lines and just two rhymes. The tercets rhyme a-b-a and the concluding quatrain rhymes a-b-a-a, with the sixth, twelfth and eighteenth lines repeating the first line, and the ninth, fifteenth and nineteenth lines repeating the third line. A tercet is a group of three lines of verse that rhyme with each other or with another group of three and it is partly the break between this 3-line stanza form and the final 4-line stanza that energizes the villanelle. The challenge for a poet is to establish two refrain lines that have equal power. These lines are kept apart from the beginning where they form the first and third lines of stanza one and though they relate to each other throughout the work, they do not appear as the couplet they really are until the end when they should come together in an unexpectedly satisfying way.

The schema can be rendered: A'bA" abA' abA" abA' abA" abA'A" or as:

A1 (line repeated)
b   (rhyme repeated)
A2 (line repeated)

a   (rhyme with A1 and A2)
b   (rhyme with b)
A1 (line repeated), and so on.

But because this explanation is difficult to imagine as poetry, it is best to begin by reading the contemporary villanelle below. If read aloud, it is easier to get a sense of how the repeated lines create a mesmeric effect that resists the forward thrust of a narrative. Instead, though they can still frame a story, they become full of insistence in their circularity:

Leavetaking

The swing of wipers like a metronome.	A'
A swirl of rain through sleeping midland towns.	b
I see The West, can't find the road for home.	A"

The surgeon's reassurance melts like foam,	a
I left you in a green theatre gown.	b
The swing of wipers like a metronome.	A'

The bouquet by your window said shalom.	a
You caught the hesitation in my frown.	b
I see The West, can't find the road for home.	A"

It was agreed, your wish to be alone.	a
Some privacy before they wheeled you down.	b
The swing of wipers like a metronome.	A'

I should have stayed, you never need have known;	a
three a.m., all logic in meltdown.	b
I see The West, can't find the road for home.	A"

Twice, three times; an eddy near Athlone.	a
Roundabout – I circle as I drown.	b
The swing of wipers like a metronome,	A'
I see The West, can't find the road for home.	A"

Gerard Hanberry

In *Leavetaking*, Hanberry answers our 'what is it?' by using the shape of the villanelle to suggest a recurring set of emotions. As two complete lines are each repeated four times, those lines carry much of the sense and the feeling. Here, the word 'metronome', a device used to mark musical tempo, is almost a comment on the way the villanelle itself works to make time cyclical. The other line of refrain matches an idea of direction, 'The West', with a sense that this West is where the speaker might escape the sense that 'home' cannot be found.

As with all the received forms, the answer to 'what is it?' is completely bound up with the history of the form. Until recently, scholarly surveys have asserted that the schema of the villanelle at 19 lines, as above, was established in Renaissance France and the first recorded example given is nearly always Jean Passerat's 'Villanelle', also known as 'J'ay perdu ma tourterelle', which dates from the late sixteenth century (though cited for publication in 1606).

This story has been woven in with the idea that our strict modern form is also associated with the songs of medieval troubadours, when in fact villanelles from the earlier period tended to have no fixed length or form and what connected them is more to do with their content. The word *villanelle* (French) comes from the *villanella* in the Italian which itself derives from *villa* (house in Latin) and *villano* (farm labourer). Therefore, prior to the villanelle acquiring its fixed form, it was understood to imply a possibly nostalgic rustic song in contrast to the 'madrigal', which had more to do with city life and courtly advancement, though 'courtly' composers of early sixteenth-century Italy would have written in both forms.

Scholars such as Amanda French, Ronald McFarland and Annie Finch (see Bibliography) have unpicked and amplified the legacy of the villanelle and their research concludes that in its early appearances it was democratic and, while based on the refrain, it had no fixed form or meter, lending itself to anonymous composition and often being packed with dialect words, bad puns and proverbial wisdom. They agree that the words would have fitted with accompanying music and there are varying reports as to whether words were fitted to pre-existing tunes or whether the verse came first.[1]

How then did the notion arise that Jean Passerat's poem (which Amanda French identifies as the only example of the period) was representative of a long tradition mapping the formal qualities of the villanelle we write today? The answer seems to be a tale of poetic gossip and rivals in prosody. The chief French popularizer of the form was Théodore de Banville who became the second person to write in the schema above (though centuries later) and can be thought of as parodying Passerat since his poem, 'I have lost my Limayrac' (1845), humorously laments the loss of a person, as Passerat's speaker bemoaned the loss of his 'turtledove' or lover.

In the 'fixed forms revival' of the nineteenth century, poet-scholars tended to claim a more ancient heritage for the forms they wanted to define. It seems that de Banville may have been led by Wilhelm Ténint to think that the villanelle was an antique form, making him perhaps more likely to write them – which he did, popularizing the form further and becoming in turn an influence on Edmund Gosse, who made the form fashionable with his 1877 essay 'A Plea for Certain Exotic Forms of Verse'.

The burgeoning nineteenth-century interest in fixed-form poetry led to other poets such as Austin Dobson, Oscar Wilde and Edith Thomas taking on the villanelle and though there continued to be variation in its length, the A'bA" form became fully established.

Our modern dual-refrain form of the villanelle, then, derives from nineteenth-century admiration of the only identified Renaissance poem in that form and this trajectory explains why there are so few examples in French of what is known as a French form, but several examples in English from the nineteenth century onwards. In terms of meter, variation continued throughout the development of the form but nineteenth-century poets favoured trimeter or tetrameter while twentieth-century poets seem to prefer iambic pentameter.

How does it work?

As the villanelle moved from its popularity at the end of the nineteenth century and on into the next century, new poets attempted the form, as this is how practising writers have always answered the question, 'how does it work?'. For W. H. Auden, William Empson, Dylan Thomas, Theodore Roethke, Elizabeth Bishop and Sylvia Plath among others, the variations in meter and especially the range of possible subject matter and tonal play were part of their answer.

Let's turn to some villanelles which show their inner workings in ways that teach the pleasures of the form.

Wouldst thou not be content to die?

Wouldst thou not be content to die
When low-hung fruit is hardly clinging
And golden Autumn passes by?

Beneath this delicate rose-gray sky,
While sunset bells are faintly ringing,
Wouldst thou not be content to die?

For wintry webs of mist on high
Out of the muffled earth are springing,
And golden Autumn passes by.

O now when pleasures fade and fly,
And Hope her southward flight is winging,
Wouldst thou not be content to die?

Lest Winter come, with wailing cry
His cruel icy bondage bringing,
When golden Autumn hath passed by;

And thou with many a tear and sigh,
While life her wasted hands is wringing,
Shall pray in vain for leave to die
When golden Autumn hath passed by.

Edmund Gosse (1878)

What we notice first is that this poem with death and loss at its centre is well served by the cyclical form of the villanelle. Is there something about the cycle of repetitions that mirrors the cycle of life from which none of us can escape? Could this be why one of the most influential twentieth-century villanelles is *Do not go gentle into that good night* by Dylan Thomas, which is also about dying and is addressed to his father? We note too that both Hanberry's and Gosse's poems are written in the form of an address to a listener. Direct address is something to consider using in your villanelle experiments, as the immediacy of a speaking voice gives a powerful contemporary feel.

As we have seen, part of the challenge is to select two refrain lines which will bear the repetitions without becoming cloying. In the best examples, these lines appear to gather more meaning as the poem develops.

In Gosse, A' (or A1) begins as 'Wouldst thou not be content to die' and A" (A2) starts out as 'And golden Autumn passes by?'. The poet helps us see that there's a shift from possible hope to a definite feeling of loss by variation on the latter. When, in the second pair of appearances, he changes it to 'When golden Autumn hath passed by', we are left in no doubt as to the finality of what has occurred. But look, there's variation on the use of the A' refrain too. While it appears where we might expect throughout, it changes in the quatrain to 'Shall pray in vain for leave to die' and this acts to emphasize that the irony in the rhetorical question about being 'content' has been answered by a fully blown death-wish by the end of the poem.

It is important to note, as shown by Amanda French, that when it first appeared, 'Wouldst thou not be content to die' had two more stanzas, making it 25 lines in total. French argues persuasively that early practitioners in English viewed the form as more stanzaic than fixed and that variation on length in fact reflected its history more completely than the latter-day idea that the form was rigidly 19 lines. Interestingly though, on subsequent printings, Gosse removed the second and third stanzas, leaving the poem as we have it above.

Edmund Gosse's friend Arthur Dobson provides examples of the form which are less finely worked. Dobson's 'Villanelle' (cited by French as appearing in the 24 October 1874 issue of *The Examiner*) has shorter refrain lines and these allow for less amplification of meaning as the poem progresses. 'When I first saw your eyes,/ You were then but a child/Time changes, Time tries.' This continues in fairly obvious steps toward the final stanza:

You are cold, you are wise;
Yet you were but a child
When I first saw your eyes.
Time changes, Time tries!

Remember what we said about the necessity of choosing refrain lines which can appear to add new layers of meaning as they continue to repeat? Dobson shows the effect of not doing just that, pointing out how a less than subtle villanelle can feel clunky and underworked.

Contrast the key lines of the above with the refrains of William Empson in his 1935 'Villanelle' with its striking combination of intelligence and emotion:

> It is the pain, it is the pain endures.
> Your chemic beauty burned my muscles through.
> Poise of my hands reminded me of yours.

Or with the mantra-like refrains of the first tercet in *The Waking* by Theodore Roethke (1953):

> I wake to sleep, and take my waking slow.
> I feel my fate in what I cannot fear.
> I learn by going where I have to go ...

The second repeated line here becomes more ironic in register as the poem continues and, as we read more villanelles, we notice how the structural opportunity for several tonal shifts is optimized by many writers. See, for example, where Sylvia Plath's *Mad Girls Love Song* uses parentheses to dramatic and ironic effect: 'I shut my eyes and all the world drops dead. / (I think I made you up inside my head.)'

You might be forgiven for thinking that the villanelle form has improved with use or that poets have found ever more subtle ways to exploit its twisting repetitive dance. And you would only be half-wrong, for it's true that contemporary writers have the whole breadth of what has gone before to choose from in their attempts to either match their poem to the strict schema or develop a variation in rhyme or refrain to amplify poetic intent.

Nigel McLoughlin's unrhymed villanelle below is an interesting example of the form being used to great effect without the necessity for the secondary drumbeat of rhyme:

The Book of Invasions

> I have come here in winter
> to watch darkness creep over Muckish
> like an invader from the north
>
> to watch the fire thole in stone
> at the stroop of two hills
> I have come here in winter

to hear the whispered notes of a white
melody strange from the stream's bed
like an invader from the north

to hear it echo, rise and dance
through rocks at the water's fall
I have come here in winter

to take the wordless air and fill it
with a populace of new language
like an invader from the north

to plunder a landscape for a refuge
to take possession and find belonging
I have come here in winter
like an invader from the north

Nigel McLoughlin

As contemporary readers of poems, we are attuned to the fact that many poems may have an underlying theme addressing the poem itself. This self-consciousness is endemic to the form, as no one ever wrote a villanelle without planning to do so. It's what Elizabeth Bishop references in her famous 'Write it!' admonishment in her poem *One Art*. With that in mind, if we look back at Gerard Hanberry's *Leavetaking*, we might be struck by the way he uses what amount to variations of the same rhyme when he might have had a more contrasting centre rhyme (foam, gown, metronome / shalom, frown, home / alone, down, metronome). The emphasis is designed to bring our ear back to the word 'metronome', and what is a villanelle except a kind of metronome where the timing set up in the first tercet is maintained until the final quatrain? Hanberry gives us a hint that this interpretation is right when he says, 'Roundabout – I circle as I drown' which may well be a comment on the form itself. Primed thus to read McLoughlin's piece as one which may address the very nature of the villanelle 'like an invader from the north', we begin to notice phrasing in almost every stanza that backs up this interpretation and it's fun to have that *aha!* moment on how the villanelle works.

'At the stoop of two hills' may be a reference to the space for the line that exists between two refrains. The sense of hearing the 'whispered notes' of the past may allow the speaker to take and adapt this 'white melody / strange from the stream's bed' (the source of the form perhaps). Strikingly, the fourth stanza confirms our reading as the speaker hears the 'echo, rise and dance' – a perfect description of the movement within this form – and we are then left in no doubt that the 'new language' of subsequent lines is referring to this poet's capacity to produce an unrhymed villanelle which works on many levels designed 'to take possession and find belonging'.

How can I use it?

You could think of the villanelle as an architectural form that can be broken down into stanza 'bricks', with 'spacers' of rhyme and the 'mortar' of refrain holding everything together.

We have seen that the pressure on the two key lines is immense, since they must dance apart but relate to one another for the whole of the piece until finally brought together in the quatrain. Read villanelles widely (see the Everyman's anthology and PoetryFoundation.org for several examples) and once you have had the heuristic pleasure of enjoying the poems, go back and closely observe how those two key lines demand attention and acquire their power.

Exercise

To begin writing your villanelle, set out the schema for the whole poem, with the *a*'s and *b*'s in the left-hand margin, as shown on the first page of this essay. Separately, begin notes on what the subject of the two refrain lines might be. If you think of an incident from life which captures a time when something changed, it can be a good place to start. Think your way into the nub of contrasting ideas related to this memory. Martha Collins' villanelle, *The Story We Know*, uses the contrast between hello and goodbye. Her refrains are variations on 'The way to begin is always the same. Hello,' (the first line) and 'Good-bye is the end of every story we know' (line 9).[2]

Another way to begin is to think of a person to whom you had things to say which were never expressed. Often, beneath the initial words you might have spoken, there's a set of complex emotions. Use the two refrains to capture first, the words themselves, and then, the underlying emotion. You may end up with two very usable refrain lines. Now begin to put these into your schema, remembering that you can vary them as you go if that seems to fit the unfolding set of meanings. Try several lines to fit in between. Read your work aloud often, as this will help you to hear new possibilities.

We've noticed that a serious form of 'play' is at work in the villanelle, something that allows the tone to change as a poem develops, even if the variation in wording is small. Play with your initial set of lines, observing what happens when you try to tell a story or what occurs when you attempt to render an atmosphere. It is always good to try the poem of 'address' when getting to grips with a form. It may be that the ruse of 'speaking' to an identified 'other' helps to solidify the 'voice' in the poem.

As you progress in building this form, the shaping of your drafts may seem to declare poetic solutions to you in ways that seem mysterious. But you now know that this experience is more to do with the cyclical patterns of the form which act, at their best, as a kind of microcosm of life.

Your reanimation of the villanelle is one of the ways in which you join the generations of poets who have returned to the form as a fascinating, sometimes maddening, but always intriguing challenge. There is no reason why your particular approach should not enhance the form further and be part of passing it on to the coming generation of poets.

Bibliography

Collins, Martha (1985) *The Catastrophe of Rainbows* (Cleveland: Cleveland State University Press)

Finch, Annie and Mali, Marie-Elizabeth (eds) (2012) *Villanelles*, Everyman's Library Pocket Poets (London: Alfred A. Knopf)

French, Amanda (2004) 'Refrain, Again: The Return of the Villanelle', Ph.D. thesis (University of Virginia), http://amandafrench.net/files/ Dissertation.pdf, accessed 15 October 2012

McFarland, Ronald E. (1987) *The Villanelle: The Evolution of a Poetic Form* (Moscow, ID: University of Idaho Press)

4
The Ballad

Paul Hardwick

History

The ballad is the narrative poetic form *par excellence*, characterized by directness of address, simplicity of language and a strong rhythm. Surviving from the late medieval and early modern periods, topics include contemporary events, love found and (more often) lost, the supernatural, military might, murder, betrayal, banditry and bawdry. The main common denominator is that all were composed to be sung, this musical origin reflected in the form's name which is derived from the Italian *ballare*, to dance. Some were no doubt sung first and recorded later, whilst others may have been composed for the growing market in cheap broadsides which flourished in the seventeenth century; in either case, the ballad was very much common property to be shared orally. Consequently, the majority of early ballads exist in numerous variants, each bearing the imprints of those through whose hands they have passed. Although there are a great many collections, the landmark remains Francis James Child's *The English and Scottish Popular Ballads*, which was published in ten volumes between 1882 and 1898, and which comprises more than 300 ballads, each with full discussion and, in most cases, variant forms. More than a scholarly work, the series has, appropriately, functioned as a key text in folksong revivals in both Britain and the United States.

An essentially popular form, the ballad was given a new 'literary' life with the 1798 publication of Wordsworth and Coleridge's *Lyrical Ballads*, which, as stated in Wordsworth's 'Advertisement', had much in common with 'our elder writers'. In the celebrated Preface to the 1800 version, this point was expanded upon, with Wordsworth noting that:

> There will also be found in these volumes little of what is usually called poetic diction; I have taken as much pains to avoid it as others ordinarily take to produce it; this I have done … to bring my language near to the language of men.

It is testament to the success of the enterprise that the first edition opened with what is undoubtedly one of the most celebrated literary ballads in the English language, Coleridge's 'The Ancient Mariner: A Poet's Reverie' (later renamed 'The Rime of the Ancyent Marinere'). Notable modern exponents of the literary ballad include Wilde and Auden, whilst songwriters such as Pete Seeger and Bob Dylan have made significant additions to the body of works that continue to be sung.

Common ballad form

As may be expected of a form historically reliant upon popular oral tradition, there are numerous variations to be found. However, the basic ballad stanza is of quatrains of alternating tetrameter and trimeter in an a-b-a-b rhyme scheme, with strong masculine endings to each line creating an assertive, declamatory diction.

The Twa Magicians[1]

1 The lady stands in her bower door,   A
    As straight as willow wand;   B
The blacksmith stood a little forebye,   C
    Wi hammer in his hand.   B

2 'Weel may ye dress ye, lady fair,
    Into your robes o red;
Before the morn at this same time,
    I'll gain your maidenhead.'

3 'Awa, awa, ye coal-black smith,
    Woud ye do me the wrang
To think to gain my maidenhead,
    That I hae kept sae lang!'

4 Then she has hadden up her hand,
    And she swam by the mold,
'I wudna be a blacksmith's wife
    For the full o a chest o gold.

5 'I'd rather I were dead and gone,
    And my body laid in grave,
Ere a rusty stock o coal-black smith
    My maidenhead shoud have.'

6 But he has hadden up his hand,
    And he sware by the mass,
'I'll cause ye be my light leman
    For the hauf o that and less.'
        O bide, lady, bide,
    And aye he bade her bide;
        The rusty smith your leman shall be,
    For a' your muckle pride.

7 Then she became a turtle dow,
    To fly up in the air,
And he became another dow,
    And they flew pair and pair.
        O bide, lady, bide, &c.

8 She turnd hersell into an eel,
    To swim into yon burn,
And he became a speckled trout,
    To gie the eel a turn.
        O bide, lady, bide, &c.

9 Then she became a duck, a duck,
    To puddle in a peel,
And he became a rose-kaimd drake,
    To gie the duck a dreel.
        O bide, lady, bide, &c.

10 She turnd hersell into a hare,
    To rin upon yon hill,
And he became a gude grey-hound,
    And boldly he did fill.
        O bide, lady, bide, &c.

11 Then she became a gay grey mare,
    And stood in yonder slack,
And he became a gilt saddle,
    And sat upon her back.
        Was she wae, he held her sae,
    And still he bade her bide;
        The rusty smith her leman was,
    For a' her muckle pride.

12 Then she became a het girdle,
    And he became a cake,

And a' the ways she turnd hersell,
    The blacksmith was her make.
        Was she wae, &c.

13 She turnd hersell into a ship,
    To sail out ower the flood;
He ea'ed a nail intill her tail,
    And syne the ship she stood.
        Was she wae, &c.

14 Then she became a silken plaid,
    And stretchd upon a bed,
And he became a green covering,
    And gaind her maidenhead.
        Was she wae, &c.

Variants upon this playful Scottish ballad have been recorded through-out Europe, attesting to its popularity, and it is in many ways an exemplum of the form. There is a clear third-person narrative which is introduced without preamble, the avoidance of 'what is usually called poetic diction' in favour of demotic speech, and the use of repetition, not just in choruses, but in figuring the magical battle of wits through incremental repetition with variation in the verses ('Then she became' … 'And he became'). Notice, however, that with few exceptions, the stanzas are not cross-rhymed but instead follow an a-b-c-b pattern, placing the greatest emphasis at the end of the second and fourth line rather than on every one. Note how the stress subtly changes in stanzas 6 and 7 which are cross-rhymed; indeed, a more self-consciously literary production would most likely have avoided the awkwardness of rhyming 'dow' with itself in stanza 7.

THE **lady stands** in her **bower door**,
As **straight** as **willow wand**;
The **black**smith **stood** a **little** fore**bye**,
Wi **ham**mer **in** his **hand**.

As may be seen, the disposition of unstressed syllables is irregular around the rhythmic beats of the stressed syllables, thereby fusing structural regu-larity with a variation in pace which reflects common speech and, in turn, creating a dynamic in the diction which holds the listener's interest as the story unfolds – something that is crucial on longer ballads.

Another feature, which is only apparent through comparative study with other ballads, is the use of common symbolic tropes. In the final stanza, for example, the smith becomes a 'green covering'. The line could be sung without any adjective – 'And **he** be**came** a **cover**ing' – yet the addition speeds the pace of the last half of the line, thus emphasizing the rapidity of motion, whilst at the same time not only adding colour but also placing emphasis upon it: 'And **he** be**came** a **green** cover**ing**'. Green is traditionally the colour of youth and vigour: in 'Tam Lin'[2] the heroine must lose either her maidenhead of her green kirtle, and chooses the former; her fruitful vigour remains. Likewise, the eponymous protagonist of 'Clerk Colvill'[3] takes the maiden by her 'grass-green sleeve' and lays her 'down upon the green'. The more one reads, the more one notices instances of this and other stock images which offer a shorthand commentary on the narrative to those familiar with the form's conventions.

The six-line ballad

A more literary variation on the form is the six-line ballad, which doubles the tetrameter in order to form rhyming couplets followed by trimeters in an a-a-b-c-c-b pattern. An early example of the form is Sir John Suckling's seventeenth-century *Ballad upon a Wedding* which begins:

I **tell** thee, **Dick**, where **I** have **been**,	A
Where **I** the **rare**st **things** have **seen**,	A
Oh, **things** be**yond** com**pare**!	B
Such **sights** a**gain** cannot be **found**	C
In **any place** on **English ground**,	C
Be **it** at **wake** or **fair**.	B

This parody of the epithalamium – the celebration of a wedding – makes use of the popular ballad form in order to satirize the lower-class nuptials which the poem describes. Notice how a steady iambic line is used in place of the dynamic play of stressed and unstressed syllables we saw in *The Twa Magicians*. The additional tetrameters also alter the rhythm, emphasizing the end of each line of the couplets and, particularly, the trimeters, which – coupled with the strong masculine endings common to the ballad – create emphatic pauses every three lines. We may, then, see this as an exaggerated form of the common ballad which, in this example, creates a jogtrot rhythm which is employed by Suckling to heighten the comic effect of the poem.

Exercise one

Write a ten-stanza ballad. A good starting point is a story we all know, but one that offers scope for narrative development; a nursery rhyme is ideal. Let's take, for example, *Little Boy Blue*, which could be rendered thus:

The **sheep's** in the **mead**ow, the **cow's** in the **corn**,
The **work**ing **day** is **through**,

The **lab**ourers **gath**er **back** at the **farm**,
Ex**cept** for **Little** Boy **Blue**.

We can see here the strong, regular rhythm coupled with the irregular use of unstressed syllables. The language is simple and direct, without any self-consciously 'poetic' diction. Note, too, the use of pararhyme for the tetrameters which, whilst strictly following an a-b-c-b pattern, nods towards cross-rhyme.

In establishing the scene based on the nursery rhyme, the stanza opens up a number of possibilities for the fate of the missing Little Boy Blue. Many broadside ballads offer sensational accounts of tragedies or murders – see, for instance, *The Twa Sisters*[4] or *Lord Randal*[5] – so perhaps Little Boy Blue could have been murdered. On the other hand, the nursery rhyme merely has him asleep. As we have seen in *The Twa Magicians*, seduction is also a common ballad theme, so he could be sleeping in the arms of the farmer's daughter (who, of course, could be wearing a green dress!).

In either developing your own work from the stanza above or starting with a nursery rhyme of your own choice, keep in mind the ballad trope of repetition with variation which we saw in *The Twa Magicians*. You could, for example, mention Little Boy Blue in the last line of each stanza, in order to keep the ballad focused upon his absence. Of course, the name does not have to be at the end of the line; this would perhaps provide too much of a challenge to come up with suitable rhyme words for the first trimeter.

Exercise two

Another source for suitable ballad material is to be found in news items, which, sadly, never seem to run out of tragedies that may be retold. Fortunately, however, there are always lighter items with which to leaven the mix and these offer ideal subjects for humour which can be developed in the manner of Suckling's *Ballad upon a Wedding*.

Look in a newspaper and find a story which makes you smile and is suitable for an eight-stanza six-line ballad. Amidst the stories of sporting success and failure reported in the newspapers during the 2012 London Olympics, I spotted an account of a publicity stunt which left the Mayor of London stranded in mid air from a faulty zip wire with a Union Jack in each hand while those below worked out how to return him to earth – the very thing:

Come **one** come **all**, come **see** the **sight**,
That's **sure** to **fill** you **with** de**light**,
A **spect**acle so **fair**.
The **no**ble **Mayor**, so **proud** and **grand**,
With **Union Jack** in **either hand**,
Is **dangling** in the **air**.

Note the hyperbolic introduction which is exaggerated through the tetra-metric couplets and how the strong rhythmic emphasis upon 'fair' makes the promise of the spectacle the core of the first half of the stanza. By the same token, the bathos of the unexpected final line punctures the dignity expressed in the second couplet and highlights the ridiculousness of the situation.

As in the first exercise, in either developing this or writing from a news item of your choice, think about the effect of repetition and variation. In the example above, for instance, focusing upon the flags could build a comic dynamic which works on the tension between national pride and personal embarrassment as different plans are tried in order to rescue the stranded Mayor. Be as imaginative and ridiculous in your narrative as you like – here a passing circus troupe could build a human pyramid, a party of Mexicans could mistake him for a piñata – but maintain a serious tone in order to provide a foil for the humour.

Bibliography

Child, Francis J. (1882–1898) *The English and Scottish Popular Ballads* (Boston: Houghton, Mifflin and Company)

Suckling, Sir John (1892) *The Poems, Plays and Other Remains of Sir John Suckling*, ed. William Carew (London: Reeves and Turner)

Wordsworth, William and Coleridge, Samuel Taylor (1800) *Lyrical Ballads*, 2nd edn (London: T.N. Longman and O. Rees)

5
Sestinas

Barbara Smith

History

The word *sestina* is believed to derive from the word *sesto*, meaning sixth in Italian. As a form, it emerged from a group of twelfth-century poets, the troubadours, in Provence, France. Particularly associated with Arnaut Daniel, the complex form was the signature form of a master troubadour.

Troubadours (in all probability from *trobar* – to invent or compose verse) were court poets. They sang, accompanied by *joglars* or jobbing minstrels, for French nobles at their courts. Thematically, the trouba- dours' poems were highly wrought lyrical poems, dealing with courtly love, and often about or respectfully addressed to the wife of their par- ticular patron. Well-written troubadour poems became popular as they were disseminated from court to court and troubadour to joglar and back again, enhancing reputation and standing for composer and patron alike.[1] Troubadours competed with one another to produce witty, sensa- tional poems.

Arnaut Daniel is credited with the development of the sestina form as we might know it now. His poetry was typically described as 'close' or 'obscure' (*trobar clus*), because of unfamiliar expressions and enigmatic allu- sions, unusual meters and rhymes. This made his work more complex than his contemporaries. The form then found its way to Italy, being taken up by Dante and Petrarch who kept the idea of courtly love and held Arnaut Daniel to be the best of the Provençal troubadours. Dante and Petrarch admired the way that Daniel's work suited form to subject, favoured intri- cacy over simplicity in expression and created subtlety in the effects of the overall complexity. Both writers absorbed this complex form into their own work. Daniel is often mentioned by Dante in his treatise *De Vulgari Eloquentia* and Petrarch named Daniel as the 'great master of love' in his *Trionfo d'Amore*.

As with the sonnet, so the sestina found its way into English poetry. There are examples by Elizabethan poets: Edmund Spenser, 'Ye wastefull woodes bear witness of my woe', part of *The Shepheardes Calender*, and Philip Sidney's 'Ye Goat-herd Gods', a double sestina. The Victorian poet Algernon Charles Swinburne used the form for 'The Complaint of Lisa' (also a double sestina), and a later example from this time period is Rudyard Kipling's 'Sestina of the Tramp-Royal', which uses vernacular English.

The sestina form

The form a sestina traditionally takes is of six stanzas with a particular rhyme scheme followed by a three-line *envoi* or *tornado* at the end. The 39 lines themselves may be of any length, although traditionally in English these sestinas have been iambic pentameters. However, modern poets often choose to use varying line lengths to add variety and texture. You choose six end-words (also known as *teleutons*). These don't need to rhyme with each other but rather the words must be used over and over in a particular pattern, creating an interlinking sense and sound to the overall poem. Initially the sestina can seem daunting, more like a complex knitting chart for an Aran jumper to be deciphered, rather than a form to experiment with, but don't let this deter: good planning and persistence will enable experimentation. The sestina provokes the writer into writing to suit the end-words: being confined by form very often takes a sestina into realms that might not have been considered without the form's constraints.

In the scheme presented below, the letters represent the stanza and the numbers show how the rhyming scheme should be followed. For example, the end-word from the last line (line 6) of stanza A should be at the end of the first line of stanza B. For clarity, you should number the end-words from each line of the first stanza and use them as your overall guide for the entire poem.

Stanza A	1, 2, 3, 4, 5, 6
Stanza B	6, 1, 5, 2, 4, 3
Stanza C	3, 6, 4, 1, 2, 5
Stanza D	5, 3, 6, 2, 1, 4
Stanza E	4, 5, 1, 3, 6, 2
Stanza F	2, 4, 6, 5, 3, 1
Envoi G	5, 3, 1 or 1, 3, 5 (and variants, see below)

The observant will have noticed that once used to the form, it is just as easy to use 6,1,5,2,4,3 from the second stanza on, but perhaps to begin with the sestina should follow the pattern outlined above.

The best way to understand the sestina form is to take one and transcribe the pattern beside it to see how it works:

Sestina

To F. H.

'Fra tutti il primo Arnaldo Daniello
Gran maestro d'amor.' – Petrarch.

In fair Provence, the land of lute and **rose**,	1
Arnaut, great master of the lore of **love**,	2
First wrought sestines to win his lady's **heart**,	3
For she was deaf when simpler staves he **sang**,	4
And for her sake he broke the bonds of **rhyme**,	5
And in this subtler measure hid his **woe**.	6
'Harsh be my lines,' cried Arnaut, 'harsh the **woe**	6
My lady, that enthorn'd and cruel **rose**,	1
Inflicts on him that made her live in **rhyme**!'	5
But through the meter spake the voice of **Love**,	2
And like a wild-wood nightingale he **sang**	4
Who thought in crabbed lays to ease his **heart**.	3
It is not told if her untoward **heart**	3
Was melted by her poet's lyric **woe**,	6
Or if in vain so amorously he **sang**;	4
Perchance through cloud of dark conceits he **rose**	1
To nobler heights of philosophic **song**,	2 *
And crowned his later years with sterner **rhyme**.	5
This thing alone we know: the triple **rhyme**	5
Of him who bared his vast and passionate **heart**	3
To all the crossing flames of hate and **love**,	2
Wears in the midst of all its storm of **woe**,—	6
As some loud morn of March may bear a **rose**,—	1
The impress of a song that Arnaut **sang**.	4
'Smith of his mother-tongue,' the Frenchman **sang**	4
Of Lancelot and of Galahad, the **rhyme**	5
That beat so bloodlike at its core of **rose**,	1
It stirred the sweet Francesca's gentle **heart**	3
To take that kiss that brought her so much **woe**	6
And sealed in fire her martyrdom of **love**.	2

And Dante, full of her immortal **love**,   2
Stayed his drear song, and softly, fondly **sang**   4
As though his voice broke with that weight of **woe**;   6
And to this day we think of Arnaut's **rhyme**   5
Whenever pity at the labouring **heart**   3
On fair Francesca's memory drops the **rose**.   1

Ah! sovereign **Love**, forgive this weaker **rhyme**!   2, 5
The men of old who **sang** were great at **heart**,   4, 3
Yet have we too known **woe**, and worn thy **rose**.   6, 1

Sir Edmund Gosse (1849–1928)

For the most part, Gosse follows the scheme (*with that exception in the third stanza, likely done for the sake of sense) and the expected layout in the envoi. In choosing this poem as an example, it can be seen that it is a homage to the Provençal troubadour tradition of the twelfth century, as well as the Italian poets who took the form forward. The subject is that of courtly love and the tradition of poets writing about courtly love. This sestina honours those who have come before in that tradition. Gosse refers to Arnaut Daniel throughout the poem as well as quoting Petrarch's own homage to Daniel in the epigram. He also links the tradition to Dante, neatly squaring tradition and modernity for the Elizabethan ear. The meter throughout is iambic pentameter (discussed further in Chapter 13).

Study of more recent sestinas shows how this tricksy form can lend itself to some very playful results. Modern poets such as John Ashbery and Elizabeth Bishop took the sestina and put it to work in the modern idiom. Particularly worth reading are Bishop's *Sestina* and Ashbery's *Farm Implements and Rutabagas in a Landscape*, both of which are widely anthologized and readily available online.

As Ezra Pound noted in *The Spirit of Romance*, the sestina can be like 'a thin sheet of flame folding and infolding upon itself'. Bishop's *Sestina* utilizes exactly that circularity to present the claustrophobic atmosphere of a grandmother, a small child and the cast of objects in the house – what particularly draws attention in this example is the end-word 'tears'. Bishop's use of regular meter in this poem also sets an easy conversational tone. Conversely, John Ashbery's *Farm Implements and Rutabagas in a Landscape* uses the characters from *Popeye*, a popular American cartoon from the early to mid twentieth century, giving a surreal, choking feeling to the narrative proceedings, with a great round-up of his end-words (particularly 'scratched') in the final envoi. Also effective is his use of 'spinach' as a repeating end-word, which in the original cartoons conferred 'superpowers' on Popeye when he consumed it.

Moving forward in time, Jonah Winter has a most amusing version: *Sestina: Bob*, which undercuts the whole form by taking the word 'bob' as the sole end-word for each line of the entire poem. A more recent example is that of Christine Webb, *Seven Weeks*, the Poetry London 2007 competition winner, which uses the trope of moving backwards through time across seven weeks to a bereavement, as well as five seemingly ordinary end-words – sheets, breath, garden, finished and wind – to carry the poem's sense of grief and loss.[2] In this case, using the circularity of form helps the poem to govern a highly emotive subject to great effect.

Other examples of the sestina show its versatility and the ambition of poets who have used the form. As mentioned above, Algernon Charles Swinburne's 'The Complaint of Lisa' uses a double sestina, using 12 end-words, each stanza being double the normal length, as too is the envoi. Swinburne even goes as far as rhyming his end-words, making the job even more difficult. The contemporary poet Marie Ponsot is credited with developing the *tritina* (from 'three') form which uses three recurring words, and an example of this is 'Living Room', with three stanzas and a one-line envoi. One last example of innovation is 'The Shrinking Lonesome Sestina' by Miller Williams, where the lines in each subsequent stanza shrink in length until the penultimate stanza simply uses the end-words: 'Time / goes / too / fast. / Come / home' – an example of a careful choice of end-words and formidable planning indeed.

Some considerations when composing a sestina might be:

- Consider using homographs as end-words, or words that double as nouns and verbs – for example row, as in to fight or as in to use oars, or rose, as used by Gosse in the example above, to mean flower and also the past tense of rise.
- You might try altering end-words using slant-rhymes to add variety and flexibility.
- Choose your end-words carefully, as they set the tone for the entire sestina. Try not to let the form dictate the poem, but rather the words. Either use ordinary words or extraordinary words. Remember, govern the form rather than let the form govern you.
- Try writing the envoi before the main sestina. This can give you a chance to establish the sestina's tone. Notable examples include Elizabeth Bishop's 'Sestina', or Miller Williams' 'Shrinking Lonesome Sestina'.
- Alternatively, you could drop the envoi altogether, as Donald Justice does in 'The Metamorphosis'.

Exercise

Take either a subject you know well outside the realm of poetry or perhaps one you would like to know well. Choose something that has unusual vocabulary, say, for example, cooking or rock climbing. Brainstorm a short-list of ten concrete nouns and active verbs associated with this activity: stew, simmer, braise; or rappel, crampon, scale, and so on. From your lists choose the six that appeal the most. Dive in and write the first stanza or write the envoi as suggested above. Either way, once you have a first stanza written, work out the pattern in which the end-words will sit for the subsequent stanzas. Once the pattern is established, see where you can go with the chosen words.

Bibliography

Pound, Ezra (1910) *The Spirit of Romance: An Attempt to Define Somewhat the Charm of Pre-Renaissance Literature of Latin Europe* (London: J. M. Dent & Sons)

Smythe, Barbara (2000) *Trobador Poets: Selections from the Poems of Eight Trobadors* (Cambridge, Ontario: Old Occitan Series) www.yorku.ca/inpar/trobador_smythe.pdf, accessed 30th June 2014

Webb, Christine (Autumn 2007) 'Seven Weeks', *Poetry London*, Issue 58, www.poetrylondon.co.uk/magazines/58/poem/seven-weeks, accessed 30th June 2014

6
The Ode

Tony Williams

What is it?

The ode is an ancient form of lyric poetry originally used for celebration. Its roots are classical: *ode* derives from the Greek *ōdē*, meaning 'song', and the Greek ode was performed simultaneously with music and dance. The Latin ode developed a distinct identity and these two classical forms provide the basis of the modern ode, which extends far beyond these origins. Typically the ode is elaborately or showily formal, elevated in tone and addressed to a person or object. It is a poem 'about' something, rather than a dramatic or expressive piece.

The Greek or Pindaric ode, associated with the poet Pindar, was a highly public form performed by a chorus with dancers and used to praise or celebrate athletes. The elaborate structure consists of three parts: the *strophe*, *antistrophe* and *epode*. The strophe introduces a subject, the antistrophe develops it and the epode provides a conclusion. Metrically the strophe is a complex stanza with lines of varying lengths; the antistrophe repeats this stanza, but the epode uses some different stanza form. The set of three stanzas may then be repeated. There are very few true Pindaric odes in English; the term comes to be used of any elaborately formal ode divided into stanzas, even where the strophic structure is not used.

In Latin the Horatian ode, associated with Horace, is more meditative and private in demeanour. The poem often concerns itself with the pleasures and tribulations of private life, as opposed to the Pindaric ode's interest in public deeds. The subject may still be addressed directly, but the tone is less expansive and the form, too, is simpler. The same stanza shape is used throughout: usually a number of longer lines followed by a number of shorter ones.

Horace's regular stanzas represent an example of the homostrophic ode, that is, a poem in which each stanza has the same metrical and/or rhyming structure. Several of John Keats' famous odes (such as 'Ode on Melancholy' and 'Ode to a Nightingale') display the elaborate formality of the Pindaric ode in the homostrophic structure of the Horatian tradition.

The development of the classical ode into increasingly irregular and cross-fertilized forms reaches its latest stage with contemporary poets who may not use regular formal patterns of stanzas at all, but who continue to write poems which are recognizably odes because of their overt ceremoniousness, high register and choice of subject. By being 'about' a particular item, by addressing or celebrating it they invoke the history of the form. Antony Rowland's 'Pie' is an excellent example.

How does it work?

Whatever its form, an ode has a particular topic; it is 'about' someone or something. It may be addressed directly *to* the object (as in Keats' 'Ode to a Nightingale') or it may simply concern itself with describing and meditating on it (as in his 'Ode on Melancholy'). In any case, the idea of address is important: the ode is a performance, a more or less public utterance pretending to get to the truth of things.

Odes have been used to address an astonishing variety of subjects. Keats wrote odes on autumn, a Grecian urn and the nightingale; Shelley to the west wind. Robert Lowell wrote an ode on 'The Quaker Graveyard in Nantucket'; Kit Wright on 'Didcot Power Station'; and Bernadette Mayer wrote an 'Ode on Periods'. I have written odes to Tuesdays, garden sheds and urban dereliction. The very formality and ceremony of this traditional form gives the poet licence; odes are not 'realistic' or 'objective' truth-telling, but performances to savour.

The celebratory tone of the early odes may or may not be present in later examples; the tone may be ambiguous, and many great odes use irony or a range of different views and ideas in order to build up a complex picture of their subject. And, while an ode tends to keep its focus steadily on its subject, it also uses this as an occasion to speak of wider cultural, social or philosophical concerns.

Horatian Ode

1. Regular stanzas (the same structure repeated in each stanza – so the Horatian ode is *homostrophic*).
2. Usually a pattern of long lines followed by short lines (for example, two lines of iambic tetrameter followed by two lines of iambic trimeter).
3. Often metrically regular, though it may not be.
4. Often uses end-rhyme, though it may not.
5. Usually adopts a meditative or reflective tone.

6. Usually concerned with, or addressed to, a single subject which it celebrates or interrogates.

An Horatian Ode upon Cromwell's Return from Ireland

The forward youth that would **appear**	A
Must now forsake his Muses **dear,**	A
Nor in the shadows **sing**	B
His numbers **languishing.**	B

'Tis time to leave the books in dust,
And oil the unused armour's rust,
   Removing from the wall
   The corslet of the hall.

So restless Cromwell could not cease
In the inglorious arts of peace,
   But through adventurous war
   Urgèd his active star:

And like the three-fork'd lightning, first
Breaking the clouds where it was nurst,
   Did thorough his own side
   His fiery way divide:

For 'tis all one to courage high,
The emulous, or enemy;
   And with such, to enclose
   Is more than to oppose.

Then burning through the air he went
And palaces and temples rent;
   And Cæsar's head at last
   Did through his laurels blast.

'Tis madness to resist or blame
The face of angry Heaven's flame;
   And if we would speak true,
   Much to the man is due,

Who, from his private gardens, where
He lived reservèd and austere
   (As if his highest plot
   To plant the bergamot),

Could by industrious valour climb
To ruin the great work of time,
    And cast the Kingdoms old
    Into another mould;

Though Justice against Fate complain,
And plead the ancient rights in vain—
    But those do hold or break
    As men are strong or weak—

Nature, that hateth emptiness,
Allows of penetration less,
    And therefore must make room
    Where greater spirits come.

What field of all the civil war
Where his were not the deepest scar?
    And Hampton shows what part
    He had of wiser art;

Where, twining subtle fears with hope,
He wove a net of such a scope
    That Charles himself might chase
    To Caresbrooke's narrow case;

That thence the Royal actor borne
The tragic scaffold might adorn:
    While round the armèd bands
    Did clap their bloody hands.

He nothing common did or mean
Upon that memorable scene,
    But with his keener eye
    The axe's edge did try;

Nor call'd the gods, with vulgar spite,
To vindicate his helpless right;
    But bow'd his comely head
    Down, as upon a bed.

This was that memorable hour
Which first assured the forcèd power:
    So when they did design
    The Capitol's first line,

A Bleeding Head, where they begun,
Did fright the architects to run;
    And yet in that the State
    Foresaw its happy fate!

And now the Irish are ashamed
To see themselves in one year tamed:
    So much one man can do
    That does both act and know.

They can affirm his praises best,
And have, though overcome, confest
    How good he is, how just
    And fit for highest trust.

Nor yet grown stiffer with command,
But still in the republic's hand—
    How fit he is to sway
    That can so well obey!

He to the Commons' feet presents
A Kingdom for his first year's rents,
    And, what he may, forbears
    His fame, to make it theirs:

And has his sword and spoils ungirt
To lay them at the public's skirt.
    So when the falcon high
    Falls heavy from the sky,

She, having kill'd, no more doth search
But on the next green bough to perch;
    Where, when he first does lure,
    The falconer has her sure.

What may not then our Isle presume
While victory his crest does plume?
    What may not others fear,
    If thus he crowns each year?

As Cæsar he, ere long, to Gaul,
To Italy an Hannibal,
    And to all States not free
    Shall climacteric be.

The Pict no shelter now shall find
Within his particolour'd mind,
   But, from this valour, sad
   Shrink underneath the plaid;

Happy, if in the tufted brake
The English hunter him mistake,
   Nor lay his hounds in near
   The Caledonian deer.

But thou, the war's and fortune's son,
March indefatigably on;
   And for the last effect,
   Still keep the sword erect:

Besides the force it has to fright
The spirits of the shady night,
   The same arts that did gain
   A power, must it maintain.

Andrew Marvell

Marvell reproduces the Horatian stanza form with two lines of iambic tetrameter followed by two of iambic trimeter, rhymed AABB. The result is a highly dynamic form which constantly renews its momentum: the reader's ear keeps having to adjust its expectation of when the rhyme will arrive. This makes the poem reproduce aurally the intellectual complexity of the poem: Marvell's sense, and his attitude to the poem's subject, is continually shifting. The two pairs of lines do function as couplets: in most stanzas, lines 1 and 2 express a distinct thought and then lines 3 and 4 express another thought which builds on the first one while remaining distinct from it:

The forward youth that would appear
Must now forsake his Muses dear,
   Nor in the shadows sing
   His numbers languishing.

The metrical tightness and the overt end-rhyme (a feature completely absent from Horace) combine to give the poem a feeling of cleverness which departs from the reflective, relaxed-seeming classical model.

The ode is addressed obliquely to Oliver Cromwell, a major figure in the Commonwealth republic of England following the English Civil War.

Cromwell led a brutal military campaign in Ireland, and Marvell's poem affects to celebrate his return to England and praise his actions and qualities as a soldier and statesman. However, Marvell's political sympathies were changeable and unclear, and in fact the poem is a masterpiece of irony, innuendo, ambiguity and satire. For example, in praising Cromwell's 'industrious valour' in overthrowing the monarchy, Marvell seems equally to be lamenting the fact that 'Justice' and 'ancient rights' mean nothing in the face of military and political power:

> Though Justice against Fate complain,
> And plead the ancient rights in vain—
>> But those do hold or break
>> As men are strong or weak.

Pindaric/homostrophic ode

1. Poems about, and often directly addressed to, a person or thing, either to celebrate them or to reflect on them.
2. Usually elevated in tone and formally ornate.
3. True Pindaric ode uses a three-stanza structure of strophe–antistrophe–epode, but these are extremely rare in English.
4. More often a Pindaric ode is one which uses irregular stanzas (each stanza uses a different structure of line length, rhyme and number of lines). A famous example is William Wordsworth's 'Ode on Intimations of Immortality from Recollections of Early Childhood'.
5. A homostrophic ode is one in which the same stanza structure is used throughout. Many Pindaric odes in English are homostrophic, for example John Keats' 'Ode to a Nightingale'.
6. Usually uses both regular meter and end-rhyme, often in complex ways, but the exact patterning varies from poem to poem.

Ode to a Nightingale

My heart aches, and a drowsy numbness pains	A
My sense, as though of hemlock I had drunk,	B
Or emptied some dull opiate to the drains	A
One minute past, and Lethe-wards had sunk:	B
'Tis not through envy of thy happy lot,	C
But being too happy in thine happiness,—	D
That thou, light-winged Dryad of the trees	E
In some melodious plot	C
Of beechen green, and shadows numberless,	D
Singest of summer in full-throated ease.	E

O, for a draught of vintage! that hath been
       Cool'd a long age in the deep-delved earth,
Tasting of Flora and the country green,
       Dance, and Provençal song, and sunburnt mirth!
O for a beaker full of the warm South,
       Full of the true, the blushful Hippocrene,
              With beaded bubbles winking at the brim,
                     And purple-stained mouth;
       That I might drink, and leave the world unseen,
              And with thee fade away into the forest dim:

Fade far away, dissolve, and quite forget
       What thou among the leaves hast never known,
The weariness, the fever, and the fret
       Here, where men sit and hear each other groan;
Where palsy shakes a few, sad, last gray hairs,
       Where youth grows pale, and spectre-thin, and dies;
              Where but to think is to be full of sorrow
                     And leaden-eyed despairs,
       Where Beauty cannot keep her lustrous eyes,
              Or new Love pine at them beyond to-morrow.

Away! away! for I will fly to thee,
       Not charioted by Bacchus and his pards,
But on the viewless wings of Poesy,
       Though the dull brain perplexes and retards:
Already with thee! tender is the night,
       And haply the Queen-Moon is on her throne,
              Cluster'd around by all her starry Fays;
                     But here there is no light,
       Save what from heaven is with the breezes blown
              Through verdurous glooms and winding mossy ways.

I cannot see what flowers are at my feet,
       Nor what soft incense hangs upon the boughs,
But, in embalmed darkness, guess each sweet
       Wherewith the seasonable month endows
The grass, the thicket, and the fruit-tree wild;
       White hawthorn, and the pastoral eglantine;
              Fast fading violets cover'd up in leaves;
                     And mid-May's eldest child,
       The coming musk-rose, full of dewy wine,
              The murmurous haunt of flies on summer eves.

Darkling I listen; and, for many a time
    I have been half in love with easeful Death,
Call'd him soft names in many a mused rhyme,
    To take into the air my quiet breath;
        Now more than ever seems it rich to die,
To cease upon the midnight with no pain,
        While thou art pouring forth thy soul abroad
          In such an ecstasy!
Still wouldst thou sing, and I have ears in vain—
    To thy high requiem become a sod.

Thou wast not born for death, immortal Bird!
    No hungry generations tread thee down;
The voice I hear this passing night was heard
    In ancient days by emperor and clown:
Perhaps the self-same song that found a path
        Through the sad heart of Ruth, when, sick for home,
        She stood in tears amid the alien corn;
          The same that oft-times hath
Charm'd magic casements, opening on the foam
    Of perilous seas, in faery lands forlorn.

Forlorn! the very word is like a bell
    To toll me back from thee to my sole self!
Adieu! the fancy cannot cheat so well
    As she is fam'd to do, deceiving elf.
Adieu! adieu! thy plaintive anthem fades
        Past the near meadows, over the still stream,
        Up the hill-side; and now 'tis buried deep
          In the next valley-glades:
Was it a vision, or a waking dream?
    Fled is that music:—Do I wake or sleep?

John Keats

This ode is Pindaric in spirit, with a highly rhetorical register and a complex stanza form. It is homostrophic, since the same stanza form is repeated each time. Every line is iambic pentameter (allowing for some variations), except the eighth line of each stanza, which is iambic trimeter. The effect of this is to complicate and add interest to the rhythm; often enjambment is used to fuse this short line with the one before or after. For example, in the first stanza 'in some melodious plot of beechen green' forms a complete phrase, hurrying the reader's eye and ear over the line ending and the rhyme of 'plot' on 'lot'. This sort of tension between lines and syntax is extremely important.

The rhyme scheme is also complex: after the relatively stable ABAB of the first four lines, the stanza turns to a CDE pattern which it then repeats. Hence the distance between the rhymes changes between the beginning of the stanza and the end, and this is one reason why rhymes might surprise the ear even in such a formally constrained poem. More generally, end-rhyme represents only the most obvious form of sound patterning in the poem: internal rhyme and its variants knit together Keats' ode into a famously musical piece of language.

The poem is addressed, as the title suggests, to a nightingale; addressing a bird is just the sort of imaginative opportunity that the ode allows. But, as is typical with a great ode, though the bird and its song remains the central focus to which the poet continually returns, it also offers an opportunity for a more wide-ranging reflection on nature, death and poetry itself.

How can I use it?

Today few poets pursue the elaborate structure of a Pindaric ode or the regularity of a Horatian ode (although both represent excellent challenges which you would learn from). In contemporary writing the ode tends to lose its formal complexity, but it still represents an opportunity to address a specific subject, such as the humble pie, in detail and with an enjoyable theatricality.

Contemporary Ode

1. May or may not draw on traditional formal features of the ode.
2. Tone may be meditative, drawing on the Horatian tradition, or more elaborately formal and rhetorical, drawing on the Pindaric.
3. A common feature is the use of the poem to address or interrogate a specific item or subject, often shedding light on a wider topic by implication.
4. The ode represents an opportunity for contemporary poets to indulge in theatricality and ornateness, tendencies which may be otherwise difficult to accommodate in contemporary practice.

Pie

'Will you go to the pie-feast ?'
— Dodsley, 1550

Singing herb singe roast vapours Fray: Saturday
pie-floater in Rawson market; waxy peas island
gelatine-coated pink flush before comic stall.

Passionate friendship wanted with a Bentos,
good sense of meat to gravy ratio. Slim,
attractive suet looking for pudding love
with like-minded crust: no tin wasters;
Swiss-slapped pâté on the brawn of pigley
-pie, ridged with needle precision and oh,
so delicately browned at the knobs, bow-tie
at the centre hot-puddled, pie *de pundio*,
fayre buttys of Porke smyte with Vele welcome.
Mint-chopped sausage baguette found abandoned:
police are savouring bent *expenditum*
at Bolton Priory in pyis et pastellis. Pie-purrs
undercut by cholesterol scam: police support nut diet.
Sought in attractive wastes of Uppermill: chips just so,
clay-coloured dish Delia-thick in hot top-slick
— 'That's not a pie, it's boo-gloop with a bin lid' —
pastry chocked round oval but peels off faced with fork.
'Hote pies, hote! Goode gees and grys, Gowe dyne, Gowe!'
Bramble for afters? No, two would be spoiling us.
Policy wonks hit pies with fat tax, fatties
who puttis fast at their vly pyiss, headlines
Yorkshire chippies' favourite rag, *The Fryer*.
Finger buffet threat to national health:
Blair's babes weaned on focaccia and lamb's lettuce
forced into Mowbray tour of the bow-walled pie,
northern one-portion growlers and stand-pies
that stand-pipe Roberts's pie-house in Bradford:
Jerry bombs cobweb the glass but daily displays
defiantly steam. 'Every puff', puffed Priestley,
'was defying Hitler. Keep your pie level
to avoid ungelled gravy dribble incident.'
The Fryer pastes the government's attempt
to ration meat dripping — 'Animal fat
for the dominant race. Animal fat
for the dominant county within that race.'
Cold balls lovingly brisked with milk yolk: Sunday chow
brought family together not gristle niblets
in bad butchers' pork cast-offs. Bison pies
go missing in Salford posse mix up. Small shops'
warmers in sausage roll chaffage scandal:
police inspect gluten levels, mustard lovers,
cuckoo mayonnaise run off with sheer pie.

Antony Rowland

Formally speaking, few features of the classical odes may be evident: no strict meter is used, and no end-rhyme. But the poem's rich patterning of sounds and images, its celebratory tone and, above all, its insistent focus on a single subject, gradually accumulating into a poem which speaks of larger matters, mark it out as derived from the ode tradition.

The poem uses collage: unlike most odes, which discuss their subjects in a sustained argument, this poem simply accumulates phrases, images and ideas associated with the pie. The language often reproduces the abbreviated syntax of newspaper headlines and other media: 'Small shops'/ warmers in sausage roll chaffage scandal'. The lack of strict meter and full rhyme does not mean that formal features are absent; the single line 'clay-coloured dish Delia-thick in hot top-slick' uses alliteration, several types of rhyme and a noticeable rhythm, all showily. In its own way it is as formally elaborate a poem as any Pindaric.

The accumulation of details serve primarily as a celebration of the pie, but a range of historical and cultural connotations make the pie stand as a symbol for something larger: the poet's West Yorkshire regional identity. The survival of 'Roberts's pie-house in Bradford' through the Second World War connects cultural details such as cuisine with the wider values of the culture, and the juxtaposition of the beloved pork pie with a scornful reference to trendy 'focaccia and lamb's lettuce' stake a claim for rooted regional identity against the fashionable metropolis. The poem is a classic example of how the ode's focused light can illuminate a much larger area than its literal subject.

Bibliography

Keats, John (2005) 'Ode to a Nightingale' in *The Norton Anthology of Poetry*, 5th edn, eds Ferguson, Salter & Stallworthy (New York: W. W. Norton)

Marvell, Andrew (2005) 'An Horatian Ode Upon Cromwell's Return from Ireland' in *The Norton Anthology of Poetry*, 5th edn, eds Ferguson, Salter & Stallworthy (New York: W. W. Norton)

Rowland, Antony (2008) 'Pie' in *The Land of Green Ginger* (Cambridge: Salt)

7
Modern Syllabics

Claire Crowther

What is it?

In the twentieth century, English language poetry began to include poems which were syllabically measured but not otherwise metered. Every syllable in the line was counted and a pattern of syllable counts established. Previous to the twentieth century, poems with lines of a regular syllabic number were also metered.

Shaping a line simply by counting the number of syllables in it has been done through many centuries in a wide variety of poetic traditions – for example in Welsh, French and Japanese poetry. The syllable is the single respiratory event in the spoken material of a poem. It is sound-based, typically a consonant plus a vowel plus perhaps another consonant. But it can be as simple as 'O' and as convoluted as the word 'trench'. Many languages use syllable count in the poetic line because there are no stresses in the language. But English is a stressed language, so it developed meters, ways of measuring a line which use the common stresses that English words carry. But is modern syllabics a meter? Some critics say yes; others believe such a form is not measured at all because you do not hear the count of syllables. Those critics would call it free verse. But if measure is defined as a count of some kind, then syllabics must be seen as metered and at least there is more measure in a syllabic line or set of lines than in prose. In fact, if you use, for example, a regular 5-syllable line you will hear a 2-beat meter in the background, as poet A. E. Stallings has pointed out. Indeed, if you read enough 13-syllable lines you start to recognise them. But the rhythm of syllabics is, in a way, discounted and, says Timothy Steele, there being no pattern of accent is a principle of syllabic verse.

Syllabics simply insists that the line or stanza reminds the reader of its programmed nature. Many poets use it occasionally or even as part of their process. Thom Gunn said that his way of teaching himself to write free verse was to work with syllabics.

How does it work?

A great strength of modern syllabics is its variety and flexibility of form. A simple version has the same number of syllables on every line throughout the poem. The number chosen by the poet will dictate the personality of the poem. An even number, for example, will have more bounce and tend to sound metered. An odd number will jump and judder.

A development of this simple form is the stanza with varying line syllable counts matched in every stanza. Marianne Moore is famous for devising subtle and complex patterns of syllabically counted lines through her many-stanzaed poems. The following are the final three lines of the first and second (final) stanza of Moore's *No Swan So Fine*:

> as the chintz china one with fawn-
> brown eyes and toothed gold
> collar on to show whose bird it was
>
> ...
>
> it perches on the branching foam
> of polished sculptured
> flowers at ease and tall. The king is dead.

Note the pattern of the syllable count. Did you find that the final line can be counted as having either nine or ten syllables? That is because 'flowers' can be counted as either one or two syllables, a decision you will need to make occasionally in the syllabic poems you write. You need to consider the regional accent your narrating persona/voice is using and the impact on a reader of what they might see as a change in the pattern. In Moore's line, 'the king is dead' suggests that while art remains, power does not. 'Power' like 'flower' can be pronounced with one or two syllables.

Philip Levine's poem *Animals Are Passing From Our Lives* makes a feature of this device of syncope, pronouncing two syllables as one:

> In my dreams
> the snouts drool on the marble,
> suffering children, suffering flies,
>
> suffering the consumers
> who won't meet their steady eyes
> for fear they could see.

Note that the word 'suffering' must have two syllables in the first two instances, but three in the third to fit the regular seven-syllable line. Among the several effects of altering the syllable count of 'suffering' are the suggestions that the consumers are the heaviest weight for the condemned pig to bear and that the death of a pig is the death of an enslaved creature who, if it could speak, might sing of its suffering. Levine includes other syncopated words in this poem: 'ivory', 'discovering' so that the reader can feel squeezed, uncomfortably at times, by the voice of the noble pig. Levine's practice here of adjusting syllables was popular in past ages. Poets dropped syllables from the beginning of words (apheresis) or the end (apocope) in ways once thought beautiful but that now sound unacceptably poetic.

Some poems make simple and non-visual metaphoric use of syllable count. Sylvia Plath's poem, *Metaphors*, describes a pregnancy in nine lines of nine syllables each. Here are the first three lines:

I'm a riddle in nine syllables,
An elephant, a ponderous house,
A melon strolling on two tendrils.

Plath's last line refers to a 'train there's no getting off' but syllabics should not be thought of like that. The poets I have mentioned have felt able to break their syllable pattern when necessary. Basho, a famous Japanese poet, is quoted by Jane Hirshfield as saying that if a line of haiku has perfect syllable count yet sounds wrong, 'look at it hard'. But if the poet realizes more syllables will make the best sound, then they must break the syllable count.

Carrie Etter's poem *The Trapeze Artist's Dear John Letter* makes a syllabic pattern that reflects the content in a wholly contemporary way:

The Trapeze Artist's Dear John Letter

I recede like a vanishing point on my ribboned trapeze
and trust hamstring and calf's steady marriage
when I hang from my knees.

Physics can name the force that pushes the bar away again.
I'd call it *Fortune's wheel* or *Tantalus's fruit*,
but then I'm the company tragedienne –

all good trapeze artists are. I no sooner arrive than leave.
I love you, I'm quitting you. I live my life between
the two meanings of cleave.

The voice in the poem explains the way her life moves to and fro, from trapeze act to daily behaviour to love. The long 15-syllable bar of the first line in each stanza provides a hanger for the final two lines. The third line is short and makes the stanza look upside down. The last lines of the first and third stanza are almost one-third the number of syllables of the first line: 6 to 15. Close up, a body is large; far off it is small. As a trapeze artist creates a predictable rhythm in her work so the syllabic lines are predictable and safe. She is in control – syllabics are a very controlled medium. But she is about to spring into an apparently dangerous action; the audience does not know when she will do this.

But there are 'two meanings of cleave': to join and to cut away from or cut in half. The central line of each stanza is thus unpredictable or a rather subtle pattern: the first stanza's central line has ten syllables; the second stanza's central line has eleven and the third stanza has a central line of thirteen syllables. The gap between syllable count increases, in these lines, by doubling. Thus each stanza 'cleaves' its first line in half for its last line, yet shows a central line that dithers between the first and last lines, as if finding it hard to let go of the first line – 'cleaving' in the second sense. As the narrator says: 'I live my life between / the two meanings of cleave.' Syllabics here offers both a metaphoric and a structural dimension to this poem.

Did you notice that the syllabic structure of Etter's poem varies between odd and even syllabic measures? Marianne Moore pointed out that:

> when one follows a ten-syllable line with a nine syllable line, or any alteration of odd with even, the main pause comes in the middle of the line (not at the end); and the long pauses between stanzas come in the middle (of each stanza)... I do not try to make this kind of pattern, it is instinctive and usually I would prefer not to divide words at the end of the lines but am willing to for the sake of the larger and more inclusive symmetry.

The frequent use of apparently careless enjambment in syllabic poems is striking. But it contributes to a special effect. Moore's mid-line pausing and the common end-of-line running on make what Glyn Maxwell refers to as a breathless quality, typical of syllabic poetry.

How can I use it?

There are many ways of playing with syllabics. Poems can be devised in monosyllables. Syllable count can be increased or diminished from line to line. A set number of syllables per stanza can be spread through a poem. In that variant, each line could have a different syllable count and the poem would sound more like free verse.

There are some famous syllabic variants. The haiku, in recent English poetry, has had 17 syllables spread as 5-7-5 over three lines. The tanka has five lines with a 5-7-5-7-7 pattern. Adelaide Crapsey, at the beginning of the twentieth century, is credited with devising the cinquain, a five-line poem with a 2-4-6-8-2 syllable pattern.

Here is one of Crapsey's cinquains, written between 1911 and 1913:

Release

With swift
Great sweep of her
Magnificent arms my pain
Clanged back the doors that shut my soul
From life.

Haiku, tanka and cinquain are as well known for their shape on the page as for their syllabic pattern. Syllabic poems offer the possibility of a visual equivalent to a strong metrical experience for the reader. Marianne Moore and Dylan Thomas made good use of this potential. In Thomas's sequenced poem *Vision and Prayer*, the lines run from one to nine syllables, which contributes to the highly structured symbolism of the piece and shows either a diamond or a cross on the page. This is not easy to do. In a letter to his publisher, Thomas complained that the layout was all wrong: 'the lines are not spaced as they must be... Up to line nine, each line should be one exact space to the left of the preceding line, the line above it, & should then decrease space by space...' This sounds simple but is a nightmare for typesetters and you will find it challenging if you make a concrete poem using syllabics.

There are many reasons to choose syllabic form for your poem. Marianne Moore wanted to replace meter with a pattern less suggestive of the social establishment. Though meter is far less frequently used today there is something subversive about a form which is arguably invisible. You may want to employ the rich symbolism of number or shape for your poem. Most importantly, you can use syllabic form as one draft in the process of shaping and finishing a poem. It is a powerful sweep through, taking redundant syllables and whole words with it.

While it does not offer strong meter as a guide to meaning, as the iambic pentameter does for example, nor autonomy to the line as free verse does, the unstated order of syllabic poems soothes an era of philosophic change.

Bibliography

Crapsey, Adelaide (1922) *Verse* (New York: Alfred A. Knopf)
Etter, Carrie (2009) *The Tethers* (Bridgend: Seren)
Hirshfield, Jane (2007) *The Heart of Haiku* (Kindle edition)
Levine, Philip (1968) *Not This Pig* (Middletown, CT: Wesleyan University Press)

Maxwell, Glyn, 'Review of Thom Gunn's *Collected Poems*', *Times Literary Supplement*, 18 March 1994

Moore, Marianne (1982) *The Complete Poems of Marianne Moore* (London: Macmillan)

Moore, Marianne (1997) 'Letter to Marianne Craig Moore, May 5 1942', *Selected Letters*, ed. Bonnie Costello (London: Penguin)

Muldoon, Paul (2006) *The End of the Poem,* Oxford Lectures in Poetry (London: Faber & Faber)

Plath, Sylvia (1981) *Collected Poems*, ed. Ted Hughes (London: Faber & Faber)

Stallings, A. E. (2009) *Eratosphere* online discussion forum 19 March 2009 and 20 March 2009

Steele, Timothy (1999) *All the Fun's in How You Say a Thing* (Ohio: Ohio University Press)

Thomas, Dylan (1952) *Collected Poems* (London: J. M. Dent)

Thomas, Dylan (1987) *The Collected Letters*, ed. Paul Ferris (London: Paladin)

8
Blank Verse

Ros Barber

What is it?

Blank verse, sometimes confused with free verse, is a metrical form, being unrhymed iambic pentameter. It is flexible enough to lend itself to a number of uses, but has most commonly been employed in long narrative and epic poetry (when it is sometimes known as heroic verse), dramatic monologue and drama.

At the time *Hamlet* was written, blank verse was only around 60 years old. It can be dated to circa 1540, when it was first developed by Henry Howard, Earl of Surrey, who also – with Thomas Wyatt – was responsible for adapting an Italian form into the English (often called Shakespearean) sonnet. Howard, who was executed at the age of 30, translated two books of Virgil's *Aeneid* into unrhymed iambic pentameter, creating a form that has proved itself the only English corollary of Latin heroic verse.

The first blank verse play, *Gorboduc*, was written in 1561 by Thomas Sackville and Thomas Norton. It is monotonously end-stopped. It was Christopher Marlowe who wrote the first consistently successful blank verse dramas in the late 1580s and early 1590s, and his techniques were developed further by Shakespeare, who used increasingly more enjambment and feminine line endings, as well as variation within the line, to break up the meter's regularity.

Milton's *Paradise Lost* is written in blank verse; later exponents include Wordsworth, Shelley, Browning, Tennyson, Frost, Yeats and Wallace Stevens. Modern blank verse poets include Howard Nemerov, Richard Wilbur and Anthony Hecht. A comprehensive and very readable guide for further study is *Blank Verse: A Guide to Its History and Use* (2007) by Robert Burns Shaw.

How does it work?

Blank verse consists of five metrical 'feet'. A foot is a pattern of syllables, which may be stressed or unstressed. The six most common metrical feet are as follows:

- iamb: weak-STRONG

- trochee: STRONG-weak
- anapaest: weak-weak-STRONG
- dactyl: STRONG-weak-weak
- spondee: STRONG-STRONG
- pyrrhic: weak-weak

Four feet make a line of tetrameter, five is pentameter, six is hexameter and so on. For a line to qualify as iambic pentameter, the majority of the five feet must be iambs.

In natural human speech we stress some syllables more than others. Before we can use meter effectively, we must develop an ear for the way that words fall into stressed and unstressed syllables. In my experience, some students have difficulty determining how many syllables a word has, and indeed, this cannot always be agreed upon. *Actually*, for example, can be pronounced with either three or four syllables (act-chuh-lee / act-u-al-lee) and one of these will feel more natural to you. Neither is wrong, and only in analysing the contextual meter of the line will the poet's intended pronunciation become apparent. Though some students will easily hear the stresses in a line, others will have trouble determining which syllables are stressed and which are unstressed. As with most skills, the only remedy is practice.

Whether a syllable is stressed or unstressed is not fixed and will depend to some extent on its context and the words around it. *Happily*, when sounded on its own, falls naturally into a dactyl: HAP-uh-lee. (We often pronounce unstressed vowels as 'uh'.) When placed into an iambic line, however, we find the final syllable will take a stress:

I WENT/ to FIND/ my MIST/ress HAP/pilLY

Not all syllables, however, can take a stress. We would always pronounce the word *orphans* as ORphans, not orPHANs, and woe betide any poet who places that word in a metrical line such that a stress seems to fall on the second syllable. If we are not to throw our readers off the poetic horse, we must only place words within a stressed syllable pattern they can naturally bear.

We will also stress different syllables for emphasis and meaning. In speech:

i WANT to take you

(it's not duress) means something different from

i want to take YOU

(and not some other person) or

I want to take you

(don't go with Dave), or even

i want to TAKE you

(saucy).

Thus how we place a phrase into an iambic line (and how it throws stresses on to certain syllables) must be borne in mind if we are to communicate what we intend.

Iambic pentameter creates alternating stresses:

i WANT/ to TAKE/ you...

The next syllable would likely be stressed to continue the iambic pattern:

i WANT/ to TAKE/ you DANC/ing...

If the poet wished to throw the stress on 'you', creating a rather different emphasis, they must make it possible to read 'to take you' as an anapaest by following it with a weak syllable:

i WANT/ to take YOU/ to DANCE/...

But it is still possible to scan this phrase as:

I WANT/ to TAKE/ you to DANCE...

Thus other factors (in terms of context, meter or perhaps internal rhyme on the 'oo' sound) may be needed to ensure the reader understands where the stress was intended to fall. Heavy-handed, perhaps, but

I WANT/ to take YOU/ to DANCE/, and YOU/aLONE/

would do the trick. You will notice that the anapaest gives this line eleven syllables.

A line of blank verse, or indeed any line of iambic pentameter, need not have ten. And a ten-syllable line will not necessarily be a line of blank verse. Syllable counting is the most common error of those attempting to write iambic pentameter for the first time. The essence of a line of iambic pentameter is not how many syllables it has, but how many metrical feet.

A line of completely standard iambic pentameter has five iambic feet and can be scanned:

de-DUM / de-DUM / de-DUM / de-DUM / de-DUM

Clearly this has ten syllables. But if one were to write iambic pentameter sticking rigidly to iambs, the poetry would soon be in danger of becoming monotonous. Thus there is a degree of allowable variation, with a rule of thumb being that so long as the majority (that is, three out of five) of the feet are iambic, the verse will maintain the characteristics of iambic pentameter. Since iambs produce a 'rising' rhythm (as opposed to the 'falling' rhythm of trochees), the most common substitution is the anapaest, which has three syllables. An iambic line with the allowable variation of two anapaestic feet, therefore, has twelve syllables.

Another additional syllable can arise from what is called a feminine line ending. In a regular iambic line, the final syllable is strong; this is known as a masculine line ending. An additional unstressed syllable at the end of the line is known as a feminine line ending, and the extra syllable known as hypermetrical, that is, beyond the meter.[1] Thus a line of iambic pentameter may have as many as 13 syllables. A ten-syllable line, by contrast, even if it contains five stresses, will not qualify as a line of iambic pentameter unless it can be scanned into five metrical feet, at least three of which are iambs.

There are two other common variations in iambic pentameter. One is to reverse the first iamb into trochee. This is used most often in the first two feet of a line, to introduce a new idea or movement: 'THIS is/the THING'. The other variation worth mentioning is the pyrrhic–spondee combination, where the strong syllable of the first iamb is 'pushed' into the second foot: 'like a/BIG BOOT'.

For ease of reference, we will denote the allowable variations to the iambic line as follows:

A – anapaest (de-de-DUM) substitutes for an iamb
B – feminine line ending/hypermetrical syllable after the final iamb (de-DUM/de)
C – trochee–iamb pair (DUM-de/de-DUM)
D – pyrrhic–spondee pair (de-de/DUM-DUM)

As well as varying the line by these methods, the poet may choose to break up the regularity of blank verse by employing enjambment, so that a phrase runs over the end of a line into the next, rather than being end-stopped. Generally, you can read the amount of end-stopping by noting the quantity of end-of-line punctuation.

To explore the notion of allowable variation, as well as exploring the role of enjambment, let's take for illustration perhaps the most famous passage of blank verse ever written, Hamlet's famous soliloquy from Act III, Scene 1. Scanning the first line, we get:

To BE/ or NOT/ to BE,/ THAT is/ the QUEST/ion

In this 11-syllable line, three iambic feet are followed by variation C, a trochee–iamb pair. There is also a feminine line ending, resulting in a hypermetrical syllable. Someone not familiar with the conventions of blank verse might scan this line with the last two feet as a dactyl and a trochee:

> To BE/ or NOT/ to BE,/ THAT is the/ QUESTion/

but this is to misunderstand that the final weak syllable is considered to be outside the meter.

The next line begins with a trochee–iamb pair and ends with a hypermetrical syllable:

> WHEther/ tis NOB/ler IN/ the MIND/ to SUFF/er

The third is entirely regular apart from that feminine line ending:

> The SLINGS/and AR/rows OF/outRAG/eous FOR/tune

'Of' would not bear any stress in normal speech, but in an iambic line it will bear some; not as much, though, as the other strong stresses in the line. Line 4 demonstrates a pyrrhic–spondee pair before again ending with a hypermetrical syllable:

> Or to/ TAKE ARMS/ aGAINST/ a SEA/ of TROUB/les

The next line has an anapaestic substitution in the fourth foot:

> And BY/ opPOS/ing END/ them? To DIE,/ to SLEEP

It is the first line of the speech to have a masculine ending, but is it softened by enjambment? Punctuation makes a great deal of difference here. Though modern editors sometimes insert a comma or a dash here, making the line end-stopped, the Second Quarto (1605) and First Folio (1623) versions have no punctuation between this and the following line, meaning the phrase can be read through the end of the line – 'to sleep no more' – softening that masculine line ending. Note we have not yet had a ten-syllable line.

The next line

> No MORE/ and BY/ a SLEEP/ to SAY/ we END

is the first line of regular iambic pentameter, and the soliloquy now continues in a regular vein (with only one hypermetrical syllable) until the line

> Must GIVE/ us PAUSE./ THERE'S the/ reSPECT

There is a trochaic reversal in the third foot of this line, but there are only four feet. In other words this is a line of iambic tetrameter, rather than pentameter. Given the author's general facility with creating an iambic line, it can only be seen as an error.

How can I use it?

It is most important, if you are writing blank verse for the first time, to get a feel for the rhythm: this will help it come more naturally. So begin by reading a couple of pages of blank verse from any Shakespeare play you have handy (there are texts freely available online). Ideally, read them aloud in order to *hear* the rhythm. Then begin to write with your only objective being to continue that rhythm. The essence of it can be as prosaic as you like: you are not aiming for great poetry at this stage, only to write some lines that qualify as blank verse. They can be about what you did when you woke up this morning. When you have eight lines, stop.

Now scan your lines into metrical feet.

- Remember that a weak syllable at the end of a line is a hypermetrical syllable and is not to be counted within the meter.
- Ensure that you have five feet in every line (it is common to have less – we naturally fall into tetrameter – and sometimes more). Where a line has more or less than the required number of feet, do what is necessary to turn it into pentameter. If you add a foot and you can make it *not* seem like padding, so much the better.
- Ensure that at least three feet in every line are iambs.
- Mark any variations you have used as A, B, C or D.
- Notice how many of the eight lines are end-stopped and how many use enjambment.
- Now you should have a short piece of blank verse. Read it aloud and ensure that you have marked the stressed syllables correctly. Are stresses being thrown onto syllables that cannot bear a stress? Is it overly regular? Is it overly end-stopped? How natural does it sound?
- Try your hand at a short dramatic monologue – speak as a character from history, or a fictional character, telling their side of the story. Use the techniques above to ensure you are correctly maintaining blank verse, and use enjambment and allowable variation as appropriate.

Bibliography

Jerome, Judson (1980) *A Poet's Handbook* (Cincinnati, OH: Writer's Digest Books)

Shaw, Robert B. (2007) *Blank Verse: A Guide to Its History and Use* (Athens, OH: Ohio University Press)

9

Vers Libre/Free Verse

Todd Swift

What is it?

If you are from Canada or the United States and are reading this chapter, then you might almost wonder why it needs one of its own. Probably more than 95 per cent of contemporary North American poetry is written in what was once called 'free verse' – though the term is increasingly outdated and is often replaced with the broader 'open form'.

What is of interest to creative writing students and poets is the recognition that in other parts of the English-speaking world, such as Ireland and the UK, it is by no means certain that most poems are in free verse at all. This is because free verse has often been seen (incorrectly) as a foreign form, derived either from nineteenth-century French practitioners of *Vers Libre*, such as Rimbaud or Laforgue, or Americans such as Walt Whitman – somehow unnatural to the English poetic tradition. Many contemporary Irish and British poets enjoy writing in forms that tend to work better with some sort of rhyme or meter, and free verse needn't have those; it is almost like walking naked.

Free verse can be quickly traced back, at least in English, to the King James Bible translation, where, for instance, the psalms sound like this:

[1] Blessed *is* the man that walketh not in the counsel of the ungodly, nor standeth in the way of sinners, nor sitteth in the seat of the scornful.
[2] But his delight is in the law of the LORD; and in his law doth he meditate day and night.
[3] And he shall be like a tree planted by the rivers of water, that bringeth forth his fruit in his season; his leaf also shall not wither; and whatsoever he doeth shall prosper.
[4] The ungodly are not so: but are like the chaff which the wind driveth away.
[5] Therefore the ungodly shall not stand in the judgment, nor sinners in the congregation of the righteous.
[6] For the LORD knoweth the way of the righteous: but the way of the ungodly shall perish.

Free Verse is also used by eighteenth-century poets such as Christopher Smart who used the form in a manner that leads to it sometimes being called 'list poetry'. The part of his long poem *Jubilate Agno* that readers today tend to enjoy the most is the excerpt where he praises his cat, in touching and sensitive ways that sound very contemporary to most cat lovers:

> For I will consider my Cat Jeoffry.
> For he is the servant of the Living God duly and daily serving him.
> For at the first glance of the glory of God in the East he worships in his way.
> For this is done by wreathing his body seven times round with elegant quickness.
> For then he leaps up to catch the musk, which is the blessing of God upon his prayer.
> For he rolls upon prank to work it in.
> For having done duty and received blessing he begins to consider himself.
> For this he performs in ten degrees.
> For first he looks upon his forepaws to see if they are clean.
> For secondly he kicks up behind to clear away there.
> For thirdly he works it upon stretch with the forepaws extended.
> For fourthly he sharpens his paws by wood.
> For fifthly he washes himself.
> For sixthly he rolls upon wash.
> For seventhly he fleas himself, that he may not be interrupted upon the beat.
> For eighthly he rubs himself against a post.
> For ninthly he looks up for his instructions.
> For tenthly he goes in quest of food.
> For having consider'd God and himself he will consider his neighbour.
> For if he meets another cat he will kiss her in kindness.
> For when he takes his prey he plays with it to give it a chance.
> For one mouse in seven escapes by his dallying.
> For when his day's work is done his business more properly begins.
> For he keeps the Lord's watch in the night against the adversary.
> For he counteracts the powers of darkness by his electrical skin and glaring eyes.
> For he counteracts the Devil, who is death, by brisking about the life.
> For in his morning orisons he loves the sun and the sun loves him.
> For he is of the tribe of Tiger.
> For the Cherub Cat is a term of the Angel Tiger.
> For he has the subtlety and hissing of a serpent, which in goodness he suppresses.

For he will not do destruction, if he is well-fed, neither will he spit with-
out provocation.
For he purrs in thankfulness, when God tells him he's a good Cat.
For he is an instrument for the children to learn benevolence upon.
For every house is incomplete without him and a blessing is lacking in
the spirit.

This sort of poem can be described as a 'list poem' because it works by simple statement (and repetition).

Each of the lines offers one notable idea or image, more or less, and the
whole lends itself to repetition or some form of repeated start to the lines.
Free verse, then, looks and sounds a lot like prose, but also still has something of poetry to it. Most definitions in fact suggest that what free verse
loses is the metrical regularity, but retains the rhythm, of poetry. As such,
it seems more able to follow the flow of a thinking and reactive mind,
in terms of syntax and diction: that is, it can often sound more like how
people really talk, because most people don't speak in heavily accented
meter. To test this claim, however, may prove challenging, because when
one listens to actors performing Shakespeare's lines in iambic pentameter, a
common enough meter for poetry, it sounds very lifelike indeed (if a little
archaic).

This has more to do with actors naturalizing the lines, I think, than with
the meter itself – though some UK poets like to claim that the speaking
voice does fall into a meter on its own. Most American poets wouldn't think
so, and in fact, it was to escape the narrow limitations, as they heard them,
of meter that free verse was adopted by the time of the early twentieth century as the default mode for most poets across the pond. William Carlos
Williams even spoke of there being an 'American grain' for poetry, but even
anglophiles such as T. S. Eliot used free verse in much of his work, including
his most famous early (Laforguean-style) poem, 'The Love Song of J. Alfred
Prufrock', which remains one of the greatest free verse achievements.

Walt Whitman though is the American master of free verse, as can be
heard in this wonderful excerpt from 'Crossing Brooklyn Ferry':

The impalpable sustenance of me from all things at all hours of the
day,
The simple, compact, well-join'd scheme, myself disintegrated, every
one disintegrated, yet part of the scheme,
The similitudes of the past, and those of the future,
The glories strung like beads on my smallest sights and hearings, on the
walk in the street and the passage over the river,
The current rushing so swiftly and swimming with me far away,
The others that are to follow me, the ties between me and them,
The certainty of others, the life, love, sight, hearing of others.

Others will enter the gates of the ferry and cross from shore to shore,
Others will watch the run of the flood-tide,
Others will see the shipping of Manhattan north and west, and the heights of Brooklyn to the south and east,
Others will see the islands large and small;
Fifty years hence, others will see them as they cross, the sun half an hour high,
A hundred years hence, or ever so many hundred years hence, others will see them,
Will enjoy the sunset, the pouring-in of the flood-tide, the falling-back to the sea of the ebb-tide.

Immediately, we note the repetitions, the listing, such as Smart employed – which is a rhetorical, and oratorical, strategy derived from the Bible. Reading this, one can hear the way the poet's humanity – and desire to be one with his future readers and the common person – is usefully carried across by the flow of this manner. One of Britain's greatest mid-century poets, F. T. Prince, was influenced by both Milton and Whitman and often wrote in something akin to free verse.

How does it work?

Free verse poetry needn't be long, though, like parts of the Bible, or Whitman, or even Prince. Some of the earliest free verse poets were imagists, inspired by Ezra Pound to severely limit the scope of their poems, verbally and visually, to approximate the potent simplicity of a Chinese or Japanese character. Arguably the most famous free verse poem in English is only two lines long: 'In A Station of The Metro', by Pound, where he simply describes 'the faces in the crowd' as apparitions that look like 'petals' on a dark tree branch in the rain. The first line of this famous brief poem has 12 syllables; the second, 7. This is free verse at its purest, where the irregularity of the meter is replaced, instead, by a strong visual sense, which guides the meaning of the lines (each line is an instant, an image, one bit of information).

In the chapters in this book on lineation and prose poetry you will naturally encounter aspects of free verse. Free verse also lends itself to typographical experiment, for, once the line of a poem is not measured by a strictly regular beat, the unit of the line can be determined by other things instead: the breath, for example, or the unit of sense or image. The Russian poet Mayakovsky is an example of the more experimental aspects of free verse, as in this excerpt from his poem 'At The Top of my Voice' translated by Max Hayward and George Reavey:

My most respected
                    comrades of posterity!
Rummaging among
                    these days'
                              petrified crap,
exploring the twilight of our times,
you,
      possibly,
            will inquire about me too.

And, possibly, your scholars
                    will declare,
with their erudition overwhelming
                              a swarm of problems;
once there lived
            a certain champion of boiled water,
and inveterate enemy of raw water.

Professor,
      take off your bicycle glasses!
I myself will expound
                  those times

Other masters of free verse in the twentieth century would include H. D., Marianne Moore, D. H. Lawrence, David Jones, Langston Hughes, George Oppen, Charles Olson, Allen Ginsberg, Elizabeth Bishop and Sylvia Plath, and note that some of these poets also wrote metrical verse from time to time. Plath is an example of a poet who, cutting her teeth on meter, sought out the more ferocious and urgent, energized properties of free verse for some of her late, tragic poems of rage and suffering.

What can I use it for?

The key idea behind free verse – which famously is not 'free for the man [sic] who wants to do a good job', as Eliot said – is just that: freedom. It was a blast of liberating air, arguing for the poet to determine how and where and why words would appear on the page. As open form poetry – as developed by post-modern poets such as Charles Olson and Charles Bernstein – it takes on a variety of forms and looks and is constantly shifting according to various poets and their poetics.

As well as list poems, free verse can become letter poems or recipe poems or poems shaped to look like the subject of the poem (an altar, a cross, a candle, a swan, a heart, a gun). The lines and words can dash and

zip and trip across the page. The poet – or the language of the poem perhaps – gets to determine where the words will go. At times, free verse even
begins to look a lot like concrete poetry – at which point, you may have a
different topic on your hands.

Bibliography

Acheson, James and Romana Huk (1996) *Contemporary British Poetry: Essays
in Theory and Criticism* (Albany, NY: State University of New York Press)

Beach, Christopher (1947) *The Well Wrought Urn: Studies in the Structure of
Poetry* (New York: Harvest Book)

Beach, Christopher (1992) *A Poetics* (Cambridge, MA: Harvard University
Press)

Beach, Christopher (2003) *The Cambridge Introduction to Twentieth-Century
American Poetry* (Cambridge: Cambridge University Press)

Bernstein, Charles (2011) *Attack of the Difficult Poems* (Chicago: Chicago
University Press)

Brooks, Cleanth (1939) *Modern Poetry and the Tradition* (Chapel Hill, NC:
The University of North Carolina Press)

Dowson, Jane and Alice Entwistle (2005) *A History of Twentieth-Century
British Women's Poetry* (Cambridge: Cambridge University Press)

Forrest-Thompson, Veronica (1978) *Poetic Artifice: A Theory of Twentieth-
Century Poetry* (Manchester: Manchester University Press)

Fussell, Edwin (1973) *Lucifer in Harness: American Meter, Metaphor and
Diction* (Princeton, NJ: Princeton University Press)

10
The Prose Poem

Carrie Etter

History

While critics cite a number of possible antecedents for the prose poem in poetic prose, it first appears as a discrete form in 1842, with the publication of Aloysius Bertrand's *Gaspard de La Nuit* in France. Thirteen years later, Charles Baudelaire publishes his first prose poems, and in a later letter turned preface, he cites Bertrand's work as the source of his inspiration for the form, though Bertrand never used the term prose poem. Baudelaire's prose poems do not appear in book form until after his death, but nonetheless proceed to popularize the form in French, most famously with Stéphane Mallarmé and Arthur Rimbaud.

In the United States, Baudelaire's influence led to the occasional use of the prose poem by individual writers such as Gertrude Stein, but it does not appear more widely until employed by a handful of American writers in the 1950s and 1960s, including Robert Bly, Russell Edson and Allen Ginsberg. In Britain, as N. Santilli explains, after the appearance of 'the first identifiably prose poetic texts in England' in the Romantic era,

> From there the genre appears in somewhat bloodless imitations of Gallic imagism, fake scripture, or Ossianic gasps before Eliot finally scolds Richard Aldington in his 'Borderlines of Verse' for attempting an impossible genre and since then the prose poem has proved more of a pathological itch for some experimental writers.[1]

Thus from the 1960s to the new millennium, prose poetry in Britain was largely segregated to writers working outside of the mainstream. It appears another option for experiment alongside using the page as an open field, among other approaches. Such authors include Roy Fisher, Lee Harwood, Rupert M. Loydell, David Miller, Christopher Middleton, Geraldine Monk, Peter Reading and Peter Riley, among others. While a few of these poets later enjoyed a somewhat wider audience, there was little critical discussion or other apparent interest in the form as such.

Only in the twenty-first century has the prose poem begun to obtain a broader following in Britain. Important milestones in this development include, in 2005, the first publication of a prose poem collection by a mainstream press with Patricia Debney's *How to Be a Dragonfly* (Smith Doorstop); the 2007 Forward Prize shortlisting of Luke Kennard's *The Harbour Beyond the Movie*, whose third of three sections consists entirely of prose poems; and the 2011 publication of the first British-only prose poetry anthology, *This Line Is Not for Turning: An Anthology of Contemporary British Prose Poems* (edited by Jane Monson, Cinnamon Press). Prose poems have begun to appear more regularly in the full spectrum of poetry-publishing periodicals and individual collections, and workshops and seminars devoted to the form have become increasingly common.

Definition

While some poets and critics insist that we must resist defining prose poetry for it to retain its subversive, genre-blurring character, some basic distinctions seem crucial for its appreciation. While a lineated poem's development requires some sort of progression as it moves down the page, most reductively a movement from point A to point B, a prose poem develops without 'going' anywhere – it simply wants to inhabit or circle A. To see how the prose poem focuses on a single idea, consider Linda Black's 'Maze':

Maze

I've an etching, one of a series, loosely based on Pandora. A woman kneels on the earth, head in hands, above her in the sky a fine tangle; a knot of ribbons so interlocked it is impossible to unravel. Clearly, a pretty burden. In another she sits on a sofa, hands folded in her lap; lightning streaks across her face, a crevasse opening beside her. In yet another she is seated on a high stool, her long hair plaited and crossed at the ends like an open pair of scissors, across her thighs, a cat-o'-nine-tails. Beside her on the dressing table, perfume bottles, sharp and angled, a pair of evening gloves almost alive; in the mirror she faces, naught but a passing cloud.

Here, Black explores the myth of Pandora by juxtaposing three different contemporary representations of her. Each shows Pandora and her world under threat, but through varying images with their own implications. As the poem progresses, the evils Pandora has released become increasingly interior, from out of doors in the sky to a place that seems to bring together both inside and out with the sofa and the lightning and, finally, a menacing domestic space. The end does not come to a particular conclusion or resolution; rather, the poem as a whole inhabits or circles the idea of Pandora and her legacy.

If the prose poem takes narrative form, that narrative operates to represent or suggest a single idea or feeling; the story or plot is there *at the service of* an idea. Otherwise the piece is a form of narrative prose, such as a flash fiction or an anecdote, rather than a prose poem. To clarify this distinction between a narrative prose poem and a piece of narrative prose, read Antony Rudolf's 'Perfect Happiness'.

Perfect Happiness

I am ten years old. We have arrived at the house of my grandparents in Stoke Newington, 47 Manse Road, London N16, after driving here in our little Standard car from our own house, 41 Middleway, London NW11. I run upstairs and kiss my grandparents, Josef Rudolf and Fanny Rudolf. As usual, my grandfather is wearing his suit. His watch is in the waistcoat pocket, at the end of a chain. My grandmother is dressed in black. She is large, not like my other grandmother. I smell chicken soup. I go downstairs and wander around the house. The house is tall and narrow. My grandfather works at home. He deals in second-hand clothes and army surplus. The ground floor is full of great coats and other items of men's clothing. The basement is full of comics, published by my Uncle Leon Rudolf. One of them is called *The Merrymaker*. I like looking at the advertisements: toby jugs, packets of assorted stamps, magic charms. I go outside and throw my tennis ball against a wall. Where I live there are no walls like that. Here there are even shops close by! My grandfather speaks in English with a funny accent. Sometimes he speaks Yiddish. He gives me sixpence. It is time to go home.

The poem begins with the announcement that the speaker is ten years old and has just arrived at his grandparents' house; he goes on to relate his activities over the course of the day: wander about, look at comics, throw a tennis ball against a wall, and so on. The poem's momentum derives from this succession of events. The point of the poem, however, is not the story so much as the way these simple events add up, either in retrospect and/or as they are experienced, to an overall sense of 'Perfect Happiness', to that single idea or feeling. That quality distinguishes the poem from anecdote or flash fiction.[2]

Composing prose poetry

One of the best ways to accustom yourself to the prose poem in all its variety is to read widely in the form, beginning with either Monson's *This Line*

Is Not for Turning or the excellent *No Boundaries: Prose Poems by 24 American Poets*, edited by Ray Gonzalez (Tupelo Press, 2003).

Here are two exercises to try:

Exercise one: the object prose poem

Choose an object and try to imagine its existence in a description that either does not anthropomorphize the object at all or that fully indulges in ascribing human qualities to it. For example, in one response to this exercise, a student portrayed a kettle's heating to a boil as though it were a person reaching orgasm. Alternatively, another described a kitchen table in such close physical detail that for some sentences the object was unclear, and once its identity was realised, the description appeared the more original for that unexpected revelation. In *This Line Is Not for Turning*, some examples of object prose poems include Linda Black's 'E J Arnold & Co, Stock No 201194', which begins with a precise description of a note-book and then imagines the woman who writes in it influenced in her composition by those characteristics; Lucy Hamilton's 'A Road in Berlin', detailing all the rich activity the speaker has seen in that place; and Jean Long describing the slow decline of some helium balloons in 'Balloons'. Sometimes it helps to 'overwrite' in response to this prompt, writing as much about the object as you can think of and then cutting back to the strongest passages and revising to connect them.

Exercise two: the single feeling prose poem

Regarding Rudolf's 'Perfect Happiness' as a model, choose a specific feeling – ennui, fear, excitement – for your title and then compose a narrative that demonstrates it. It need not come from your own experience; indeed, this exercise can prove more successful with a fictionalized account. In my prose poem, 'Melancholia', in *This Line Is Not for Turning*, I invented the story of a stranger's increasingly long speeches at a bus stop as a way to evoke a species of urban exhaustion, where one is as tired of other people as physically fatigued.

After you have drafted your response to one of these exercises, use the following points to guide your revision:

1. A shorter length generally helps prose poems to be more cohesive. Until you become comfortable with the form (and perhaps thereaf-ter), strive to keep your prose poems to a single typed page of one to three paragraphs.

2. Ask yourself how well the poem is focused on a single idea, removing any elements that appear tangential or irrelevant. The stricter you are about the poem's degree of focus, the more effective it is likely to be.
3. One can create fluency in prose by varying sentence type and length. If, when read aloud, your prose poem does not seem effortless, revise it to give greater variety to your sentence length and structure.

Bibliography

Gonzalez, Ray (ed.) (2003) *No Boundaries: Prose Poems by 24 American Poets* (North Adams: Tupelo Press)

Monson, Jane (ed.) (2011) *This Line Is Not for Turning: An Anthology of Contemporary British Prose Poems* (Blaenau Ffestiniog: Cinnamon Press)

Santilli, Nikki (2005) 'The Prose Poem in Great Britain', *Sentence: A Journal of Prose Poetics* 3

11
Taking Form: Experimental and Avant-Garde Forms

Robert Sheppard

What was free verse? What is an experimental form?

Traditional forms work by making the form of the final poem (its unique formation) a variation of the ideal form. Think of the sonnet frame and then of the form of any sonnet; it differs from it, while demonstrating it at the same time. Free verse and Olson's Projective Verse were reactions against that.[1] The form of the free verse poem develops as it is formed, the better to register the mind's thought or the body's movement, it is often said. It may be improvised or carefully constructed, but in both cases (and in combinations of them, of course) the line – whether short or long, visually scattered or in paragraph blocks – becomes the unit of the poem. For a long time, free verse remained the most radical technique in the toolkit of the formally inventive poet and it certainly hasn't been rejected as a look at Harriet Tarlo's anthology *The Ground Aslant* will show.[2] Indeed, despite its thematic focus upon rural landscape, even a flick through its pages will demonstrate the vitality and variation of visual forms in page space, to use a more accurate way of phrasing these things. In this chapter I make reference to available books, anthologies and online works, which I hope you will follow up from the bibliography.

The critic Derek Attridge says readers – and what is a writer but a reader who writes? – must apprehend 'the eventness of the literary work, which means that form needs to be understood verbally – as "taking form" of "forming", or even "loosing form",' and I intend to trace this eventness through techniques and clusters of techniques (even 'schools' of writing) which either ignore, re-form or attempt to supersede both the traditional and the free verse understandings of form.[3]

Concrete poetry

What is it?

Concrete poetry, both in its forms as *sound* poetry, which uses the sounds of words, part-words and even non-words in performance by one of more voices – sometimes with musical accompaniment or electronic manipulation – and *visual* poetry, which uses the shapes of words, part-words and even non-words in visual configurations or constellations, has been around since radical modernism (and enjoyed a resurgence in the 1960s). Look at Bob Cobbing's anthology *Verbi Visi Voco*.[4] While sound and shape are elevated over meaning this does not imply that fragmented forms do not have meanings of their own. The conceptualist Kenneth Goldsmith has recently opined that the Internet has only now – with its flexible visual displays and its audio files – provided concrete poetry with its perfect medium, which is why there is a resurgence of interest in this work.[5] While I think technology has indeed made this work accessible, I think recent generations of young people, because of TV, advertising and the increasingly interactive new technologies, *think visually* and are open to manipulating page and screen (and possibly sound files).[6] If we look back to 1960s concrete poetry, British poet Bob Cobbing is exemplary because he practised both visual and sound poetry, for *both* eye and ear, as his title 'Sonic Icons' anagrammatically confirms. Cobbing could 'write' a text in the morning, print it as a booklet in the afternoon (which in some cases was another stage of 'writing', perhaps involving moving the original while photocopying it) and perform it (often with other voices or musicians) in the evening, and attempt to sell the booklet from his own small press to the audience. His earliest work *ABC in Sound* (republished in 2015) is the place to start, because as an alphabet book its structure is obvious and its play various, between the austere gothic grimness of 'G' with its play on words such as 'grin', 'grim' and 'gangrene', and 'T' with its hymn-like permutations of the non-words 'tan', 'tandita' and 'tanrata' in complex combinations.[7]

The website of the contemporary Norwegian-French-British writer and performer Caroline Bergvall (www.carolinebergvall.com) demonstrates some of the multi-media work being done in the wake of concrete poetry. Bergvall is a major practitioner (and theorist) of a mode of artistic production somewhat inaccurately called 'performance writing'. Performance, indeed collaboration with musicians and sound artists, is important to her, but so is operating in space, with installations and environments, peopled or not. This work, with its roots *in* language, is sometimes called 'off the page' writing, but this implies that printed text is merely a 'score', and Bergvall, as her website proves, has been most insistent that her work can be versioned as a printed booklet just as well as it can be transformed inside a gallery. (The word 'trans*form*' reminds us how forms are indeed open to metamorphosis.)

How can I use it?

Read Bob Cobbing's *ABC in Sound* or listen to it on the CD *The Spoken Word: Bob Cobbing* or online.[8] Design your own sound poem by working with alphabetical alliteration.

Look at Caroline Bergvall's website and consider ways to make your work *transform* between media, presentation style and environment. Perhaps your work works better on the page. If so, why?

Oulipo

What is it?

An increasingly influential group of experimenters is the French Oulipo.[9] The French name stands for the Workshop of Potential Literature, the word 'potential' signifying that they devise forms which may be actualized in a number of ways. At the heart of their practice is a distinction between forms that are conventions and those that are constraints. A convention is a form that has been bequeathed by tradition; the sonnet is a very good example – and it is one that this group has been interested in using and misusing.

How does it work?

A constraint is a rule that is self-invented and is then tested. Their famous N+7 technique instructs users to take an existing text and sub-stitute every noun (N) with the seventh subsequent one in the diction-ary. So Shakespeare's 'My mistress' eyes are nothing like the sun' becomes 'My misventure's eye-openers are nothing like the sundries,' which has the virtue of being, like a lot of N+7s, suggestively comic. Another of the Oulipeans' contentions is that the best source-texts make the best results. At the very least, it is important to carefully select your origi-nal. Built into the constraint is often the notion of the 'clinamen' (or swerve), something that will throw an absurd spanner into the works of the mechanical process. In the case of N+7 the clinamen derives from the fact that different dictionaries yield different results. N+7 is one exam-ple of what I call versioning, which involves taking an existing text and transforming it in a predetermined way or ways. The American Harry Mathews, in his 'Trial Impressions', takes a song by John Dowland and transforms it 29 times: for example, he attempts a 'double' N+7 (all the lines versioned twice from two dictionaries); a Chinese version in haiku-like brevity; and a simple 'up to date' which replaces Dowland's doleful Jacobean love lyric with modern (and rude) ejaculations! He transforms it into a sonnet, a sestina and squeezes it through the cadences of the King James Bible. There is a bravura palindrome (a text that reads the same backwards and forwards) and many others.[10] The British poet Philip Terry has done something similar, not with one text repeatedly, but with most of Shakespeare's sonnets, which he even appropriates as his title.[11] On one occasion he 'subtracts' a sonnet to a minimum numbers of words; on another, he rewrites the poem through anagrams. His 'up to date' consists of the use of newspapers, *The Sun* and *The Times*, not because they are both owned by Rupert Murdoch, but because 'sun' and 'time' are suggestive motifs in Shakespeare's poems. It's another constraint, but a productive one.

One mustn't lose sight of *potentiality* at the heart of these processes. Raymond Queneau's famous *A Hundred Billion Sonnets* operates like a child's head-body-legs book, except that it's cut 14 times and across 10 pages. The effect of the cuts is that what originally might be read as simply 10 sonnets become texts of so many possible combinations that it would take the reader over 300 years to read them out loud! (The clinamen in this case is somewhat existential, I think you'll agree.) The forms invented can be as complex as this, or as simple as Metro Poems, whose rule is simply to think between tube (or train or bus) stops and write one line only during each stop. (The clinamen is that if the train ever stops between stations you have to decide what to do!) The implicit invitation of Oulipo's existing techniques (listed well in books and websites) is to make up your own constraints and then experiment with them. This is what the Oulipo do: they meet monthly to discuss new techniques; being French they do it over dinner and fine wines.

How can I use it?

Try one of the Oulipo techniques described above or in any of the sources listed in this chapter. Oulipo has its own French website at www.oulipo.net but another site has English versions of Queneau's sonnets.[12]

Try to invent your own constraints and clinamen. Ask yourself why a constraint might *need* a clinamen.

Try to 'version' another text, like Mathews and Terry.

The sonnet is a favoured form for the Oulipeans but also for recent British, American and Australian formally investigative poets. Look at the sonnet forms in Jeff Hilson's anthology *The Reality Street Book of Sonnets*,[13] compare them to those described in this book and adapt your own free verse or experimental versions of them. Use it as a textbook of innovative sonnet forms.

Conceptual writing

What is it?

The most recent avant-garde is 'conceptual writing'. Kenneth Goldsmith, the most flamboyant member of this grouping, calls it 'uncreative writing' (the title of his critical poetics) and is involved in the teaching of these forms, which are antagonistic to the emphasis upon good form, pattern, meaning and convention in straight 'creative writing', with its supposed emphasis upon originality and craft.[14] These don't matter to Goldsmith: instead of asking his students to write a story in the *style* of Jack Kerouac, he asks them to write out (word for word) a Kerouac piece and lets them describe the effects of the process (from cramp in the hand to noticing certain patterns in the text). Obligingly, one British writer has blogged the book page by page, but Goldsmith's prime exemplar is his own *Day*, a 700-page writing out of an edition of the *New York Times*, with no images and no change of type-size for headlines or adverts. The result *feels* like a weighty masterpiece and is weirdly fascinating in parts as well as deeply and deliberately boring in others (pages of stock exchange statistics).[15] In its mechanical way, it's like Joyce's *Ulysses*, a panoramic presentation of one day, minus the genius of the writing. (You need to decide if that last part bothers you and, if so, how much it bothers you.)

How does it work?

Goldsmith says the reader doesn't have to read his books (this isn't true as I hope my description above suggests) but it's his way of emphasizing how conceptual writing works. The concept is often more important than the result. This means it must be a good one. Your readership is a 'think-ership', admiring your conceptual acuity, your conceptual forms rather than your literary skills (although I think the forms are often fascinating). The ultimate in appropriative text is to take somebody else's and sign it as yours. Plagiarism and plundertextualities underwrite many of these experiments. However, the irony for me is how quickly conceptual writing has taken hold of the avant-garde imagination and then infiltrated the mainstream – Goldsmith has read at the White House and wowed the audience with his rendition of appropriated traffic news broadcasts – and how rapidly forms of uncreative writing have become exercises in creative writing.

How can I use it?

Dwoskin and Goldsmith's *Against Expression: An Anthology of Conceptual Writing* operates like a textbook for new writers and its formal experiments include rewriting texts (last night's TV or the Bible) from memory; taking the first page/sentence/word of one text and joining it to the first of another and so on; taking a text and re-arranging all the sentences (or the words, or even all the letters) alphabetically or through some other arbitrary formal principle; listing every book/possession/trademark you own or see; recording every word you (or somebody else) utters for a set period of time; and amassing every document about you (official and private) to compose a re-formed self-portrait (using any or some of the techniques listed here).[16]

You should carry out the task(s) as mechanically as possible. Try any of these ideas listed above (or others in *Against Expression*, on Goldsmith's Ubuweb website or the ones I list in my 'How to Produce Conceptual Writing'.[17] Work out a clear *concept* and achievable *procedure*. Theoretically, absolute repetition of somebody else's work or technique is quite in order, though perhaps you will discover something new about language and form. What is it? Is boredom the new interest? If you think of a concept but cannot then be bothered to actualize it, is that a failure on your part? Or have you become post-conceptual?

Language poetry and poet's prose

What are they?

The American language poets of the 1980s were – and still are – theorists of how the investigation of language (which they take on dubious trust is an instrument that doesn't merely describe but constructs the world and its ideological structures) is the primary responsibility of the poet. But they were also great formal experimenters who invented new forms for these investigations.

I want to focus on two prose forms that are often found in a form of writing called 'poet's prose' by writers and critics who find the old term 'prose poetry' too poetic for the kinds of prose that can change register sentence by sentence. A specific term, 'the new sentence', is used by US poet Ron Silliman to describe the collaged prose many writers now produce.

The second technique is called 'writing-through' and is perhaps most associated with the prose pieces by Rosmarie Waldrop, which produced a kind of consistent meta-discourse or commentary on another text, famously Wittgenstein's philosophical writings (which are treated as though they are the one-sided utterances of a self-obsessed lover!).[18]

How do they work?

The New Sentence develops not by logic or narrative (or even by associative content or sound) but by the reader's propensity (Silliman calls it 'the parsimony principle') to want, to *need*, to make sense, to track the shortest distance between two sentences that are placed together. Silliman makes work by writing down observations and linguistic oddities and composes them into longer units as new sentences, but he uses numerical (sometimes alphabetic) orderings, most famously counting sentences in paragraphs using the Fibonacci number sequence in his *Tjanting*.[19]

The term writing-through is now used of any kind of sequential tracking through a text. I was doing it (with Superman frames, with sequences of photographs and other images, even with a whole novel) long before I knew it had a name or pedigree. Indeed, Waldrop calls the result a 'palim-text' and explains: 'Whether we are conscious of it or not, we always write on top of a palimpsest. Like many writers, I have foregrounded this awareness of the palimpsest as a method: using, trans-forming, "translating" parts of other works.'[20]

How can I use them?

Work your way through Charles Bernstein's online 'Experiments'. Bernstein's extension of Bernadette Mayer's famous 'experiments' list is a popular online resource for young formal experimentalists. Ranging from writing the worst poem you could think of to producing a homophonic translation (one that works with sound similarities rather than meanings) from a language you don't read or speak, from Google poetry to Flarf, there is much to explore here; the last (ninety-fourth) one runs: 'Make up more experiments', which expresses well the formal restlessness that drives innovative poetry.[21]

Attempt a new sentence work. Write or collect a lot of unrelated sentences (impressions, thoughts, found texts) and juxtapose them by chance (using a dice) or by a strict method (for example, the longest first) or by alphabetical or numerical ordering, like Silliman. Notice how the parsimony principle works to bring order to it.

Conversely, 'write-through' existing material (whether your own, such as diaries, or through graphic novels in a foreign language, or simply through your photograph collection spilt onto your floor or through a biography of a famous person), one sentence per unit (page, paragraph, frame or image). Notice how, far from being mere description, it becomes a text with its own energies – and forms.

You could explore David Miller's 2012 anthology *The Alchemist's Mind* for British and other poets who have been drawn to various prose forms. My own text 'The Given' is included, which is a writing-through of my diaries largely cataloguing all the things I couldn't remember on re-reading; it's an odd kind of autobiography.[22] Like me, you may take the forms described here, making your own constraints where you find them, losing form and finding form in the most unlikely of places.

Bibliography

Attridge, Derek (2004) *The Singularity of Literature* (London and New York: Routledge)

Bergvall, Caroline (2015) official website: www.carolinebergvall.com, accessed 11 June 2015

Bernstein, Charles (1996–2014) 'Experiments', http://writing.upenn.edu/bernstein/experiments.html, accessed 11 June 2015

Cobbing, Bob (1965) 'D, P and T' from *ABC in Sound*, at www.ubu.com/sound/cobbing.html, accessed 11 September 2012

Cobbing, Bob (2005) [1965] *ABC in Sound* (London: Veer)

Cobbing Bob (2007) British Library CD: *The Spoken Word: Bob Cobbing* (NSACD 42)

Cobbing, Bob (2012) 'Group Reading at The Other Room, Manchester' at http://vimeo.com/52068018, accessed 5 October 2014

Cobbing, Bob and Bill Griffiths (eds) (1992) *Verbi Visi Voco* (London: Writers Forum)

Dworkin, Craig and Kenneth Goldsmith (eds) (2011) *Against Expression: An Anthology of Conceptual Writing* (Evanston, IL: Northwestern University Press)

Goldsmith, Kenneth (2003) *Day* (Great Barrington, MA: The Figures)

Goldsmith, Kenneth (2011) *Uncreative Writing* (New York: Columbia University Press)

Joyce, James (1969) [1923] *Ulysses* (Harmondsworth: Penguin)

Hilson, Jeff (ed.) (2008) *The Reality Street Book of Sonnets* (Hastings: Reality Street)

Mathews, Harry (1992) *A Mid-Season Sky: Poems 1954–1991* (Manchester: Carcanet)

Miller, David (ed.) (2012) *The Alchemist's Mind: A Book of Narrative Prose by Poets* (Hastings: Reality Street)

Motte, W. F. Jnr. (ed.) (1986) *Oulipo: A Primer of Potential Literature* (Lincoln, NE: University of Nebraska Press)

Olson, Charles (2000) 'From "Projective Verse"', in Herbert, W. N. and Matthew Hollis (eds) *Strong Words: Modern Poets on Modern Poetry* (Tarset: Bloodaxe Books)

Oulipo official website (2015) www.oulipo.net, accessed 11 June 2015

Queneau, Raymond (2012) 'Hundred Billlion Sonnets', in English at www.bevrowe.info/Queneau/QueneauHome_v2.html; in the original French at www.growndodo.com/wordplay/oulipo/10%5E14sonnets.html, both accessed 11 September 2012

Perloff, Marjorie (1991) *Radical Artifice: Writing Poetry in the Age of Media* (Chicago: Chicago University Press)

Perloff, Marjorie (2010) *Unoriginal Genius: Poetry by Other Means in the New Century* (Chicago: Chicago University Press)

Rothenberg, Jerome and Pierre Joris (eds) (1998) *Poems for the Millennium: Volume Two* (Berkeley: University of California Press)

Sheppard, Robert (2012) 'The Given', in Miller (2012) *The Alchemist's Mind*, pp. 75–80

Sheppard, Robert (2015) 'How to Produce Conceptual Writing' at www. robertsheppard.blogspot.co.uk/2015/06/robert-sheppard-how-to-produce. html, accessed 14 June 2015

Silliman, Ron (2002) *Tjanting* (Cambridge: Salt Publishing)

Tarlo, Harriet (ed.) (2011) *The Ground Aslant: An Anthology of Radical Landscape Poetry* (Exeter: Shearsman Books)

Terry, Philip (2010) *Shakespeare's Sonnets* (Manchester: Carcanet)

Ubuweb official site (2015) www.ubu.com, accessed 11 June 2015

Waldrop, Rosmarie (2006) *Curves to the Apple* (New York: New Directions)

Waldrop, Keith and Rosmarie Waldrop (2002) *Ceci n'est pas Keith/Ceci n'est pas Rosmarie* (Providence, RI: Burning Deck)

12
Spatial Form

Mario Petrucci

Initializing questions

What is the meaning of poetic form? What is meant by 'meter'? Or 'iambic rhythm'?
What is concrete poetry? What do you understand by 'free verse'?
Are you able to plunder the poetry canon to find examples of each?

Free verse; *spatial form*

Whenever poets or critics discuss free verse they often imply (whether or not they actually mean to) some deep relaxation of form by the poet or suggest that there is little *apparent* form to be had. That is to say, they might seek form that is present in some subdued or 'organic' way. Free verse (or *vers libre*) is certainly a move away from traditional or conventional forms such as the sonnet or ballad. It suits many modern poets who prefer to explore rhythms and scansions that are more personal, more flexible. These poets, one supposes, wish to discover – poem by poem, line by line – forms that are appropriate to their voice and to the particular content of each statement.

I sometimes refer to free verse as 'using ragged lines'. It's my tongue-in-cheek way of making a more serious point about the dangers of free verse. For a start, free verse can get lazy. Anything goes. Form can be overlooked or given only cursory attention. Now, I'm not saying that poems can't 'splurge'. Some of the greatest poets have, in some sense or other, splurged. What I'm saying is that, actually, composing in free verse needs a sharp ear and an experienced eye. You don't have the scaffolding of an established form to climb up, so you have to have, instead, an incredible sense of linguistic balance and an acute sensitivity to the more subtle aspects of form, rhythm and the arrangement and length of lines.

Spatial form is one such aspect.[1] It's rarely given much thought in the study of poetry. I developed the idea because I believe the eye (as opposed to the ear) is far more interested in space than it is in meter or rhythm. Behind and beyond the sound of that inner voice we use when we read, our eyes are busy registering the shapes made by poems on the page – the promontories and vacancies of words, lines and stanzas. That's why our eyes can instantly tell apart (most) poems from (most) prose, without having to read a word of either. Usually, we can simply *see* (from the way it's laid out) whether something is a poem or a piece of prose.

Well, I think you probably knew that already! So, why all this fuss? What is so special about *spatial form*? One way to begin to answer that, is with a simple exercise. First, make a transparency of a poem on clear plastic or acetate. You can use a poem on the syllabus, but make sure it's one you've not yet read or studied. The exercise works better (and is more revealing) if you don't know what the poem is about. Now place the transparency on an overhead projector and quickly de-tune the focus; that is, blur the text slightly, so you can't quite read it. What you should see is a clear but unreadable shape (see Figures 1 and 2). (If you don't have access to an overhead projector, you can scan your chosen poem into your PC and then resize the image to suitably diminish its resolution, or just take an out-of-focus photo.)

In a sense, you are now looking at the poem's *spatial form*. It's astonishing just how much information can be carried by that shape. To see what I

Figure 1 'Shadow', in *Heavy Water: a poem for Chernobyl* by Mario Petrucci

Figure 2 'Couchette', in *Shrapnel and Sheets* by Mario Petrucci

mean, simply ask yourself how you react to it. Some students, for instance, point to a sense of uncertainty, or raggedness, in some poems. Others pick up on a 'martial' or obsessive quality, usually if there are ordered ranks of lines or stanzas. That last observation shows how *spatial form* and conventional form can be linked. It is probably true, for example, that most traditional sonnets will look rather similar when viewed on the overhead projector; many modern poems, however, will not. That's one reason, I believe, why *spatial form* is now important: because the way poets are arranging their poems on the page has become a complex (though key) aspect of what they want to say to us. Still unconvinced? Well, for the time it takes, why not give Exercise one a try?

Exercise one

Look at Figure 1. What is the blurred poem saying to you (if anything) through its shape? Whatever you do, don't read the poem until you've had a good chance to brainstorm and share impressions.

The blurring exercise described above might show up only one or two prominent or obvious visual cues in whatever text you've chosen to use (for example, a diptych poem or the presence of lines that are more or less even in length) but not being able to read the text can actually help us to weigh up the significance of these visual cues with a little more clarity.

One further thought here, regarding performance poems, is that poetry designed primarily for oral delivery can sometimes suffer a little on the page, perhaps because the author felt less need for the above visual cues. In some cases, these poems might lack (what one might term) spatial confidence. I should add that the visual and oral are, of course, linked in many ways and cannot be separated in the way my observations might imply; moreover, performance poems needn't be lacklustre on the page at all; but the problems of 'performance on the page', where these occur, may sometimes have something to do with the text (as a spatial entity) not having been orchestrated, or thought through, *visually*.

Shadow-development

Once you tune into *spatial form*, the discussions can get quite involved. Sometimes, students can detect an emotional or psychological development at work in a poem, simply through its changing shape. I call this the poem's 'shadow-development' (or *sub-textual shadow*). But don't worry (when you eventually do read the poem) if your thoughts on its *spatial form* or shadow-development took you in a very different direction from the poem's actual message. That's okay. It doesn't mean you've got it wrong. In fact, you might have spotted something interesting. What if, for instance, the poet is using the visual clues of *spatial form* (either consciously or unconsciously) to undermine the poem's content? Why might they do that?

Exercise two

First, repeat Exercise one using the unfocused poem in Figure 2. Now look at the way the shape of the poem evolves. Is there any 'shadow-development' in the poem? When you've discussed this fully, read the poem. Compare and contrast the shadow-development with the actual message of the poem.

Spatial form: the outs and ins

I hasten to add, these first two activities certainly don't define what *spatial form* is, nor do they exhaust all the ways you might talk about it. *Spatial form* is a new idea – I don't want to surround it in its cot with technical definitions or sets of things you have to search for so you can tick them off on a list. I'd much rather you experienced the poem's shape and then responded to it, both intellectually and intuitively. Decide for yourself what *spatial form* really means. I believe, though, you'll get the gist of it from the above activities, which should elicit at least some of the key elements. I hope, too, you'll discover that *spatial form* (however you choose to understand it) can sometimes communicate with the reader quite effectively.

Exercise three

In groups, study Figures 1 and 2. Make a list of characteristics you think are important to *spatial form*. For instance, the raggedness or regularity of the lines and stanzas; the thinness or fatness of the poem; the use of left or right justification, indents; and so on. In your opinion, is *spatial form* a useful idea?

I'm entirely happy if your answer to this exercise is a resounding 'no' – as long as you have your reasons. You might feel, for instance, that *spatial form* is a pretty blunt instrument for examining poems. Its characteristics aren't very well defined and the interpretation of those characteristics is rather subjective. There are obvious limits to how much it can tell us: insights are usually quite general and you might disagree over what those are anyway! There's a real danger of reading far too much into what is, after all, just a shape. So, why bother with it at all? I'll attempt to answer all that in a few different ways.

First of all, *spatial form* is just another tool. It is not meant to replace all the other ways of appreciating, studying or looking at poems. If it doesn't help, move on. But it might just give you a crucial, or unexpected, insight into the poem's intentions or structure.

Secondly, *spatial form* helps us to examine, closely, one of the poem's most mysterious and fascinating moments: that moment we turn the page *onto* a poem, and recognise it *as* a poem. At that instant, we haven't yet started to read. We haven't broached the poem's linear sequence of words. Our typewriter-carriage brain is not yet enabled. The poem hovers there, as an aggregation of geometrical lines and symbols set against white canvas. Before it can flare into comprehension, it must first present itself to us (albeit instantaneously) as a primal, patterned bulk on the chalky cave wall of the page. In fact, most poems (unlike the majority of prose) *are* mostly the blank of canvas or wall. This is the instant in which we see the poem as a whole – as a Gestalt. It is a crucial moment, because it can frame how we take the poem in. It's a bit like love or hate at first sight, or the way some people make a powerful first impression on us. It colours, for us, everything they subsequently do.

Thirdly, it's only part of the story to say that a page of poetry is – initially – usually taken in as a whole. In our eyes' hunt for meaning, there are also many local features of *spatial form*. One such feature is the visual impact of typeface. Some poems just look wrong in certain fonts. Then there's the visual texture created by the letters themselves. This can come to the fore in poems heavily structured by alliteration, assonance or some other sonority. For instance, look carefully at the lettering in Dylan Thomas's poem: 'Do Not Go Gentle Into That Good Night'. Can you see its typographic 'nap' – that is, those patterns in the letters, like the fibres in velvet or on a snooker table? What about that visual tension between the lines' long vowels and their terminating consonants? Line endings, as well, make a crucial local contribution to the spatial energy of a poem. True, they can signal a pause in the thought or where to take a breath. But they tell us much more than how our lungs should breathe the poem; line endings are also intimately concerned with how the eye 'breathes' it. There is, we know, a natural iambic heartbeat in speech and breath; but it's also worth considering (particularly in such a visual age as ours) that more erratic heartbeat of the scanning eye.

Finally, *spatial form* doesn't just switch off when we start reading a poem. Why should it? I believe it's like a ghost shaking its chains down the corridors of every line. And it's precisely where there isn't any obvious or conventional form (as in free verse) that *spatial form* can take over. Concrete poetry provides a good, though extreme, example of this. At its most banal, concrete poetry will make a poem about a fish – well – *look* like a fish; though, of course, it can be far more subtle and sophisticated than that. I only mention concrete poetry at all because it provides absolute proof that *spatial form* does exist, that it can add information to a poem. What I hope, however, is that the above activities have convinced you of a little more than that: namely, that *spatial form* is at work, at some level, in *all* poetry. Even where a poem is completely regular or visually uninteresting on the page, that still tells us something. Maybe it serves to calm us or encourages us to accept the poem as 'proper' literature; perhaps it helps to set up some kind of expectation or repetition or passivity in our minds. In any case – whether what we're reading is precisely metered or in free fall – the productive murk of *spatial form* will haunt us even as we delight in the poem's most brightly lit parts.

Based on a talk first delivered at the 'Words by the Water' Cumbrian Literature Festival, March 2004. Variations on this piece were published in Writers' Forum *(November 2004) and* Writing in Education *(issue 40, Winter 2006).*

Appendix 1: full texts for Figures 1 and 2

Shadow

She came. I just know she
  came. At nightfall I'd place

our boy's wet things under
   her pillow. Each morning

    they were dry and folded.
     I contrived once – to stay

      awake. Saw her slow shape
       cast by the moon. Saw it

        pass a shoulder-bone of wall.
        His cot. Those tiny fists

        shadow-boxing the dark.
        I called her – but had left

      the key in the door so
       she vanished. I can't be

    sure – even now – if that
     first small cry came from

the boy. Outside was all
moon and snow. And nothing

  to give him. Nothing. Just
my thumb to suckle.

From *Heavy Water: a poem for Chernobyl*, Mario Petrucci
(Enitharmon, 2004)

Couchette

Summer. Dreary Calais
left behind - and the day.
Through half-sleep crescents I see
print on white fluorescence: "Lyon".
Heat. Flesh merged with air I am

this entire cabin, the interminable sliding
of doors. Sweat. The thirst for merest breath
of cool. The window is my mirror. Hard
to swallow. Jolted through the dark
through the struck anvil of junctions
to eventual
sleep
to turn up
in morning green, among mountains
rearing up from the glass-blur. Alps. Whitefaced
chalets flash between limestone, sudden
tunnels channel an ache for light.
Then the gradual withering
of grass to embankment straw, and the home straight
that never comes. In the corridor
children squeal, drench their hair
with wind. I dangle promises
before myself: the orange glow
of evening; the airborne tang of citrus;
and a strange-tongued aunt ladling Latinate soup,
offering lemons
still warm from the sun.

From *Shrapnel and Sheets*, Mario Petrucci
(Headland, 1996)

Appendix 2: some alternative texts for study

I've used my own poems in the figures for copyright reasons. By all means substitute suitable poems of your own choice. Here are some productive alternatives for further study of *spatial form*, with a few observations:

- Sylvia Plath, 'The Fearful'. The hourglass shape (albeit sliced in half, Damien Hirst-style) reflects the shifts in emotional intensity through the poem.
- Philip Larkin, 'For Sidney Bechet'. After its pitter-patter heartbeat of near-regular tercets, the poem's closing couplet suggests something cut short.
- Ken Smith, 'Fox Running'. The line lengths in the opening stanzas generate a kind of spatial acceleration before adjusting themselves into a regular trot.

Bibliography

Larkin, Philip (1964) *The Whitsun Weddings* (London: Faber & Faber)
Petrucci, Mario (1996) *Shrapnel and Sheets* (West Kirby: Headland)
Petrucci, Mario (2004) *Heavy Water: a poem for Chernobyl* (London: Enitharmon)
Plath, Sylvia (1981) *Collected Poems* (London: Faber & Faber)
Smith, Ken (1982) *The Poet Reclining: Selected Poems 1962–1980* (Newcastle upon Tyne: Bloodaxe Books)

PART II: TROPE & DEVICE

13
Prosody

J. T. Welsch

What is it?

One frosty night, not too long after Christmas Day, 1066, with William on the throne and England duly conquered, the most typical Norman teenager you can imagine muttered a quick slew of choice Old French swear words and slipped out to meet her new heavier-tongued Anglo-Saxon friends. And the rest, as we English-speakers say, is history. In coming to terms with prosody and the rhythmical nature of anglophone poetry, it may help to bear in mind these two main forebears of our messy language. Even now, the combination of Germanic Anglo-Saxon (or Old English) and Old French sounds gives modern English its particular texture.

Anyone who has ever looked up a word in a dictionary and found one or more of its syllables marked with an accent or in bold knows that language has such a thing as *stresses*. It's the property that makes Americans say 'AD-dress' when they mean 'ad-DRESS'. Broadly speaking, every syllable in English is either stressed or unstressed. What you may not realize, however, is that the difference between stressed and unstressed syllables varies significantly between languages and that this variation has a profound effect on different poetic traditions. That's because poetry, by most definitions and for most of its history, has been a game of numbers. Beyond these traditions, whether or not you decide to construct your lines according to the number of stresses or syllables in their words, the fact of their existence remains. In that sense, *prosody*, or the occurrence of these rhythmic stresses in all language, can be understood as a physical phenomenon, rather than mere convention. And in terms of measuring that rhythm, you have three options: count every syllable, only stressed syllables or both.

These options bring us back to English's ancestors, and the effect of different levels of stress we see, even in their modern counterparts. Where German (to which Old English is more similar than it is to modern English) has a stronger stress, much of its poetry has been built by counting the stresses in a line, regardless of the number of unstressed syllables between these. It is, for this reason, a type of *accentual verse*. Even if you don't read

German, you need look no further than *Beowulf* or any number of nursery rhymes for examples. Modern French, on the other hand, has a lighter stress accent, or a subtler difference between stressed and unstressed syllables. As a result, French verses have more often been measured according to total syllable count, making it *syllabic verse*. Finally, as you might have guessed by now, our modern English has a bit of both parents, with a degree of stress accent somewhere between the two. Thus, we're left keeping track of both stresses and syllables in our *accentual-syllabic verse*.

How does it work?

I start with this slightly fanciful history because it helps broaden the scope beyond the definitions of 'meter' or 'iambic pentameter' you may have learned in school, emphasizing the rhythm intrinsic to all language. Whatever sort of poetry you like reading or writing, these beats are pulsing away in every line. So it will be in your best interest to learn to appreciate, analyse and maybe manipulate these little thumps. More than anything, that means *listening*. After all, stress is a surprisingly tough thing to define. In ancient Greek or Latin, where the notion of prosody originates, it was a case of longer versus shorter syllables. But in English, what makes a syllable stressed is partly volume – the latter syllable of *ad-DRESS* is a bit louder – but it is also partly to do with pitch, so that the stressed syllable is actually voiced ever-so-slightly higher than those around it. In this sense, you might think of all speech (including the speech in your head as you read this) as musical, following its own subtle rhythms and melodies.

Learning to hear stresses in meter isn't easy, but we are surrounded by opportunities to practice. I wouldn't advise it in situations where your well-being depends on the content, but next time a politician graces your television screen, or an actor or lecturer or any other professional speaker hits their stride, I give you permission to tune out a little. Let the content fade into the background, close your eyes if you have to and feel the material rhythm of their words. Tap your finger or toes as it bops along. Sometimes the beat will be fairly regular, as in 'The ON-ly THING we HAVE to FEAR is FEAR it-SELF'. More often, a bit of irregularity will be part of the line's power: 'TAKE your STINK-in' PAWS OFF me, you DAMN DIRT-y APE!'.

Normally, this effect goes unnoticed. We think it is the meaning of Roosevelt's line that reassures us or Charlton Heston's delivery that is so forceful. But the music of the words themselves is quietly working on our unconscious all the while, in either its steadiness or its syncopation. Becoming aware and then training your sensitivity to that rhythm is the first step in learning to evaluate and make use of it in poetry, where the play between content and form is everything. You may have had a vague sense of it already, perhaps feeling that a line would 'sound better' with a two-syllable word in the place of a monosyllabic one, but without being able to diagnose the specific problem. That's prosody. The word is sometimes used as a synonym for *meter*, but in the more general – and to my thinking, more useful – sense, the art of prosody is the art of rhythm.

Meter

I've been making my way rather circuitously towards the more technical aspects to do with meter because I hope this broader, more fundamental notion of prosody will prove relevant to a wider range of poetry. However, this more basic idea of rhythm also offers a less convention-bound approach to meter. If I repeat the definition of iambic pentameter in the factual way you may have heard or read a dozen times elsewhere – a line of ten syllables and five stresses, with every other syllable stressed – we can now ask whether there isn't something intrinsic about that pattern which makes it the most common metrical baseline in English verse. First though, we may want to remind ourselves what the name 'iambic pentameter' actually means. And this takes some backtracking.

This is the bit with the jargon. It is also the bit where I can't invoke anything but pig-headed, stuffy old tradition to explain why we're still using terms derived from Ancient Greek via Latin for what really aren't such complicated phenomena. I refer to the naming of the building blocks of meter commonly known as *feet*. And as any nineteenth-century schoolmaster could have told you, you'll do yourself a favour by simply memorizing them. The idea is that every line of poetry can be divided up into a number of these units or feet, usually made up of either two or three syllables. Because the individual syllables in those feet are either stressed or unstressed, there are a finite number of combinations for any given foot. With only the two options – stressed or unstressed – it is sort of like Morse code and even looks a bit like Morse code when notated above a line, with ´ marking stressed syllables and ˘ for unstressed. This notation, or the act of scanning metrical rhythm, is called *scansion*; and the names for the two-syllable feet are as follows:

iamb:	˘ ´	(unstressed, stressed)
trochee:	´ ˘	(stressed, unstressed)
pyrrhus:	˘ ˘	(unstressed, unstressed)
spondee:	´ ´	(stressed, stressed)

Those are the only four possible combinations for a two-syllable foot. And since most two-syllable words are made up of one stressed syllable and one unstressed syllable, the word itself will be either an **iamb** or a **trochee**. To use the example from before, for most British speakers, the word 'address' is pronounced as an iamb (ad-DRESS) and for most Americans, it is a trochee (AD-dress). Easy peasy.

For three-syllable feet, there are more possible combinations of stressed and unstressed syllables (eight, to be exact), but only three are commonly used:

anapaest:	˘ ˘ ´	(unstressed, unstressed, stressed)
dactyl:	´ ˘ ˘	(stressed, unstressed, unstressed)
amphibrach:	˘ ´ ˘	(unstressed, stressed, unstressed)

To finish with the terminology then, we see how the name iambic pentameter or, for instance, *dactylic hexameter* provides a very simple description of a poem's baseline meter. The first word tells us what the basic foot is and the second word tells us how many of them there are. Thus, monometer has one foot, dimeter two feet, then trimeter, tetrameter, pentameter, hexameter, and so on. And, therefore, iambic pentameter has five iambic feet – which is to say, as before, ten syllables, and five evenly placed stresses. It might help to think of the feet as something like musical bars, the way the phrase of longer and shorter words runs across them.

Exercise: iambic pentameter hunt

Find what sounds like a well-written excerpt from a newspaper article or a paragraph or two from a novel you admire – something with lush, meaty language. Now, 'scan it'. First, mark the stresses with ´ or another clear accent. Then mark the unstressed syllables between with ˘. You may need to retype the passage and print it double-spaced to give yourself room for the scansion marks – retyping or rewriting something is also a good way to listen to the rhythm more closely and slowly. Now, looking back over the scanned passage:

- How often does language fall into fairly regular iambs?
- Is there anywhere where the phrasing seems to fit into ten-syllable groups?

This isn't a Derren Brown guessing trick, and given the enormous variety of writing you might have chosen, I'm not willing to put any money or percentage on how much iambic pentameter you happen to find naturally occurring in the wild, as it were. But I assure you it is out there in abundance if you look for it. Learn to hear it, tap it out – that's why we have five fingers, right? – and you'll find it everywhere, even in, dare I say it, a lot of so-called 'free verse' (regardless of whether the poet has cheated and split it over a line break).

How can I use it?

The main lesson here is the notion of a baseline rhythm. There's something about iambic pentameter that feels quite natural in English. It must be partly to do with tradition, of course, and the sheer amount of Shakespeare and Milton with which our culture inundates itself. But that tradition also seems contingent on the balance of stressed versus unstressed in the English language. The ten-syllable or five-foot length seems to have something to do with its physical weight as well, where anything longer (for example, French alexandrines or the hexameter of ancient epics) proves unwieldy or seems to break in two in the ear. But the more important point about establishing a baseline rhythm – whether it is iambic pentameter, dactylic hexameter or amphibrachic tetrameter (all of which have fine examples in English verse) – is that once you establish the beat, you are free to deviate from it. That's one thing pure, unmetered free verse (if there is such a thing) can never offer: the groovy effects of metrical syncopation.

The corresponding notion is *substitution*. No one but an absolute pedant would write something that was *entirely* within a fixed meter. The whole point, as I've said, is variation. Go back to Shakespeare's sonnets or the blank verse (that is, unrhymed iambic pentameter) of his plays. How does Milton keep us riveted over the more than ten thousand lines of *Paradise Lost*? Partly by content, yes, and partly by his masterful use of enjambment and caesura, but also in no small part by his equally deft play with and against the basic iambic pentameter. It might not be obvious at first, but copy something out, use your scansion, divide up the iambs and see for yourself where a different kind of foot has been subbed. Then see how it is working with the content.

Because the art of prosody deals with such physical, non-literal characteristics of language, its mostly unconscious effects are hard to define. But that doesn't mean they are any less real. Sure, a vague rule of thumb is that unstressed syllables are quicker than stressed ones and that, as a result, pyrrhic substitutions speed things up, while spondees slow things down. But the ideal, whether the lines of your poems are in a regular meter or not (come on, have a go!) is, as Alexander Pope suggests, that 'The sound must seem an echo to the sense'. In Greek, and in another English definition, prosody refers to the relationship between words and music. As we've seen though, the music is already there, in the language itself, so you may as well learn to love it and see what it can do for you. Learn to hear its accompaniment and trust your ear to fine-tune it.

Exercise: mimetic meter

Write a short poem about something in motion – part of a landscape, an animal or even a piece of instrumental music. Pay special attention to the play of stressed and unstressed syllables as you write (and rewrite), seeing how you can make the rhythm imitate the things you describe. For an example, find the Pope line quoted above in his poem 'Essay on Criticism' and see what happens in the few lines that follow.

Bibliography

Fussell, Paul (1976) *Poetic Meter and Poetic Form,* rev. edn (New York: McGraw-Hill)

Milton, John (2003) *Paradise Lost* (London: Penguin Classics)

Pope, Alexander (2008) 'Essay on Criticism', in *Selected Poetry* (London: Oxford World Classics)

Sansom, Peter (1994) *Writing Poems* (Tarset: Bloodaxe Books)

Strand, Mark and Eavan Boland (2000) 'Meter', in *The Making of a Poem: A Norton Anthology of Poetic Forms* (London: Norton)

Turco, Lewis (2000) *The Book of Forms: A Handbook of Poetics,* 3rd edn (Hanover, NH: University Press of New England)

14
Rhyme

Angela Topping

Rhyme, the deployment of words with matching sounds, is a useful and popular device in poetry. So popular in fact, that there are people who feel that poems must rhyme. People who hold this view are invariably thinking of masculine end-rhymes in a set pattern. However, there is far more to rhyme than this. It is essential to experiment with different ways of making music with words to master your craft. Ruth Padel articulates a truth in *The Poem and the Journey*:[1]

> The poet's job is to get syllables to belong to each other so ear and mind are satisfied; so that readers, even if they don't understand at once, can trust the words and feel they belong together musically and emotionally, and feel that meaning will flower from their relationships.

Rhyme is one tool in the poet's grasp for accomplishing this task and those who take the trouble to learn skills beyond hammering masculine end-rhymes into place (although they do have their uses) can extend their work so that it rhymes in more subtle ways. The practice of making unnatural inversions to accommodate rhyme is a serious error made by proponents of rhyming at any cost. Poets such as Elizabeth Bishop, Robert Frost, Carol Ann Duffy and many others are examples of using the tool of rhyme effectively to delight the reader and build confidence in the music of the poem. However, as Geoffrey Hill stated in his second Oxford lecture as Professor of Poetry:

> The basic fact to be understood about this strange art, is that it is an art of invention. Rhyme stimulates one to invent even more wildly.[2]

So, sometimes, using a complex and tricky rhyme scheme can strengthen the poem and force the poet to seek ways of following the pattern while saying what is wanted. The imposition of rhyme can lead to exciting lexical choices and imagery.

A brief history of rhyme in English poetry

English poetry traditionally used alliteration rather than end-rhyme, for musicality and memorability. *Beowulf* and the Anglo-Saxon riddles make extensive use of alliterative patterns and rhythmic movement with a central caesura. Chaucer, however, wrote *The Canterbury Tales* in rhyming couplets, an innovative departure from the norm. This was made possible by the Norman invasion and the influence of French upon Anglo-Saxon. The effect of a Romance language colliding with a Germanic one was to round out the sounds, provide new suffixes such as 'ment' and make rhyming easier. Rhyme is a continental technique and is a strong tool in European forms such as sonnets, pantoums, ballades and villanelles. However, the great poem *Paradise Lost* by Milton is written entirely in blank verse, as is much of Shakespeare. Blank verse is close to English speech because of its iambic thrust. It is also highly flexible in terms of line breaks.

Types of rhyme

The skill of using rhyme can be divided into two different aspects. Firstly, there are different ways of forming rhymes. Secondly, there are different places a rhyme can occur within a poem, to minimize predictability, offer an element of surprise or allow the poet to place line breaks more flexibly. Free verse can often include rhymes which are not in a set pattern or which are formed by less restrictive methods.

Ways of creating a rhyme

The most common form of rhyme is the single syllable, full rhyme such as cat/bat/hat/gnat/sat. These are known as single or masculine rhymes. If there are two perfectly matching syllables, the rhyme is called double or feminine: getting/setting/wetting/betting. It is even possible to use triple rhymes, though it is easy to see that they lend themselves to comic or light verse: beadier/needier/speedier/greedier and so on, because they draw attention to themselves. A good example can be seen in a comic poem by Gwen Dunn, 'Flo, the White Duck', which ends with the couplet:

> Her ducklings dip and paddle
> And try to spraddle.[3]

The full feminine rhymes capture the awkward movements of the duck-lings as they try to copy their mother. Ogden Nash creates comic effect with skilful multisyllabic rhymes, for example:

> The local shops were all out of broccoli
> Loccoli

The way he deliberately changes the spelling of 'luckily' to emphasize the rhyme, adds to the wit of the epigram.

Sometimes feminine rhymes are useful to create a dying fall, an offbeat ending which can supply a sorrowful tone, a fading cadence. Feminine rhymes can also be half rhymes, where only the final syllable matches, as in this poem by Gwendolyn Brooks, about a lover going off to war:

> And he will be the one to stammer, 'Yes'
> Oh Mother, Mother, where is happiness?[4]

From full, perfect rhymes as discussed above, the natural progression is to half rhyme, sometimes called pararhyme, slant rhyme or imperfect rhyme. Not only are these more subtle, but English offers many more of them, so that the poet is less restricted. The reader hears the chime but it falls on the ear almost unnoticed by the conscious mind at first. For example, in Heaney's 'Blackberry Picking', some of the rhymes are half rhymes:

> We hoarded the fresh berries in the **byre**.
> But when the bath was filled we found a **fur**,
> A rat-grey fungus glutting on our **cache**.
> The juice was stinking too. Once off the **bush**
> The fruit fermented, the sweet flesh would turn **sour**.
> I always felt like crying. It wasn't **fair**

The half rhymes – byre/fur, cache/bush, sour/fair – are closely related musically, yet are not clanging full rhymes, which here, Heaney reserves for the final couplet (rot/knot) to give a sense of finality at the hopelessness of keeping blackberries fresh. Full rhymes can give a clinching force to a poem's ending, which is one of the reasons Shakespeare will often end a blank verse speech with a full rhyme. The Heaney example also shows how different types of rhyme can be blended, keeping the patterning fresh and flexible. Another type of half rhyme is apocopated rhyme, in which the penultimate syllable of a two-syllable word is rhymed with a monosyllabic word on the next line, for example wordless/bird, singing/ring.

Amphisbaenic rhyme is another method of forming half rhyme. It was invented by Edmund Wilson and relies on anagrams to produce a rhyme sound, so that the order of letters is reversed. The phrase which concludes Heaney's well-known poem 'Digging', 'snug as a gun', is an example of this. Naturally, reversing syllables will result in assonance and consonance.

Assonance and consonance are important aspects of creating pararhyme. When the vowel sounds match, the device is assonance, whereas consonance is when the consonantal sounds match. These two are often found together, for example in one of my poems,[5] I use the phrase 'boozy juice'. Not only do the *oo* and *u* sounds rhyme, the sibilance of the *zy* and *ce* sounds chime to create a pleasing sound, suitable for the happy memory of blackberry pie. The opposite of this is dissonance, when sounds which clash are deliberately placed together. Consonance which includes a lot of *s, c* and *z* sounds is called sibilance. Most of these technical terms are derived from music, so thinking in terms of harmony or clashing might be helpful when considering when to use them. Alliteration (or head rhyme) is a kind of consonance which appears at the start of words placed in close proximity. Macaronic rhyme uses more than one language; for example Wilfred Owen, in his poem 'Dulce et Decorum Est' rhymes 'glory' with 'Pro Patria Mori'.

Exercise one

Take the first line from any poem, for example Keats':

> When I have fears that I may cease to be

and experiment with using different types of rhyme, as detailed above, to create a suitable couplet to rhyme with it. The best way to find lines to use is to look at the first lines index of a poetry book; then how the poem continues will not influence you. You can make your second lines amusing or serious.

Exercise two

The poem below has had all its line ending words removed. Fill them in as though you were writing the poem yourself, using different methods of rhyming. Your version of the poem must make sense. When you have finished, look up the poem and compare your own choices with the ones made by Frost.

> Tree at my window, window _____,
> My sash is lowered when night comes _____;
> But let there never be curtain _____
> Between you and _____.
>
> Vague dream-head lifted out of the _____,
> And thing next most diffuse to _____,
> Not all your light tongues talking _____
> Could be _____.

But tree, I have seen you taken and _____,
And if you have seen me when I _____,
You have seen me when I was taken and _____,
And all but _____.

That day she put our heads _____,
Fate had her imagination _____ _____,
Your head so much concerned with _____,
Mine with inner, _____.

Exercise three

Read this short poem:

The Red Wheelbarrow by William Carlos Williams

so much depends
upon

a red wheel
barrow

glazed with rain
water

beside the white
chickens.

Free verse poem, right? Apparently simple in meaning? Read it a second time to observe the poet's rhyme sounds: 'depends/upon' with its repetition of *p* links the words through consonance. They are both iambic two-syllable words, so the rhythm supports the rhyme sounds. Then note the consonance between 'wheel' and 'barrow' again iambic two-syllable words. A pattern is emerging which helps the reader trust the poet's meaning. The third stanza creates a similar effect, this time using assonance: both 'glazed' and 'rain' have a long *a* sound. And in the final stanza, all three nouns are linked by assonance in the short *i* sound. Because of the sounds in the poem and the deliberate placing of line breaks and stanza breaks, and the stanza design of a line of three syllables followed by a line of only one syllable, the reader slows down and takes in each word. The poet is clearly saying something important; beyond the surface there are questions to be asked. What 'depends'? The rhyme sounds make the poem memorable, so it haunts the reader and makes she/he want to interrogate it, reflect on it, meet it eye to eye.

Placements of rhyme

The effect of any of these methods of creating rhyme can vary enormously depending where they are placed in a poem. The most common place is end-rhyme, but head-rhyme, or rhymes at the start of the line, can have a similar effect. When the end-rhymes are in a pattern, the rhyme words can be labelled *a* for the first, *b* for the second and so on, so that quatrains, for example, may be referred to as ABBA or ABAB and so on, as a handy shortcut.

When rhymes occur during a line, they are referred to as internal rhyme. These can occur in a pattern or randomly. Different placements are known by different names. Leonine rhyme occurs when the rhyming words are placed at the caesura (break) in the middle of a line and at the end. Internal rhymes can form interesting patterns and shift the emphasis from the line-endings.

With all rhyme, the poet's accent must be considered. Tony Harrison cites Wordsworth's rhyming of 'water' and 'matter' as full rhymes, which they would be in a Cumbrian accent.[6] As far as is possible, listen to poems read by their authors to appreciate the function of rhyme fully.

Exercise four

Look at one of your own poem drafts and experiment with placing rhymes within lines instead of letting end-rhymes bully you.

Bibliography

Blunden, Edmund (1931) *The Poems of Wilfred Owen* (London: Chatto and Windus)

Harrison, Tony (1984) *Selected Poems* (London: King Penguin)

Heaney, Seamus (1966) *Death of a Naturalist* (London: Faber & Faber)

Latham, Edward Connery (ed.) (1972) *The Poetry of Robert Frost* (London: Cape)

Nash, Ogden (1994) *Candy is Dandy* (London: Carlton Books)

Orme, David and James Sale (eds) (1987) *The Poetry Show 2* (London: Macmillan)

Padel, Ruth (2008) *The Poem and the Journey* (London: Vintage)

Topping, Angela (1999) *The Fiddle* (Exeter: Stride)

Topping, Angela (2013) *Letting Go* (Nottingham: Mother's Milk Books)

Williams, William Carlos (1991) *Collected Poems* (New York: New Directions)

15
Simile

Andrea Holland

Simile has been described as the sensible older sibling of metaphor. The suggestion here is that simile takes less risk in the act of describing something, is more judicious or well reasoned than metaphor and emerging writers can often feel more 'secure' in using a simile in a poem in order to show, suggest or denote an object or feeling; where metaphor insists, a simile suggests...

Poets have long understood that the purpose of simile is to describe something as it stands in comparison to another thing or object, thus Robert Burns' famous simile 'O my Luve's **like** a red, red rose,/ That's newly sprung in June'. It is a simple comparison yet it has endured over centuries because, in part, the simplicity is intrinsic to its appeal. Simile can help an abstract idea (in this case, love) appear concrete, tangible, even sensual. The simile conjures the rose's colour (red) but also enables readers to bring other senses to visualize the rose; we can smell its deep rich odour, we can feel the fabric of petal and the pierce of the thorn. It has a synesthetic quality. Unfortunately, not all lyric comparisons to flora or fauna manage to create such a sensual, memorable image. It is unlikely anyone can hear the clichéd simile 'fresh as a daisy' and respond in the same way as they might to Burns' simile, comparing love to a rose. So, the idea or concept (such as love, in Burns' poem) has to have a recognizable emotion or quality of understanding. Being clean, or 'fresh as a daisy' is nice, but ephemeral; however, being in love, or feeling love has a deeper, more universal, perpetual quality. Of course this does not mean all similes that try to compare love to a physical object are going to be successful; there is more behind the thought in Burns' poem and this is part of its appeal and longevity.

Carol Ann Duffy's poem 'Text' begins 'I tend the mobile now/ like an injured bird'; the mobile phone is held by the speaker as one holds an injured bird and the simile is tender, restrained. There is an odd juxtaposition between the metal, solid, recent man-made object – a mobile phone – and the fragility, warmth, naturalness of the bird. But the simile of the injured bird allows us to see the concern, wariness and emotion in the communication – now by text message where once (in Burns' day and until recently) it was by letter and most often by hand.

Simile is not only employed to make concrete an abstract idea; for many poets an ordinary object can, by way of simile, be viewed in a new way – the simile allows us to re-evaluate the way we understand something as simple, domestic. In one poem by Sylvia Plath it is a mirror which speaks: 'In me she has drowned a young girl, and in me an old woman/ Rises toward her day after day, like a terrible fish.' Or in Charles Simic's poem 'Fork' an ordinary household object is compared to part of a bird:

> It resembles a bird's foot
> Worn around the cannibal's neck

But the simile is then conflated so that, ultimately, it is something human:

> As you stab with it into a piece of meat
> It is possible to imagine the rest of the bird:
> Its head which like your fist
> Is large, bald, beakless and blind.

The fork grows into a bird with a head like a human fist. Yet the fist, so often a part of the body associated with threat or aggression, is made vulnerable, 'bald, beakless and blind'. As in Plath's and Duffy's poems, something cold, metallic, man-made is transformed into something natural: the mirror to a fish, the phone to a bird, the fork to a fist.

The discernment of simile is part of its charm; it can be simple, straightforward or more complex. It can offer a shrewd observation while making a well-reasoned comparison. In Don Paterson's 'A Private Bottling' the speaker drinks 'a chain of nips' late at night and ponders how

> each glass holds its micro-episode
> in permanent suspension, like a movie-frame
> on acetate, until it plays again.

The simile here, of preservation and repetition, serves the theme of the poem, whereby the lengthy ageing process of whisky is compared to the maturation of a marriage. The speaker describes the bottling and observes: 'The trick of how the peat-smoke/ was shut inside it, like a black thought.' Here the simile ('like') acts to both accommodate and restrain the image – if the peat smoke was described AS rather than LIKE a black thought (that is, via metaphor) the adjective *black* would over-awe the noun, *thought,* and the peat smoke would no longer be compared to, but actually become a black thought, something inherently negative. Instead, as a simile, *black* and *thought* stand together to describe the peat smoke's containment, just as a black thought may be contained within a skull.

It is possible, if simile is used well, to create plausibility with precision in describing something. In Craig Raine's 'A Martian Sends a Postcard Home' the alien speaker, observing human behaviour and writing about this strange race (our quirky habits, our odd weather) in a card home to Mars, describes mist as

> when the sky is tired of flight
> and rests its soft machine on the ground:
> then the world is dim and bookish
> like engravings under tissue paper.

This simile is ironic in its precision of detail; it heightens the irony of the voice – the words of a Martian, who does not appear to know the word *book* but uses the words 'bookish' and 'engravings under tissue paper'. This is one clever Martian and one important simile.

Although simile is most often used to make a simple comparison, within poetry and literary tradition there exists the epic simile, an extended or elaborate simile sometimes known as the Homeric simile, as employed by Homer in the *Odyssey* and the *Iliad.* Epic similes often run to several lines and appear typically in epic poetry to intensify the heroic stature of the subject and to serve as decoration or even distraction from the main event. Similes may have been employed to illuminate or decorate creative writing since antiquity, but it must be said that epic similes fit more naturally into Homer's ancient narratives than they do in a contemporary poem.

So, when does simile not work in a poem? Sometimes similes can announce themselves; it becomes obvious that the poet is trying too hard to be clever with the image. It is particularly a danger when the poet is tackling abstract concepts such as love and death, for example 'our love was as stale as bread/ as corroded as a rusty roof/ as rotten as autumn leaves' and so on. None of these are clichés per se, but neither are they fresh, inviting us to view the love-slash-relationship in a new way. The simile in a poem also has to be believable. Take a seemingly original line such as, 'your touch as rough as a cat's tongue'. While it may be that a cat's tongue is quite rough (all the better for grooming with) it is such an unusual way to describe the texture of the touch of something that the likelihood is that most people will read the line and fix on the simile rather than the thought behind it.

Practising comparisons: a simple simile exercise

This exercise works for individual practice but can also be used by individuals within a group – in a class or workshop setting:

First, create a series of adjectives (five to six usually works best) to use to compare things (nouns) by using simile. Here are some examples:

As blank as _____

As cold as _____

As rough as _____

As red as _____

and so on (a tutor can put the adjectives on a board or individuals can choose some themselves). Each student/writer fills in the blank; usually it is better if they don't think too much about the word they have chosen. The simpler, the better.

The interesting thing about this exercise is whether individuals will choose 'clichés' – for example, 'as cold as ice' – or try to come up with something a bit more unusual, perhaps 'as cold as a cave' or 'as cold as carrion'. Generally, it is helpful to avoid longer similes as these often veer into abstraction, or worse, pretension, for example 'as cold as the day you walked out my door'.

If the exercise is practised in a group setting, when they have finished filling in the nouns individuals can read out their similes, each one at a time, so everyone in the group shares/hears the first simile, for example 'as blank as a door', followed by 'as blank as a face' or the inevitable 'as blank as a white sheet of A4'. Participants enjoy hearing the variations in comparison as each one goes round, seeing if anyone else has come up with the same simile. But this exercise can go further if, after reading out all five or six similes, the group then spends a little time (another ten minutes is usually more than enough) on individually switching the endings; the similes are shifted around. Thus the first two similes ('as blank as ___' and 'as cold as ___') could be swapped. So 'as blank as a plate' and 'as cold as a slug' become 'as blank as a slug' and 'as cold as a plate'.

The group can then discuss whether the similes that have been switched work as similes; decide which ones make 'sense' and observe how some comparisons are easy or obvious, others less so. What about the similes that are simply implausible? This exercise allows participants to both practise and evaluate the ability of simile to convey emotion, idea or something more everyday through a simple figure of speech.

A good simile simply offers the reader imagination not explanation. The world is less 'dim and bookish' and more accessible; the reader can smell the red rose fresh as new love.

Bibliography

Burns, Robert (2011) *The Complete Poems and Songs of Robert Burns*
(Glasgow: Waverley Books)
Duffy, Carol Anne (2005) *Rapture* (London: Faber & Faber)
Paterson, Don (1993) *Nil Nil* (London: Faber & Faber)
Plath, Sylvia (2002) *The Collected Poems* (London: Faber & Faber)
Raine, Craig (1979) *A Martian Sends a Postcard Home* (Oxford: Oxford Poets)
Simic, Charles (1971) *Dismantling the Silence* (London: Jonathan Cape)

16
Metaphor

Nigel McLoughlin

Metaphor is defined by Baldick as a 'figure of speech in which one thing, idea or action is referred to by a word or expression normally denoting another thing, idea or action so as to suggest some common quality shared by the two'.[1] An example might be: the sky was an abstract painting. Obviously 'the sky' isn't 'an abstract painting' in actual fact. What the metaphor does is force the reader to imagine in what set of circumstances or in what way the sky might appear like an abstract painting or what qualities of the abstract painting can be applied to the sky and under what conditions.

This relies on perceptions – the reader's perceptions of abstract painting might be different to the writer's. If the writer is describing a fireworks display in which streaks and bursts of different colours litter a black background for instance, that will say something about how the writer perceives abstract painting. If on the other hand the writer uses the metaphor to describe fields of colour melding into one another in a spectacular sunset, then clearly the metaphor relates to a different type of abstract painting. The reader will be required to work out the exact way the metaphor applies using the surrounding context. The metaphor might fail to transfer across to the reader in certain cases – say where the reader has no experience of abstract painting.

I. A. Richards described a metaphor as being made up of two basic parts: the tenor and the vehicle. The tenor is the thing that is being described, the sky in the above example. The sky (the tenor) is the thing onto which attributes are being projected. The vehicle is the thing from which the attributes are taken, the abstract painting in our case. The image constructed in the reader's mind of the abstract painting (the vehicle) is being used to describe certain visual qualities of the sky. In what is called Conceptual Metaphor Theory, Lakoff has a similar idea but uses different terminology. He refers to target and source instead of tenor and vehicle and the formula is target IS source.[2, 3] In this system metaphor is thought to arise through our human experience of the world. We map across direct basic experiences to abstract concepts, for example, affection is warmth or relationships are containers.

Two further terms are used in relation to metaphors: the ground or the similarity between the two objects being compared; and the tension, which is the difference between them. In our example the ground of the metaphor is the colour and beauty of the scene that has been conjured in the mind of the reader as they picture a sky that has all the colours and energy that they might associate with abstract painting. The tension is that the sky is not made of canvas, does not have a frame and has not in fact been painted by a gigantic artist and therefore cannot possibly really be an abstract painting.

What kind of metaphor?

There are a variety of different types of metaphor:[4] dead metaphor is the term given to metaphors which have become so overused that we stop recognizing them as metaphors. They now fail to make the reader enter into any imaginative relationship with the thing they describe. An example is a 'table leg' – to refer to the piece of wood which supports a table as a 'leg' is to use 'leg' as the vehicle for a metaphor the tenor of which is the 'support'. However, no one now thinks of a 'table leg' as a metaphor – it is simply what the structure is called – the metaphor is dead.

Dormant metaphor is the term sometimes given to metaphors which are in the process of dying. An example might be 'the bottom line' when referring to the 'end result' or 'the final analysis'. This metaphor is not quite dead; it will still conjure up the image of someone drawing a line under a sum on a blackboard and calculating the result (the bottom line of the sum), but it is now so clichéd it is well on its way to being a dead metaphor.

Active metaphors are, as the name implies, metaphors which still act as metaphors and which continue to ask the reader (or listener) to make the connection between the two elements (the tenor and vehicle) in their imagination. These can be further subdivided into a number of different classes of metaphor:

A complex metaphor is one that uses a metaphor as one or both of its objects. For instance, if one were to say that 'the dark horse was top notch', then one would be using a complex metaphor. There is no actual horse and no actual notch. The tenor is itself a metaphor meaning the unknown quantity or the surprise contender, while the vehicle is also a metaphor for the best available.

Many people are commonly aware of what are called mixed metaphors and often they can have quite a humorous effect. These occur where the metaphor moves to use a comparison with a second vehicle, which is at odds with the first. For example where one might say 'he rose through the ranks by sitting on the fence'. The implication is that he was promoted through refusing to take sides but the act of rising is semantically at odds with the act of sitting. That makes it a mixed metaphor.

A compound metaphor on the other hand works on more than one ground. 'She has the feet of a mountain goat' implies small dainty feet but is also used to describe agility and surefootedness (and may be used in the physical or figurative senses of these). This contrasts with a simple metaphor that applies on only one ground. Asking someone to 'rewind and run that by me again' for example signifies the need to reverse and is usually used when the hearer doesn't quite understand and wants the speaker to repeat what they've said. The vehicle of the metaphor 'rewinding and replaying a tape recording' and the tenor 'repeat that' can only be grounded by that function.

Synecdochic metaphors occur where the vehicle is represented by one part of a greater whole. For example, 'the gears in his head had finally ceased up'. Here the underlying metaphor of 'mind is machine' is represented by the gears of the machine, and the breakdown of the machine is related to mental breakdown. Pataphor, which is a term derived from pataphysics (an absurdist trope), is a type of metaphor that extends the description of the vehicle in order to create a vivid idea of the tenor, but without actually naming either, so a hangover is a group of devils might become 'a thousand red-hot forks jabbed at his head, each one in a pulsing movement, while iron hooves danced behind his eyes the morning after the final.'

Implicit metaphors are those where the tenor is not overtly stated but the reader (or hearer) can fill in the gap. Phrases such as 'get that mop cut', when referring to someone's hair, the absent tenor that the vehicle 'mop' refers to, will fall into this category. The contrary case is called a submerged metaphor. In this type it is the vehicle that is hinted at rather than stated. Such phrases as 'a thought zoomed through her head' ask the reader to generate the implied image of a rocket, the submerged vehicle for 'thought'.

Two further types are used less often in common parlance but may be of particular use to poets: the first type is the paralogical or anti-metaphor where there is no easily accessible ground of resemblance between the tenor and the vehicle. So when one comes across something like 'the eye is an Internet of emotions' one is dealing with anti-metaphor. Clearly a linkage holds on some level between the tenor (eye) and the vehicle (Internet). The reader may understand that the eye is a means of express communication where emotion can be seen and observed, but also through which others can observe our emotions (that is information can be uploaded and downloaded very quickly), but it is far from obvious and requires an imaginative leap. The second type is the synesthetic metaphor, which expresses the link between the tenor and vehicle in terms of two different senses. An example might be 'her blouse is a recorded scream being played backwards at full volume'. Again, clearly something is communicated at some level, but again the ground is far from obvious and requires the active participation of the reader to render it meaningful. The thought process is not unlike the anti-metaphor in that it will require the reader to imagine what a 'recorded scream played backwards' would sound like and then assign the auditory effect of hearing it at full volume to a colour which might produce the visually equivalent sensation. This type of cross-fertilization can be used effectively in poetry; by understanding the effects of a fresh and original metaphor on the reader, one will better understand how to construct metaphors which will make the reader sit up and think.

Exercise

Generate a set of metaphors that exemplify each of the different types of metaphor we have discussed. Take each one and outline the process the reader will have to go through to make the imaginative leap for each. Which prove most challenging for the reader?

Write a poem attempting to describe either your favourite piece of music or your favourite abstract painting. Use as many strange metaphors as you can, but be aware of the ground and tension of each. When you've finished the first draft of this (about 20 metaphors), read over the work – does a pattern emerge? Does this suggest a direction for the poem? Can you work it up into a hook to hang a finished poem on?

Better metaphors

In order to understand how we can construct good metaphors it is important that we consider the process by which metaphor operates, or more exactly the process by which the reader constructs meaning from the metaphor. Earlier we found that Conceptual Metaphor Theory argues that metaphor is generated by mapping across common qualities between concrete and abstract (or familiar and unfamiliar) concepts directionally from source (usually the concrete and familiar) to target (usually the more unfamiliar or abstract). Another way we can think about how metaphor operates is in terms of signs: words are arbitrary signs. There is no direct relationship between the set of letters 'table' and the item of furniture that people might sit around to eat. It is only a convention in English that 'table' has been agreed to stand for that thing. A thousand years ago the letters 'bord' signified the same object – in another thousand years it might be another word. The sign has two parts to it sometimes referred to as 'signifier' and 'signified'. The signifier is the combination of letters or sounds that make up the sign. The signified is the idea of the thing that the sign refers to. Metaphor interferes with this relationship in a very particular way. Metaphor makes a new sign by combining the signifier of one sign with the signified of another sign.[5]

In a surprising or unusual metaphor, the result of the reader's imaginative leap can lead to pleasure for the reader, especially if the result offers some insight which the reader has not grasped or has not been asked to consider before. That is the key to constructing good metaphors; there should be an element of surprise for the reader – a sense of originality. All really good metaphors have this quality. If we really get lucky our metaphor may also provide what Joyce referred to as 'epiphany'. This is a sense of seeing the thing described in a new light, all at once, in a very striking realization. An example, from Emily Dickinson, might be:

Exultation is the going
Of an inland soul to sea[6]

If a metaphor can provide this sort of fresh insight, it will also undoubtedly provide the surprise. If it provides the surprise, it may be good enough for use in a poem – it does not necessarily *have* to contain an epiphany. One way in which we can do this is to start from a base metaphor. For example, the 'recorded scream' metaphor in the last section was developed by exaggerating the more usual 'loud' in reference to colour. I simply asked myself the question 'how loud was it'? Similarly anti-metaphor and pataphor can create rich associations that may also yield unusual metaphors through elaboration of basic or conceptual metaphors.

It has been argued that as soon as we see something new we ask ourselves what it resembles. This is the most common function of metaphor: to describe something that we can't describe directly (such as an abstract concept like exultation in the Dickinson example) in terms of something else which is relatively familiar such as the experience of going out to sea for the first time. We can use the relationship with the familiar object or experience to communicate the essence of the abstract concept to someone else who is not familiar with it but who shares our knowledge of the familiar thing we describe. This communication of the tenor depends upon the common ground between author and reader in regard to their experience of the vehicle.

For instance if I was to say 'heaven is an eternal dream' one reader might take this to mean that heaven is always a dream, while another reader may take it to mean that it is a dream which lasts forever. Of these readers some might find that idea pleasurable, while others may not. If they take no pleasure in the idea of heaven as a dream that lasts forever, for them it isn't heaven at all – in fact it might be that they'd find it hellish. So depending on the interpretive community that the reader belongs to, the metaphor may well not be communicating what the author intended at all. Of course, this ambiguity can itself be exploited by the author in order to generate specific effects.

Exercise

Wallace Stevens said 'reality is a cliché from which we escape by metaphor.'[7] Pick a person and use a series of metaphors to describe them. Try and mix the description between their physical characteristics and attributes and their personality traits and what they mean to you on an emotional level. Try and look at each quality in terms of something else that also possesses it, that is, on a metaphorical level. Be as off the wall as you like, no one else need see your initial list. Pick the six most original and surprising metaphors and use them to build up a poem about this person.

Bibliography

Baldick, Chris (ed.) (1990) *The Concise Oxford Dictionary of Literary Terms* (Oxford: Oxford University Press)

Chandler, Daniel (2007) *Semiotics: The Basics* (London: Routledge)

Dickinson, Emily (2001) *Poems* selected by Ted Hughes (London: Faber & Faber)

Lakoff, George and Mark Johnson (1980) *Metaphors We Live By* (Chicago: University of Chicago Press)

Lakoff, George (1993) 'The contemporary theory of metaphor', in Andrew Ortony (ed.), *Metaphor and Thought* 2nd edn (Cambridge: Cambridge University Press), pp. 202–51.

Scully, James (ed.) (1970) *Modern Poets on Modern Poetry* (London: Fontana)

Shipley, Joseph T. (ed.) (1970) *Dictionary of World Literary Terms* (London: George Allen & Unwin)

http://changingminds.org/techniques/language/metaphor/metaphor. htm, accessed 24 May 2015.

http://grammar.about.com/od/rhetoricstyle/a/13metaphors.htm, accessed 24 May 2015.

17

How to Make a Woman Disappear: Extended Metaphor in *Waiting for Bluebeard*

Helen Ivory

Waiting for Bluebeard is an attempt to understand how a girl could grow up to be the woman living in Bluebeard's house. The collection is semi-autobiographical, and although the book is inhabited by events that are not all factually true, I was attempting to get at a more powerful truth – a metaphorical truth to show what parts of my life have felt like, and to walk the reader through those experiences. 'Making sense of experience', writes Seamus Heaney, 'is a good reason for writing poems, but not good enough reason for sharing them. We want to end up with poems ... that rose beyond their immediate occasion – that transmuted experience into art'. One of the ways of doing this is to use metaphor to carry experiences on their backs. To extend your metaphor over a poem and then further, over a whole sequence of poems, enables you as a writer to imagine a whole world analogous to the 'real' one. You do not let the reader go at the end of one poem; you invite them to stay with you. Think of Ted Hughes' epic *Crow*, or any of Vasko Popa's sequences.

Waiting for Bluebeard, my fourth book, is the first I have ever thought of as a whole piece and is also the closest I have come to autobiography. The book is in two parts – the first is made up of poems loosely based around my childhood where Ouija boards and ghost cats feature, as does a barely there father. The childhood house falls apart at the seams and by the second part of the book, the child has grown up and moves away from the childhood home. In attempting to create a grown-up life for herself, she enters Bluebeard's house and an abusive relationship. The narrative 'I' becomes an observed 'she' as the woman slowly disappears and loses herself, before she even knew what that was. She also has a child, or imagines she has had a child, which she spends much time furiously searching for around Bluebeard's house. It is the Bluebeard's house poems that I wish to concentrate on for our purposes.

119

As Bettelheim writes in *The Uses of Enchantment*, it is not uncommon for us to use fairy-tale motifs as a way of tapping into a deeper understanding of human desires and solving universal human problems. Fairy tales like myths are rich with symbolism and metaphor and are a universal language and a fruitful territory for writers (and other artists) to explore and to borrow from. Fairy tales themselves are often described as extended metaphors.

So why did I choose Bluebeard specifically? Marina Warner writes: 'Bluebeard is a bogey who fascinates: his name stirs associations with sex, virility, male readiness and desire.'[1] And Bruno Bettelheim writes: 'Bluebeard is the most monstrous and beastly of all fairy-tale husbands.'[2] The story is essentially about a man who murders his wives when they have become too curious: *Here is the key to all of the rooms in my castle. I am just going away for a little while. Use the key to explore any room you want to, but I forbid you to open THAT door.* Her brothers rescue the woman the story centres around, in the nick of time, so she doesn't befall the same fate as her predecessors. The story most people are familiar with is a 'literary fairy tale' written in 1697 by Perrault, but in a chapter entitled *Demon Lovers*, in *From the Beast to the Blonde*, Marina Warner traces Bluebeard's ancestors back to the oral tradition of beastly bridegrooms.

So when it came to finding the perfect man who would use his maleness to subjugate my female protagonist, the Bluebeard character muscled his way into my mind. The following poem, demonstrating Bluebeard's courtship techniques' is from a sequence called 'A Week With Bluebeard'. The idea for this poem came from the Pagan ceremony of Drawing Down the Moon, which is thought to empower you with all of the moon's positive qualities. Being only able to produce reflective light, I had a sense that the moon might lose her powers if she were lured from the sky by Bluebeard:

Monday – Drawing Down the Moon

He'd been calling the moon
by all of her names on his midnight walk:
Selene, Persephone, Artemis…
so she followed him home
cold light burning the back of his neck.

When the music in his head begun
he offered his arm
and they took several turns of the patio
in a stately upright manner,
till the music grew faster.

He gripped her by the waist, by the wrist,
as he spun her around.

And wolves raised their voices to the sky,
and her names fell from her
and the night blurred.

The notion that Bluebeard could lure the moon from the sky and strip her of her names suggests how powerful he is, and also points to his desire to own and destroy.

There are no literal deaths in *Waiting for Bluebeard*, yet in the series of nine poems called 'The Disappearing' – which forms the backbone to the Bluebeard poems – the woman dies a tiny part at a time. When inside an abusive relationship, one doesn't always realize it is happening because it happens slowly and insidiously. According to the Counselling Directory website: 'Abusive relationships are usually progressive; the needs of one partner escalate and those of the other disappear along with their self-esteem.'

In this first poem from 'The Disappearing' sequence, the woman goes through a kind of initiation into adulthood. There is also the sense of a painful birth and the beginning of a division of selves.

1

The tariff for crossing the threshold
was a single layer of skin.

She imagined a snake
unzipping itself in one deft move.

She imagined herself lithe
inside the house, her new home.

She didn't imagine the scarring
nor the painstaking care required

to leave the ghost of herself
on the doorstep like a cold-caller.

In the following poem from 'The Disappearing' sequence, the woman divides further like a Russian doll and cannot see how to put herself back together. The last four lines show her desire to turn back time; to make it night again.

4

She stepped out of herself
like a Matryoshka, one full moon,

looked along the row of herself,
at the hand-painted colours,
checked each pair of eyes
for what lived there.

A scarf hung about each pelvic girdle
to conceal the scar of each birth;
hearts were black hens
held in each pair of arms
and cabbages grew
from fallen seeds at their feet.

When earth spun away from the moon
she attempted to gather herself back in,
and when she could not
she drowned the sun like a sack of kittens
and threaded the rooster's song
back into his throat.

In the next stage of her disappearing, the woman tries to make herself a
new skin so that she might perhaps find a new identity and begin to reappear. One of the symptoms of domestic abuse is that one begins to exhibit
escapist behaviour. What better escape than to become a bird?

5

Each day, a new birdskin appeared on the patio,
emptied of its heart and bones and singing.
Perhaps it was the owl's meticulous work.

When she'd harvested enough skins,
she sat at her table one morning
and fashioned herself a birdskin coat.

And when she put it on, the uncured hide
grafted easily to her own skin.
And when she tried to sing, she could not.

But since the birds have been murdered, there is no hope for her voice.
Indeed, there is no room for singing in Bluebeard's house, and one of the
patterns of emotional abuse is *denying*, which includes sulking, neglecting
and withholding affection from the other person. My Bluebeard is a silent
brooding man. He spends a lot of time on his own in the dark and shows
no affections towards the woman who inhabits the rooms like a ghost. In

this poem from 'The Disappearing', the woman tries to make the silences tangible and to somehow *reappear* herself, but it's easier perhaps to just forget your heart was once a beating thing:

6

She presses missed heartbeats
into a wet plaster wall
with her wedding ring finger
measuring out silences
wide enough to fall into.

Plaster loses its flesh-tone
when it dries,
leeches moisture from skin.
The heart dives
into a well of forgetting.

In the next poem, she rejoices in her disappearing and feels empowered by her new svelte form. There are overtones here of anorexia, which is largely governed by the desire to be in control of something controllable. That a person is stripped so bare that *feeling* also vanishes is marvellous to her.

7

She already knew her bones
were there for all the world to see,
so she unpeeled her hide
in the changing rooms.

Bluebeard barely recognised
the small neat form
slicing through the footbath
like a fox through night.

In the pool, she was an electric storm,
and the water shrunk away.
She marvelled, *oh the joy!*
she could not feel a thing.

Throughout the poems in this second half of *Waiting for Bluebeard* is a great sense of seclusion. One of the methods of staying in control for the abuser in an abusive relationship, is to keep the other person isolated

– cutting off contact with friends and family, not allowing or disapproving of telephone calls or other contact with the outside world, and also keeping that person hostage to you financially. The setting for Bluebeard's house is remote countryside, which reinforces that isolation. Here the woman is forced to doubt that there was a life before Bluebeard:

8

And by teatime she couldn't recognise
a single hair on her head.
Her heart was a metal bucket
and her eyes were the spaces
where fish bowls had sat.

She talked to the chickens
and the guinea fowl, and the pheasants
in the fields, as she fed them;
she had inherited their scratchy voices;
the urge to look over their shoulders.

Nothing they could say
would set her mind at rest.
None of them knew of a road outside,
they all said they were born here;
perhaps she was too.

In the final poem of the sequence, the woman does escape the house. She happens upon the room where everything disappeared from her has been stored. She is reunited with the skin she paid with in order to enter the house at the beginning of the sequence, but it no longer fits. There is a sense of new beginnings in the nakedness, but also vulnerability. The 'I' is also reintroduced in this poem, which brings back the original narrator.

9

This time the door wasn't locked
so she saw the room's plunder
floating in the dark liquid
of neatly labelled jars –
fingernails, tangles of hair,
an unborn child.
My skin hung from a wire hanger
on the back of the door
like a wedding dress

emptied of its bride.
It was too tight to climb into
so she left the house naked.

When I was writing these poems, I didn't research the signs and symptoms of domestic abuse, as I have done to write this piece. The poems came
out of lived experience, and the writing of them was necessary and urgent.
It wasn't possible for me to show this life in anything less than the thirty-
four poems which make up the second part of this book – the poems kept
arriving as the subject kept calling: *You haven't done with me yet.* Having the
Bluebeard story as a readymade idea was essential to my finding a way in.

Exercise

Focusing on the first poem in my 'Disappearing' (*1,* above) think of a
threshold moment in your life, perhaps a decision that you made which
opened a door and a new life for you. Were there any sacrifices you had to
make from moving from one state to another? This could range from moving house to making the first ever meal for yourself. Rites of passage are
perhaps not recognized as much in this country these days, but the rituals
are in themselves physical representations of metaphors. Think of baptism
and cleansing. Also how fire is used to purify. It might be useful to do just a
little bit of research about rites and rituals, to open the subject up for you.

Tips

When I write, I begin inside the metaphor and then watch what might
happen if the metaphor were taken literally, in that way the metaphor
extends over the whole poem naturally. I also try to add some everyday
things, phrases and clutter to my poems to try to anchor them, so they do
not become too abstract and otherworldly.

Bibliography

Bettelheim, Bruno (1999) *The Uses of Enchantment* (London: Penguin)
Ivory, Helen (2013) *Waiting for Bluebeard* (Tarset: Bloodaxe Books)
Warner, Marina (1995) *From the Beast to the Blonde* (London: Vintage)

18

Irony is for Losers

Kevin Higgins

My poetry heroes – John Dryden, Alexander Pope and Jonathan Swift –
all died a while ago. The last of them to depart this often unpleasant,
but always amusing planet of ours, the venerable Mr Swift, expired on
19 October 1745. It was, funnily enough, a Tuesday. A friend of mine
says that my poetry has three recurring motifs: Tuesday afternoons, bare
backsides and mildew. On occasion all three have been known to feature
in combination. Ask a nearby psychotherapist to make of that what she
will. During the final decade or so of Swift's life, as one biographer puts
it, 'insanity overcame him'. The bulk of his fortune, which according to
Wikipedia amounted to £12,000, was left to found a hospital for the mentally ill, originally known as 'St. Patrick's Hospital for Imbeciles'. A couple
of hundred years later, when its title had – in a fit of political correctness
gone mad – been softened to simply St. Patrick's Hospital, my late grandmother was a regular and always enthusiastic guest there.

The first of Swift's works to make an impression on me was not poetry
but prose. In the autumn of 1984, as America got ready to re-elect Ronald
Reagan, RTE Television broadcast live a special variety performance to celebrate the re-opening of the Gaiety Theatre. The 1,000-strong audience,
each of whom had paid £25 per ticket – a not insubstantial sum during
what was in Ireland a time of acute pecuniary embarrassment for many –
included our then President, Patrick Hillery. The actor Peter O'Toole chose
as his party piece for the evening a reading from Swift's satirical essay *A
Modest Proposal*. First published in 1729, at a time when the combination
of new political freedoms and advances in printing technology led to a
situation where every overly earnest dullard with a few quid was busy publishing pamphlets of his thoughts on how the human condition might be
improved, *A Modest Proposal* takes issue, in the most savage way, with one
of the favourite subjects of those eighteenth-century equivalents of today's
political bloggers: what to do about the terrible, poverty stricken condition
of the native Irish and their exorbitantly sized families?

Swift's proposal was as tasty as it was immodest. An obvious remedy, he
suggested, was that the children of the native Irish poor should be fattened

and fed to the aristocracy. The audience who listened to Peter O'Toole that night in the Gaiety Theatre no doubt considered themselves to be among the most cultured people in the country. Yet two centuries after his death Swift succeeded in showing many of them up as the dumb waistcoats that they were. Several dozen of the esteemed audience stalked out in protest and there were shouts of 'disgusting', 'offensive' and no doubt a few less-considered ejaculations. The target of the satire in *A Modest Proposal* is the important little man, whose wife has, over the years, made him a few big dinners too many, who likes to shake his head while reading the newspaper and mutter things like 'isn't it terrible such a thing can happen in this day and age'; a man whose littleness would though lead him to be absolutely opposed to any real societal change because such change may well put at risk his big dinners. That night in the Gaiety Theatre the audience upon whom Peter O'Toole inflicted Swift's immodest proposal would have been full of precisely that kind of person. If then Minister for Finance, Alan Dukes, had proposed in his budget of 1985 measures to incentivize the fattening of the children of Ballymun on a diet of pig's arse and buttery potatoes until they were ready to grace the dining tables of Killiney, each with an apple placed tastefully in his or her oven-ready mouth, a good proportion of that Gaiety Theatre audience would likely have sighed into their *Irish Times* that there was no alternative given the financial mess left behind by the previous Fianna Fáil government. Swift's essay is written in the deadly earnest style that was the fashion for the pamphleteers he wanted to mock. By ironically saying what he absolutely didn't mean Swift got closer to at least part of the truth about poverty than a thousand columns by Polly Toynbee.

If I could write something which, 255 years after my wife has deposited me in the New Cemetery, or buried me beside our late cat at the bottom of the garden, still retained the ability to offend all the right people, then that would be a real achievement. Many writers dream of being given awards by oversized waistcoats in fat banquet halls. We all like to be acknowledged and, more importantly, to be fed. The ironist, though, is driven by the warped yet beautiful desire to laugh at us from beyond the grave. The world is frequently ridiculous and, if you face it with a knowing smile and a shrug, there's an outside chance you might retain your sanity. It didn't work for Jonathan Swift, of course. But to paraphrase the Samuel L. Jackson character in *Die Hard With A Vengeance*: the dude had other issues.

I've chosen three examples of contemporary poems to which irony is central. The first is the short prose poem 'We were so poor' by Charles Simic, the first line of which is:

We were so poor I had to take the place of the bait in the mousetrap.[1]

Simic's irony is a little less savage than Swift's. The sentiments implied in this poem are akin to the Monty Python sketch, 'The Four Yorkshiremen', in which each character tries to outdo the other with tales of their deprived childhood. Charles Simic was born in Belgrade in May 1938. The late Adolf Hitler ordered the forces of the Third Reich to invade Yugoslavia in March 1941, when Simic was not yet three years old. There can be no doubt that Simic had a more trying childhood than most, which knowledge of course gives particular power to his satire on those who like to yak on about the bad old days. Simic's poem exaggerates beyond the point of absurdity. But in another sense it also understates, because there were far worse roles than being the bait in a mousetrap into which one could be conscripted in the Belgrade in which the three-year-old Simic lived when the forces of the Third Reich rolled into town.

The ironies in the second poem I've chosen – Sophie Hannah's 'No Ball Games etc'[2] – are of an altogether more everyday variety.

No Ball Games etc
sign outside a London block of flats

Honestly, do we have to spell it out?
No tents, space-hoppers, orgies, Brussels sprout
enthusiasts, no sponsored squirrel fights …

So often we observe in the actual world things which are patently nonsensical. Hannah takes the 'etc.' in the observed street sign and runs with it fantastically. There is a sense that as well as satirizing the local authority bureaucrat or tenants' association busy body who likely thought up that potentially all-encompassing 'etc.', she is also taking aim at the Anglo-Saxon tendency to invent bylaws banning fun. For one woman, she implies, it may be Brussels sprouts, whereas another may prefer 'weightless floating with an auctioneer / in the small pond.' Who are we to judge? The social satire in this poem – and indeed in much of Hannah's poetry – is aided by her work's formality. She is a near genius at coming up with rhyming couples of which Pope or Dryden would have been proud.

The final example I've chosen is by Peter Reading (1946–2011), a poet who is perhaps the closest to the Swiftian sensibility of my three example poets in that he for many years gave the impression of despising most of the human race. His poem 'Soirée'[3] is social satire at its brutal best:

And all their damn fool questions 'tell me Peter,
what do you write about?' (cunts like you mate).
'Peter, you interested in history?'
(Mate, I ain't even interested in
the present.)

Many's the time I've been asked versions of that question – 'what do you write about?' – and wanted to reply: 'cunts, like you mate'. But, as is the case for the acidic narrator in Reading's 'Soirée', real life rarely allows one such luxuries. The beauty of poetry is precisely that it does allow us, if we are so minded, to dress up our loathings, our hates in the best possible words. Precision is crucial, because in the words of Oscar Wilde 'A gentleman [and I might add, a lady] never offends unintentionally'.

A friend of mine said that when he heard I had started writing poems it called to mind for him the lines from the Pulp song 'I Spy':[4]

> It might look to the untrained eye
> I'm sitting on my arse all day
> I'm biding time until I take you all on

The satire which irony properly applied has the potential to let loose is not about making the world a better place, in the way that the earnest pamphleteers of Swift's time imagined they were. It is about remaining as sane as one can, and performing the occasional act of revenge, as one hurtles towards the grave. The occasional mind might be changed along the way. You'll certainly be more successful in spreading whatever your world view may be by getting others to laugh at the absurd places their own deeply held convictions often lead them than you will by explaining yet again exactly what it is you mean in words borrowed from the *Guardian* or *Daily Mail*. But that is by the way.

In his thought-provoking book *What's Left,*[5] British journalist Nick Cohen argues that irony is always the preferred tone of the losing side in any argument. Cohen observes that in the 1920s and 1930s, when the trade union movement was a rising power in society and socialism seemed to be the future towards which the world was in some sense inevitably drifting, the leading literary ironist in England was the ultra-conservative, Catholic convert Evelyn Waugh. The 1980s, though, when Maggie reigned throughout the land and the then very left-wing Labour Party, with its promises of nuclear disarmament and nationalization, kept losing election after election, saw the rise of alternative comedy, almost all of which was anti-Thatcher in tone and content. Yet she kept getting re-elected. Thatcher may be gone, but the truth Cohen put his finger on remains. Irony is for losers. You will likely not change the world. But when the day comes that you find yourself standing on the metaphorical gallows, whatever form that occasion may take for you, you'll at least be able still to smile and tell yourself a joke, which in all likelihood will contain more truth than any prayers or petitions for clemency offered on your behalf.

Bibliography

Astley, Neil (ed.) (2002) *Staying Alive: Real Poems for Unreal Times* (Tarset: Bloodaxe)

Cohen, Nick (2007) *What's Left* (London: Fourth Estate)

Hannah, Sophie (2007) *Pessimism for Beginners* (Manchester: Carcanet)

Pulp, `I Spy' *Different Class* (Polygram / Island Records, 1995)

Reading, Peter (1995) *Collected Poems: 1970–84* (Tarset: Bloodaxe)

Swift, Jonathan (1729) *A Modest Proposal for Preventing the Children of Poor People From Being a Burthen to Their Parents or Country, and for Making Them Beneficial to the Publick* (Privately)

19
Dramatic Monologue

Barbara Smith

A dramatic monologue is a poem or narrative piece in which the poet has put on a mask, or *persona*, to give us, the listener or audience, a fuller flavour of that masked person. An audience may also be implied in a poem: for instance in Robert Browning's much anthologized 'My Last Duchess', the persona is a duke addressing an envoy who has come to negotiate a new marriage with him; the duke shows the envoy a portrait of the last woman to occupy that role, as well as revealing his own skewed personality. The outer audience, that is us, can also listen (and in a way watch) with a degree of rising horror as the monologue unfolds.

In M. H. Abrams' *A Glossary of Literary Terms*, the dramatic monologue is described as having three key features:

1. A single person, who is patently *not* the poet, utters the entire poem in a specific situation at a critical moment.
2. This person addresses and interacts with one or more other people; but we know of the auditor's presence and what they say and do only from clues in the discourse of the single speaker.
3. The principle controlling the poet's selection and organization of what the lyric speaker says is the speaker's unintentional revelation of his or her temperament and character.

The beauty of a dramatic monologue lies in this ability to take on a persona, which could be completely unrelated to the author's point of view and tell a story solely from that viewpoint.

History of the dramatic monologue

Monologues can be traced through literature back as far as the ancient Greek playwrights. Closer to our own time, Chaucer's *Canterbury Tales* could arguably be viewed as being loosely in the category of dramatic monologue, as each tale is told through a different character, with the language and the way it is told changing from persona to persona; for example the courtly love theme of the knight's tale, as compared to the bawdy miller's tale. Shakespeare often used the device as soliloquies in his plays to allow characters to convey their inner turmoil and thoughts to the audience, such as when Lady Macbeth enters the stage (Act 1, Scene 5) reading a letter from her husband, and muses aloud on its tidings and their implications with regard to her husband's character.

Elizabethan writers used the dramatic monologue: Marlowe, Drayton and Raleigh wrote examples of the form, some playing on the gap between what a reader might be expected to know and what they didn't know; thus having to include explanatory footnotes for the reader. Some were criticized for being too obscure for the reader. The eighteenth-century Alexander Pope also wrote some notable examples, such as *Eloisa to Abelard*, a long poem with heroic rhyming couplets. However, as time went on, the dramatic monologue declined. The Romantic poets wrote as though they themselves were the persona of the poem. Wordsworth's 'Tintern Abbey' and Shelley's 'Mont Blanc' offer instead an insight into psychological or philosophical observation, from the poet's point of view.

Looking towards other genres, the novel could be described as having been influenced by, and perhaps having influence on, the dramatic monologue. Mary Shelley's *Frankenstein* uses both the epistolary device (letters) and the first person to tell her story, for example. But it is really in the Victorian period that dramatic monologues re-emerged. Tennyson's often quoted 'Ulysses' tells the story of his discontent after returning to Ithaca after his adventures in 70 lines of blank verse. In turn, Robert Browning became the best exponent of the form, in his collection *Men and Women*, where 51 poems use the dramatic monologue device (excepting the last poem), the best-known being 'My Last Duchess'.

As the nineteenth century moved into the twentieth and writers explored fin-de-siècle uncertainty in their writing, the dramatic monologue came to be treated by modernist writers. Eliot used this trope in 'The Love Song of J. Alfred Prufrock' although it could be argued that there is some fusion between the persona of this poem and Eliot himself. Some critics have described this type of fusion as *mask lyrics*, which place distance between the poet and the narrator of the poem, but perhaps not as much as an actual invented *persona* does. Ezra Pound explores the dramatic monologue in works such as his 'Sestina: Altaforte', which is in the persona of Bertran de Borns addressing his jongler Pappiol. Robert Frost can also be said to have used the dramatic monologue, crossing over between poet and persona. For example 'Mending Wall' uses the iambic meter, conversational tone and a particular point in time to dramatize a scene, as well as inform the reader.

Other twentieth-century poets can be seen to blur the boundaries between the poet and persona. Sassoon used his First World War experiences to dramatize the horror of specific moments in the war, particularly the death of comrades in 'A Night Attack'. The work of Sylvia Plath also has very strong elements of *mask-lyricism* in her work, her poem 'Lady Lazarus' being a strong case in point. Because of a tendency to read modern poets in the context of their lives, and because so much of their lives are public knowledge it becomes even more difficult to separate the poet from the persona. However, with poems such as 'Lady Lazarus' and 'A Night Attack', it is the drama of the voice and the work of the meters, which both poets use to different effects, that carries the poems past those quibbles. Henry Reed, a Second World War poet, also utilizes the dramatic monologue in his sequence 'Lessons of the War' (particularly 'The Naming of Parts'), which eerily recalls the training of army conscripts before they are sent into battle. The mixture of the trainer's classroom phrases on their instructions on how to use their weapons mixed with the trainee's sensate perceptions show that use of mask-lyrics again. Once more the calm, conversational tone created by the meter, as well as the adopted speaker, makes for an unsettling read.

Moving forward in time, the poems of Thomas James, highly influenced by Plath, also show effective use of the dramatic monologue, specifically 'Mummy of a Lady Named Jemutesonekh' and 'Dragging the Lake', both of which use the personas of bodies just after death. This also has the effect of bringing the bodies briefly back to life, answering some questions about their mode of death, as well as creating many more in the mind of the reader.

Today, the dramatic monologue is alive and well and is still being successfully used by modern poets. The form has been reclaimed by poets such as Carol Ann Duffy in her collection, *The World's Wife*, with poems such as 'Mrs Midas' and 'Mrs Darwin'. Vicki Feaver has also successfully utilized the form in 'Judith' from her second collection, *The Handless Maiden*.

Close reading of a monologue

We will examine Robert Browning's dramatic monologue 'My Last Duchess' more closely to identify the key features and see how he utilizes the form.

My Last Duchess

FERRARA

That's my last Duchess painted on the wall,
Looking as if she were alive. I call
That piece a wonder, now: Frà Pandolf's hands
Worked busily a day, and there she stands.

Will 't please you sit and look at her? I said   5
'Frà Pandolf' by design, for never read
Strangers like you that pictured countenance,
The depth and passion of its earnest glance,
But to myself they turned (since none puts by
The curtain I have drawn for you, but I)   10
And seemed as they would ask me, if they durst,
How such a glance came there; so, not the first
Are you to turn and ask thus. Sir, 't was not
Her husband's presence only, called that spot
Of joy into the Duchess' cheek: perhaps   15
Frà Pandolf chanced to say, 'Her mantle laps
Over my lady's wrist too much,' or 'Paint
Must never hope to reproduce the faint
Half-flush that dies along her throat.' Such stuff
Was courtesy, she thought, and cause enough   20
For calling up that spot of joy. She had
A heart – how shall I say? – too soon made glad,
Too easily impressed; she liked whate'er
She looked on, and her looks went everywhere.
Sir, 't was all one! My favour at her breast,   25
The dropping of the daylight in the West,
The bough of cherries some officious fool
Broke in the orchard for her, the white mule
She rode with round the terrace – all and each
Would draw from her alike the approving speech,   30
Or blush, at least. She thanked men, – good! but thanked
Somehow – I know not how – as if she ranked
My gift of a nine-hundred-years-old name
With anybody's gift. Who'd stoop to blame
This sort of trifling? Even had you skill   35
In speech – (which I have not) – to make your will
Quite clear to such an one, and say, 'Just this
Or that in you disgusts me; here you miss,
Or there exceed the mark' – and if she let
Herself be lessoned so, nor plainly set   40
Her wits to yours, forsooth, and made excuse,
– I E'en then would be some stooping; and I choose
Never to stoop. Oh, sir, she smiled, no doubt,
Whene'er I passed her; but who passed without
Much the same smile? This grew; I gave commands;   45
Then all smiles stopped together. There she stands
As if alive. Will 't please you rise? We'll meet
The company below then. I repeat,

The Count your master's known munificence
Is ample warrant that no just pretence   50
Of mine for dowry will be disallowed;
Though his fair daughter's self, as I avowed
At starting, is my object. Nay, we'll go
Together down, sir. Notice Neptune, though,
Taming a sea-horse, thought a rarity,   55
Which Claus of Innsbruck cast in bronze for me!

This long poem is built using rhyming couplets, each line of which follows
an iambic pentameter meter throughout. This has the effect of lending
the voice a natural tone, almost conspiratorial, as the speaker, the Duke,
shows the envoy the picture. The language used here harks back to the
Renaissance era, being formal in its diction. The persona speaks at a specific
time, and is not the voice of the poet, thus fulfilling the first condition of
Abrams. The speaker also reveals, unintentionally, his real personality to
his intended audience, the envoy, as well as to us, the independent audience, fulfilling Abrams' second criterion. Simply from the monologue, we
can perhaps get a sense of a strong, proud, powerful man used to dealing
with people harshly, one whose family name is paramount and one who
will brook no perceived disloyalty – however slight, or imagined. It also
reveals how women were treated as goods to be traded and the harsh treatment they might expect (although never fully specified, it can be inferred)
if they do not conform to their expected roles and modes (expected from
this speaker, at least!) of behaviour. This last serves to illustrate Abrams'
third point nicely: that the narrative reveals character and temperament,
unintentionally.

Richard Howard has written a dramatic monologue which answers, or
perhaps we should say builds, on Browning's, told from the point of view
of the imagined envoy: 'Nikolaus Mardruz to his Master Ferdinanc, Count
of Tyrol, 1565'. It is couched as a letter to his master and responds nicely
to some of the points raised in Browning's original, as well as giving more
insight into the imagined grounds of the Duke; from Mardruz' side we can
see things that would not have been discussed by the Duke in the original,
illustrating the principle about monologues that they can only ever give
one side of the story.

Exercises

Trying on a mask frees you from your own ego to experiment with different aspects of the voice, to take risks. It can be a refreshing challenge.
You could take a historical figure and, after some research, write a monologue in their imagined voice *at a particular point in time* – Henry VIII after

deciding to behead a wife; Amelia Earhart after flying the Atlantic; the choice is limitless.

Equally, you could take an unknown, somebody completely imagined – a widow whose husband has drowned, or a child starting school; situations such as these require empathy on the writer's part, to really imagine yourself into the feelings that the persona will have. As Rilke points out in *Letters to a Young Poet*, poems are situations – it is the reader who will find feeling within the poem. The writer needs to find enough feeling but convey it through the voice and diction of the monologue and use a concrete situation with clear imagery.

Another way is to remember that there are always two sides to any story. Leading on from the discussion of Howard giving answer to Browning's monologue, you could take a monologue that you are familiar with or admire and draft a reply to it. Set some strictures for yourself, such as trying out meter and even couplets. Try to supply a new angle on the reply, something that sheds a brand new light on what the original monologue said. You should have read both Browning's and Howard's monologues, to see how this might work.

Bibliography

Abrams, M. H. (2015) *A Glossary of Literary Terms*, 7th edn (www.ohio.edu)
    Available at: www.ohio.edu/people/hartleyg/ref../abrams_mh.pdf,
    accessed 30 May 2015
Browning, Robert (2015) 'My Last Duchess', in *Poetry Foundation: Classic Poems* (Poetry Foundation)
    Available at: www.poetryfoundation.org/poem/173024, accessed
    30 May 2015

20
Humour in Poetry

Todd Swift

What is it?

Poetry has always had a lighter side. There is, in fact, an *Oxford Book of Comic Verse* (and many other anthologies that cover similar territory). Though epic poetry has tended to cover the so-called big subjects – war, the founding of nations, the relationship of men to the gods or God and love and death – there has been satirical poetic writing since at least the time of the Greeks and Romans. Of the ancient Roman satirists, perhaps the best known is Catullus, whose raunchy poems 'took the piss out of' any number of persons and issues of his day.

English poets have employed humour from early on, as well – one thinks of the ribaldry at the heart of Chaucer. Shakespeare allowed bawdy puns to creep into his poetic plays, to please the groundlings. Later, humour becomes 'wit' – and arguably more refined – during the age of Pope and Swift. Swift's verse was often filled with the sort of bodily, lewd, gross-out humour we associate now with Adam Sandler or Melissa McCarthy; references to bodily functions, especially those of women, were meant to shock and amuse and to ultimately remind the aristocracy of the horrific fact that everyone 'shits', as Swift famously implied more than once. Pope, whose sense of wit was less scatological than Swift's, has a famous poem actually called 'Visiting Dr. Swift'.

Up until this point, very little of this poetry would be what we might consider side-splitting. Compared to the stand-up comedy of Bill Bailey or Jimmy Carr, it is more droll than laugh-out-loud stuff. Romantic poetry, indeed the nineteenth century in general, tended to become earnest again (Byron and Wilde are the exceptions here), with very little in the way of satirical or comic poetry, until one comes to what began to become known as 'nonsense verse' during the Victorian age. Nonsense verse has many famous practitioners, but the most popular is Lewis Carroll, the author of *Alice In Wonderland*, whose 'Jabberwocky' remains a delightful exercise in seriously silly wordplay:

Twas brillig, and the slithy toves
Did gyre and gimble in the wabe:
All mimsy were the borogoves,
And the mome raths outgrabe.

Others who wrote comic poetry include Edward Lear ('The Owl and the Pussy-Cat'), G. K. Chesterton, Hilaire Belloc and Sir Max Beerbohm (who wrote a poem called 'After Hilaire Belloc'). Belloc's poems begin to become recognizably humorous to the contemporary reader, especially his *Cautionary Tales for Children*, which feature bold children finding themselves dying outlandishly gruesome deaths, such as being eaten by a lion. W. H. Auden, in his lighter verse, sometimes manages to capture something of this tone. Ezra Pound, of course, wrote brief comic poems, with a satiric edge, as did T. S. Eliot, whose *Old Possum's Book of Practical Cats* is one of the greatest collections of light verse.

Modern comic poetry as its own genre really begins, though, with Don Marquis, an American poet whose masterpiece, *archy and mehitabel*, from 1927, is about the friendship between an alley cat and a cockroach. The poet e. e. cummings is the first modern poet to combine experiment and comedy so completely that it is often hard to tell them apart – though his wry, deadpan poems veer between high lyricism and zany typography and observations, so are not usually meant to be read as comic, but as simply exemplary of the modern mind at creative play. Later, Language Poets such as Charles Bernstein explored variations on this sort of manner.

Few poets of mid-century made much of a career from comic verse – though one became hugely popular, and is pretty much synonymous with light verse in America to this day: Ogden Nash. During the fifties and sixties, one American poet, John Berryman, introduced in his long sequence of poems, *Dream Songs*, a sort of vaudeville set-up, with a character Henry speaking to his wildly inappropriate alter ego (in politically dubious black face), Mr. Bones. These poems are both tragically sad (like many clowns the poet later killed himself) but at times actually funny.

Around the same time, The Movement poets in England, especially Kingsley Amis and Philip Larkin, began to explore an 'undeceived' language that was meant to debunk the rhetoric of romantic and neo-romantic poetry. Amis, whose career was mainly as a comic novelist, penned a few notable light verse poems; and it is possible to read many of Larkin's poems as comic or tragi-comic – many open with startling, darkly humorous claims ('they fuck you up, your mum and dad') or end with last lines that smack with the impact of punchlines.

Around the same time, in America, two distinct groups, the Beats and the New York School poets, managed to develop comic-satiric modes that were in some ways original. Ginsberg's poem about encountering Walt Whitman, the father of modern American poetry, in a supermarket has something of the satirical verve of Swift; meanwhile, Frank O'Hara introduced a novel style into poetry with his camp poems about events in and around the streets and walk-ups of New York.

How does it work?

If there is one thing most of us already know, it is that being funny is one of the hardest things to fake. Like being 'good looking', a lot depends on the instant reaction and tastes of one's immediate audience. If you don't find something amusing, it won't make you laugh, simple as that, but if it is truly pants-peeingly blindingly shatteringly silly, you may well not be able to control yourself from bursting out in guffaws. To be fair, poetry is rarely that sort of funny, but it can be, and it really depends on the way in which the humour or the joke is delivered. As most professional and even amateur comics will soon tell you, a lot depends on timing and on the punchline. No one has ever laughed at a joke they didn't 'get' and so one thing a comic poem often requires is to be written in a language that is more comprehensible (ordinary language) to the ordinary reader than some other poems, that may use more complex metaphors and other devices and tropes.

One thing is certain: comedians and comic poets tend to base their work on a familiarity with that of their peers, since the best way to measure if your sense of humour, your jokes, can 'go over' with a crowd is to check out how other people use comedy and humour. Fortunately, for us, then, the news is good: in the Britain of the twenty-first century, there are a number of popular and bestselling comic poets whose work we can easily access.

The best known of these is the poet Wendy Cope. Cope, whose debut *Making Cocoa for Kingsley Amis* is a send-up of a number of famous male poets and canonical poems (it includes *The Waste Land* limericks), introduces us to the concept of pastiche – where a poet takes on the style and themes of a famous poet, mimicking them in such a way as to delight the reader, who must know the originals to be in on the joke. In this way, it is a lot like being a comic impersonator.

Other current comic poets include John Hegley and Pam Ayres. Unlike in Cope's work, which is page-based, formally brilliant and usually literary, Hegley and Ayres partly rely on their performance-poet personas – which is not to suggest their work is less successful. Indeed, many slam and performance poets use comedy as a central part of their sets and at times cross over into what would to the audience sound like pure stand-up comedy.

A few of the most respected poets now writing employ a great deal of comedy or light verse touches in their work, including James Fenton, Christopher Reid, Craig Raine, Billy Collins, Paul Muldoon, Simon

Armitage, Carol Ann Duffy and Don Paterson. Fenton's light verse is very much in the mode of Auden's. Raine and Reid, once called 'Martian Poets' due to the alienating effects in their work, derive most of their comic effects from a sort of metaphysical twist – they take everyday items and topics and complicate them in an exaggerated fashion, in the process drawing out the humour (as if a Martian was describing a phone, telly or toilet, for instance) of outlandish and ingenious metaphors.

Billy Collins, perhaps America's best-known twenty-first century poet, writes poems that rely on a likeable everyday persona encountering life's little absurdities, though his work is also literary and tends to play gently with post-modern conceits as well. Paul Muldoon, in general a more serious writer, working in the shadow of Yeats and Heaney as perhaps his only rivals in the Irish canon, deploys a brilliantly baroque style that employs outrageous rhyme, much as Byron, Auden, Cole Porter and Bob Dylan did. In this, his work is more witty, a mixture of Donne and Pope with a little Wilde thrown in. His British peers, such as Paterson, are heavily indebted to his formal ingenuity and ability to make poems, even ones with quite dark themes ('Meeting the British' is about colonial murder), feel like fun – if not funny – riddles or puzzles to tease out.

Two prominent mid-career British poets associated with comedy in their work are Simon Armitage and Carol Ann Duffy; others that could be read in this light would include John Stammers, Paul Farley and Roddy Lumsden, who all use wit and humour to good effect from time to time.

Armitage's work aims to be popular but thought-provoking and is always well written, but in a way that manages to be playful and intriguing. Duffy, the current Poet Laureate, has made it her vocation to take dramatic monologue by the scruff of the neck (come to think of it, Browning was sometimes funny) and rewrite poems in the voices of various unexpected characters using the diction and perspectives of today – 'Lady Lazarus'.

For the very youngest poets now publishing in Britain, comedy has a very important part to play. Poets such as Joe Dunthorne, Jack Underwood, Sam Riviere, Emily Berry and especially Luke Kennard are often very funny. Kennard, whose influences include French and American prose poetry and *Monty Python*, is perhaps the most humorous, and yet literary, of any poet to ever write poetry in the English language. He has influenced, stylistically and thematically, nearly every poet under the age of 40 now writing in Britain. His genius is clearly evidenced, for it is a very difficult thing to be both intelligent and laugh-out loud funny, while also managing to write poetry of the first rank. In this, he has perhaps only one rival known to me, the Canadian poet, David McGimpsey, who has written a wildly comical series of 'chubby sonnets' – overlong poems that take the measure of American slob and pop culture (TV, hamburgers, and so on) – not satirically, but in celebratory fashion.

But back to Kennard, who introduces the utterly absurd, at times almost mad, scenario and character into his poetry. He often has personae speaking. They may be animals – like The Wolf – or even a snowflake speaking to a shopping centre. Unlike almost all the other poets discussed, except perhaps Wilde or Bernstein, surely influences, Kennard regards the poem as sheer artifice, a place to stage outlandish events and eruptions of insincerity – the poem as a process of ludicrous upstaging of its own conventions.

His poems break the mould of poetry and suggest unlimited new possibilities for it. It is clear to see this ability to provoke discussions of almost anything, from any speaking perspective, inspiring the best poems of Emily Berry's, whose work is darkly humorous in the manner of Morrissey's lyrics, or those of Jon Stone, whose poems are sometimes literally comic, in how they are inspired by Japanese anime. Indeed, in 2012, several 'graphic novels' were shortlisted for a major British literary prize, occasioning a recognition of the way in which genres and walls between the comic, the popular and the literary are porous and tremulous. Stone, Berry and Kennard are doing the same sort of work in poetry as are, to a degree, Riviere and Underwood.

What can I use it for?

One of the best questions ever asked of any poem is what can it be used for, and I suppose poems can be used to entertain, amuse, seduce, charm, teach, inspire and upset people, just like any other form of art (music, drama, art, film, dance and so on). Comical poetry is most obviously meant to be funny in some way, and in the process, maybe even get people to see something in a new light. But mostly, it is to make people feel better, if even briefly, and laugh.

If you are not a naturally funny person, but find yourself Eeyore-like glum and gloomy all the time, with a tendency to the more Gothic sort of poetry, dark and romantic, you needn't embark on a lifetime career of writing silly poems about crisps or alligators. It may be you can, though, turn the mirror on yourself, your habits and 'lampoon them' – send them up by exaggeration.

The best way to be funny is perhaps to use the occasion and forms of poetry itself to suggest aspects of words, language and themes that can be exaggerated and immediately signal an intent to laugh at the loftier aims of poetry.

Rhyme, for example, if handled badly (on purpose) is often amusing or silly. So is diction, if you choose ludicrous vocabulary or make up nonsense words. Another approach is to mock a genre (as Pope did) by writing, for instance, an Ode To A Paperclip – being overly self-important in poetry can lead to Bathos, which, if planned, can create comic moments. Finally, nothing is funnier than a good silly story – that is, a narrative that leads to a ridiculous and satisfyingly humorous conclusion. You may find yourself, when thinking about it, much funnier than you thought you were. So, enjoy. If your comic poems make your friends or even one other person (not a pet but a human) laugh, you can safely say you have written a comic poem.

Bibliography

Armitage, Simon and Robert Crawford (1998) *The Penguin Book of Poetry from Britain and Ireland Since 1945* (London: Viking)

Golding, Alan (1995) *From Outlaw to Classic: Canons in American Poetry* (Wisconsin: University of Wisconsin Press)

Nowottny, Winifred (1962) *The Language Poets Use* (London: The Athlone Press)

O'Brien, Sean (1998) *The Firebox: Poetry in Britain and Ireland After 1945* (London: Picador)

Perloff, Marjorie (2002) *21st-Century Modernism: The 'New' Poetics* (Oxford: Blackwell Publishers)

Puttenham, George (1970) *The Arte of English Poesie*, ed. by Gladys Doidge Willcock and Alice Walker, 2nd edn (Cambridge: Cambridge University Press)

21
Imagery

Ashley Lister

You see a little muddy pond
Of water, never dry,
I've measured it from side to side:
'Tis three feet long, and two feet wide.

These words, from the conclusion of the third stanza of Wordsworth's 'The Thorn' published in 1798, were later rewritten:

You see a little muddy pond
Of water – never dry,
Though but of compass small, and bare
To thirsty suns and parching air.

Obviously we have no way of knowing what it was about the original that Wordsworth found unsatisfactory. But it's fair to say that the final couplet of the original lacks poetic imagery and this might have been one of his reasons for the alteration. The language in the original is as poetic as one would expect to find from an order submitted to a builders' supply yard. It simply states size and measurement in a flat, two-dimensional description. It tells us nothing about the pond that would help the reader better understand its aesthetic. It says nothing that would help the reader experience any aspect of the pond's physicality.

It should be noted here that despite the usual connotations of the word, *imagery* in a literary context is not solely associated with visual stimuli. Current etymologies do cite the word *imagery* coming from Old French: *imagier*, meaning *painter*. However, tracing the word and its root further back we encounter *image*, from the Latin term *imaginem* with a stem of *imitari* meaning *to copy or imitate*.

It is this definition of imitation that sits at the heart of our poetic understanding of imagery. Plato condemned mimesis in *The Republic* but Aristotle, in *Poetics*, declared all art as imitation: 'Epic poetry and Tragedy, Comedy also and Dithyrambic poetry, and the music of the flute and of the lyre in most of their forms, are all in their general conception modes of imitation.' Sir Philip Sidney echoed Aristotle when he described poetry as an 'art of imitation'.[1] In a similar vein, Coleridge insisted: 'The artist must imitate.'[2] Imagery within poetry is the imitation of a subject through the words of the poem. Moreover, it is a form of imitation that is not limited to the reproduction of a single sense.

Conventionally, imagery is categorized under seven headings: visual, auditory, olfactory, gustatory, tactile, organic and kinaesthetic. The first five of these refer, respectively, to the physical senses of sight, sound, smell, taste and touch. Organic images are those relating to internal sensations such as hunger, fear and tiredness. Kinaesthetic images describe movement or tension. In short, imagery in poetry is any aspect of poetic language that heightens the perceived aesthetic or physicality of a piece of writing.

Exercise

Imagine yourself to be beside Wordsworth's little muddy pond from the lines of 'The Thorn' at the beginning this chapter. You already know the dimensions – 'tis three feet long and two feet wide. All you have to do for this exercise is describe the pond (or any similar pond you can imagine) using the five conventional senses. What does it look like, smell like, sound like, feel like, taste like? Don't worry about shaping these thoughts into a poem yet. Simply write descriptive notes using the imagery of the five senses.

Literal vs. figurative

As you will have noticed from the exercise above, imagery can be presented in literal or figurative terms – sometimes referred to as concrete and abstract language. If you described the ripples on the surface of the pond, or the sound of the wet splash of stones falling into the water, you were using literal or concrete imagery to name the key features perceived in your imagining of the pond.

If you described the *mirror-like* qualities of the surface, or the *giggling cries* of splashing water as the pond *swallows* another stone, the imagery moves into figurative or abstract terminology. The pond is being abstracted and personified by these descriptions in ways that move away from the literal.

To illustrate this point, consider the following lines:

The grey sea and the long black land
And the yellow half-moon large and low;
And the startled little waves that leap
In fiery ringlets from their sleep

These opening four lines from Robert Browning's *Meeting at Night* show literal and figurative language working together. The opening two lines give literal description to set the scene. We're told about the colour of the sea, land and moon, as well as being given indicators of the position and shape of those features. These are distinct literal images presented in concrete terminology. The sea is grey; the land is black; the half-moon is yellow.

However, in the third and fourth lines the imagery becomes more figurative. Browning uses personification to have the waves being *startled* from *their sleep*. He describes their shape as *fiery ringlets* – clearly a figurative description because waves (made from water) cannot literally be *fiery*. These lines with their suggestions of someone being startled awake and heatedly roused from their sleep (along with the development of the rest of the poem) have helped many commentators suggest the poem is an analogy for an intimate tryst between two clandestine lovers. It's an interpretation that would not have been possible without the imagery that is evoked by Browning's sophisticated blending of literal and figurative language.

Exercise

Start to shape your observations from the previous exercise into a poem. Begin, like Browning, by using literal descriptions to describe shape, size, colour and contours. Continue by developing figurative descriptions. Add to this some organic and kinaesthetic imagery expressing emotional and physical responses to your vision of the pond. Select an appropriate form for this draft of the poem and consider how these various elements of imagery could potentially complement each other.

Organic and kinaesthetic imagery

> When with unkindness our love at a stand is,
> And both have punished ourselves with the pain,
> Ah what a pleasure the touch of her hand is,
> Ah what a pleasure to press it again!

The above lines from John Dryden's 'Song' include examples of organic and kinaesthetic imagery in literal terms. Dryden cites organic imagery such as unkindness, love and punishment in concrete language. He mentions the touch of his lover's hand (a tactile image) and then concludes the stanza with the kinaesthetic image of receiving pleasure from pressing her hand again.

Less literal and more figurative is the imagery in the lines below:

Seasons of mists and mellow fruitfulness,
Close bosom-friend of the maturing sun;
Conspiring with him how to load and bless
With fruit the vines that round the thatch-eaves run;
To bend with apples the mossed cottages-trees,
And fill all fruit with ripeness to the core
To swell the gourd, and plump the hazel shells
With a sweet kernel; so set budding more.

In these opening lines from 'To Autumn', Keats uses organic imagery to describe the mellow fruitfulness of the season. He uses figurative language to suggest personification of the sun and autumn as they *conspire* to make the approaching harvest bounteous. Keats goes on to make this opening passage rich with kinaesthetic images as he describes the vines running round the eaves; trees bending with apples and gourds swelling. It's a detailed passage that gives us an iconic image of a superlative autumn. It's the imitation in words of the perfect autumn.

Synaesthesia

Some of the most memorable images can come to us when one domain of description is utilized by another. We are all familiar with the distinctive scent implied when someone describes 'the smell of hospital'. We all know what is meant when someone says they enjoy 'Getting their teeth into a good book' or when they claim to have seen someone 'wearing a loud shirt'. We understand the flavours of emotions in phrases such as 'the bitter taste of defeat' or 'the sweet taste of success'. We can process the imagery in these poetic descriptions even though they shift across domains of sensory perception. This is possibly because they rely on the technique of defamiliarization.

It's suggested that the overused cliché, along with the weary dead metaphor, are the greatest challenges against vivid imagery and it's true that we're not hearing anything new, memorable or exciting when we're told 'the heavens opened' or 'it's raining cats and dogs'. For our poems we want to create the most striking, vivid and memorable images and, to this end, this means creating imagery that is innovative, original and imaginative. One of the most respected thinkers on this topic was formalist writer Viktor Shklovsky:

art exists that one may recover the sensation of life; it exists to make one feel things, to make the stone stony. The purpose of art is to impart the sensation of things as they are perceived and not as they are known. The technique of art is to make objects "unfamiliar," to make forms difficult, to increase the difficulty and length of perception because the process of perception is an aesthetic end in itself and must be prolonged. Art is a way of experiencing the artfulness of an object; the object is not important.

Shklovsky, V., 'Art as Technique'[3]

This concept, referred to by Shklovsky as *defamiliarization*, is the cornerstone of vivid, innovative imagery. It is a way of creating images that are artful in their construction and sufficiently unusual to make a lasting impression.

Take, for example, George Herbert's poem 'The Collar'. When the persona in this poem uses the phrase 'Thy rope of sands' to describe the restrictive but insubstantial bindings of religious beliefs, the reader is treated to a striking image of a rope of sands that incorporates synaesthesia, figurative language and a form of description that requires some sophisticated level of aesthetic perception to translate the 'unfamiliar' into something identifiable and relatable.

Similarly, a reader could reflect on the defamiliarization of the entire poetic conceit of John Donne's 'Elegy XX: To His Mistress Going to Bed':

License my roving hands, and let them go
Before, behind, between, above, below.
O my America! my new-found-land,
My kingdom, safest when with one man manned,

This is a poem where the male persona, in attempting to seduce his mistress, develops the extended metaphor of exploring her body like a traveller discovering new aspects of the world. It is removed from a typical love poem with tropes of affection and commitment. Instead it presents the mistress as a world to be discovered by the explorer/persona which makes the unfamiliar imagery all the more memorable.

Exercise

Take any of our previous descriptions from the previous exercises and develop them through defamiliarization. Instead of relying on familiar tropes, transform your imagery into something new and unusual. Use synaesthesia to cross boundaries between domains of sensory perception. Use striking, unusual and innovative associations to make your imagery new and memorable. Make the stones beside your pond stonier.

Bibliography

Elliott, C. W. (1909) *English Essays: Sidney to Macaulay. Vol. XXVII.* The
   Harvard Classics (New York: P. F. Collier & Son)
Shepherd, Geoffrey (ed.) (1965) *An Apology for Poetry, or, The Defence of Poesy*
   (London: Nelson)
Shklovsky, Viktor (1965) 'Art as Technique' In Lee T. Lemon and Marion J.
   Reis (1965) *Russian Formalist Criticism: Four Essays* (Nebraska: University
   of Nebraska Press)

22
Persona

Angela France

The word 'persona' derives from the Latin for 'mask'; the persona was the mask worn by an actor in Greek drama. A 'persona poem' is often used to mean dramatic monologue, where a poet takes on the voice of a particular character and speaks as them, using the first person. Dramatic monologue is explored in more detail in Chapter 19. Persona is also used to describe the narrator in narrative poems and the 'I' in lyric poems; the persona is the speaker of the poem, in any type of poem. A great deal of contemporary poetry is voiced in the apparently autobiographical first person but even in a 'confessional' poem the reader cannot assume the speaker is the same as the poet; the 'I' is a persona constructed by the poet, sometimes unconsciously, to reveal to the reader only those aspects of self the poet chooses to reveal. The psychologist Carl Jung said of persona: 'The persona ... is the individual's system of adaptation to, or the manner he assumed in dealing with, the world.'[1] Persona is not always straightforward; John Berryman, in his *Dream Songs*, uses an alter ego called Henry who sometimes speaks of himself in third person. Berryman denied any autobiographical connection with Henry but also said, in an interview, 'Henry does resemble me, and I resemble Henry' and Henry appears to work through some of the traumas that Berryman suffers such as his father's suicide and deaths of poet friends.[2]

A deliberately constructed persona can be a versatile tool for the poet: it can allow the poet to explore themes outside their comfort zone; it can say things the poet may not; and may strike unpopular attitudes or examine uncomfortable issues. The constructed 'I' of the persona can be a way for the poet to work with their shadow side or to disclose to the reader only those aspects of themselves they wish to be seen. There are no limits on what a persona may be: trustworthy or unreliable, likeable or irritating, serious or playful – whatever will benefit the poem and the poet's aim. It can be easy, or at least comfortable, for poets to fall into a habit of a default persona, leading to their poems appearing to be too similar or too comfortable. The reader perceives the persona through the language used in the poem and many writers use a relatively narrow lexicon in their work, through habit. It can be fruitful to try changing the range of language in a poem from that which you normally use – for example, if you usually use multisyllable Latinate words, try simplifying the language to Anglo-Saxon-based words, or vice versa. What effect does the change have on the poem? Is the persona different? Does the change benefit the poem? Experimenting with relatively small changes of approach can alter the persona, and how the reader reacts to it, quite dramatically. Changing the point of view to third person, second person or first person can give the persona access to different ways of approaching the poem's content – a first-person speaker, for example, can access internal thoughts and feelings, while a third person can be more observational and may provide distance from uncomfortable material, though the writer should question whether distance from uncomfortable material is beneficial for the poem.

Every poet is, in a sense, a dramatist making choices about how to present their work to an audience, however vaguely or definitely imagined, through the vehicle of the persona, and the form of address used by the speaker is an important factor in how an audience perceives the persona. In a poem where the speaker is using direct address, to a lover, friend or enemy, the audience/reader is put in a position of overhearing or eavesdropping, while a poem such as Shelley's 'Ozymandias',[3] which begins with the narration 'I met a traveller from an antique land', signals that the speaker is to tell a story directly to the audience. Much contemporary poetry is in the lyric mode – that is, speaking in the first person, the present tense and focused on the speaker's thoughts and feelings; the speaker appears to be addressing themselves or no one in particular so that the audience is again in the position of overhearing. Whatever position the speaker takes in the poem, the reader has some awareness, even if subconsciously, of the poet behind the persona; conversely, the poet has some awareness of the audience so that the persona acts as a channel between poet and audience. If this relationship and awareness does not exist, then, particularly in the case of lyric poetry, there is a risk of the poem being no more than a diary entry.

Understanding how different approaches to persona can affect poems, and their readers, is essential if a beginning poet is to make considered, writerly decisions about persona for the benefit of their work.

Exercise

Read the following poem by M. R. Peacocke and think about the persona. How do you feel about the persona? What can you surmise about the speaker from the language and tone? Do you feel you can trust the speaker? Try to identify the cues in the text that help to form your opinion of the persona.

Nameless

I do not know her name.
Clearing the trough, I found
her shadow and wore it home.
Our steps moved easily
over the broken ground,
flagstones, pineapple weed.
We paused to watch a lamb
and the first brimstone butterfly
gladdening in the sun.
    She is one and many,
my undiscerned companion;
evidence of her life
bits and pieces thrown away
or lost, like this garden fork,
roughly forged, its handle gone,
under a litter of sycamore leaf
and nettle lightly buried.
    My hands like hers have thickened,
hoping to mould time
into a good loaf;
like her I bend my back
to root out thistle and dock
and trap the rat that capers under the roof.
Jetsam on this land,
labouring to eke out the hay
through meagre February,
perhaps at best we learn
to stand and note the streak of lime
that shows where already starlings are raising a brood
in the wall badged with lichen.

                    M. R. Peacocke[4]

Tone is closely related to persona; tone, expressed through the use of language, demonstrates the attitude of the speaker towards the subject matter of the poem and the audience. Tone enables the reader to know, and engage with, the persona of the poem. If a poem is read aloud, or recited, by the poet the audience can judge the tone through inflection, expression and gesture, as well as through the language, but the reader of a printed poem only has what is on the page. Tone is mostly expressed through diction but can also be discerned through image, rhythm, cadence and punctuation. Any tone which is possible in speech is also possible in poetry: bitterly ironic as in W. H. Auden's 'The Unknown Citizen';[5] tender and wistful as in W. B. Yeats's 'When You are Old';[6] or regretful as in Robert Hayden's 'Those Winter Sundays'.[7] Just as human attitudes and feelings are complex, tone in poetry can be complex; the tone can encompass more than a single attitude and may shift in the space of a few lines of poetry. Engaging with the tone of a poem brings the reader into closer contact with the poet; tone expresses, through the persona, what the poet wishes the reader to understand about the poem, both emotionally and intellectually.

Exercise

While tone is too complex in a strong poem to define from a single line, it is possible to begin to discern an indication of tone from a line. Read the following lines carefully. What sort of tones can you hear in them? Can you get any sense of a persona from a single line?

'Do not weep, babe, for war is kind' from 'War is Kind' by Stephen Crane[8]

'I have been one acquainted with the night' from 'Acquainted with the night' by Robert Frost[9]

'Twilight bounds softly forth on the grass' from 'A Blessing' by James Wright[10]

'watch the soft blush seep through her skin' from 'Warming her Pearls' by Carol Ann Duffy[11]

'in that Amherst pantry while the jellies boil and scum' from 'Snapshots of a Daughter-in-Law' by Adrienne Rich[12]

For a poem to be successful the reader has to believe in the presenting persona, and to believe in the persona the reader needs to find it consistent and authentic. That is not to say that a persona has to speak factual truths even if a poem is based on personal memory. Following the language, image, rhythm, metaphor and other tropes will build a stronger and more authentic poem than 'what really happened'. A strong poem will carry its own internal truth which feels authentic to the reader, however fictional or strange the content is, and much of the poem's credibility is carried by the persona's authority and consistency of tone. For example, if a poem relates a childhood memory from the child's point of view then a world-weary tone or sophisticated language will strike the reader as inauthentic. A persona can easily lose authority if the poet is careless; poor spelling, sloppy punctuation or obvious errors in observation, for example mentioning a swallow in a British winter, are likely to cause the reader to lose trust in the speaker and hence in the poem.

So, why is it important for the reader to believe in the persona (even in a deliberately unreliable one)? Because, if the reader believes in the persona, they will be more willing to go along with wherever (and however) the poem takes them. Conversely, if a reader loses trust in the persona through inconsistencies or the poet's carelessness they are much less likely to be open to images, metaphors or anything else the poet asks of them. They may even dismiss the poem altogether.

Exercise

For a final exercise, take one of your own poems and change the persona and tone. Aim to create three different versions of the same poem; try to identify the different affects each version will have. Share the versions with your peers and get their reactions to the different versions; this will help you understand the effect that your deliberate decisions about persona may have on your work as it develops.

Bibliography

Auden, W. H. (1940) *Another Time* (London: Random House)
Ferguson, M., M. J. Salter and J. Stallworthy (eds) (2005) *The Norton Anthology of Poetry*, 5th edn (New York: W. W. Norton)
Jung, Carl (1999) *Four Archetypes*, 3rd edn (Abingdon: Routledge)
Peacocke, M. R. (1995) *Selves* (Calstock: Peterloo Poets)
Stitt, Peter, *Excerpts from Interviews with John Berryman*. www.english.illinois. edu/maps/poets/a_f/berryman/interviews.htm, accessed 28 August 2012
Yeats, W. B. (1993) *Early Poems* (Mineola, NY: Dover Publications)

23
Voice

Andrea Holland

When we talk of the voice in a poem, we understand that it has extended metaphorically far beyond its original sense of the vocal qualities of a particular speaker. Often learners studying poetry conflate the voice in the poem and the writer of the poem; indeed, historically, the dominant poetic mode has been one in which the speaker in a poem is seen as the poet – for example, Wordsworth's 'Tintern Abbey' or Walt Whitman's 'I Sing the Body Electric'. The other approach is to see the poet constructing a persona via a dramatic monologue, perhaps most famously in Robert Browning's 'My Last Duchess', in which the Duke is 'speaking' to an unnamed and silent valet. The Duke narrates and manipulates through his single voice. Of course, unless a poem is polyphonic, most poems will offer a single voice speaking to us, the readers. But the occasion of a dramatic monologue suggests that the speaker in the poem is talking to an unnamed other, present within the dramatic moment or occasion:

> How such a glance came there; so, not the first
> are you to turn and ask thus. Sir, 't was not
> her husband's presence only, called that spot
> of joy into the Duchess' cheek ...

The narrative mode in this poem – how the story is told – is dependent on voice and is particularly significant in a poem such as Browning's; this fictive narrator affects our understanding of the subject of the poem, just as an unreliable narrator may do in a short story. However, the relationship that 'voice' has with the idea or conceit of a poem is perhaps not so tied to narrative as it may be in prose fiction, and that can be liberating when writing a poem. Poems do not always tell stories, but they always reveal a voice.

In poems such as those by Wordsworth or Whitman, in which the speaker, or voice, in the poem can be confidently assumed to be the poet, readers are offered a view, a tone of voice in which the poet's lyrical observation invites us to share this often expansive vision. This position (of privileged observation by the poet) often leads the reader to witness a self bigger than the self; at an extreme, for example, we have Walt Whitman's claim 'I am huge, I contain multitudes'. More quietly, but with as much power, Elizabeth Bishop declares 'Everything was rainbow rainbow rainbow/ and I let the fish go'.

In the twentieth century, there began to be a shift in ways of speaking, most closely observed as a result of modernist poets such as T. S. Eliot, William Carlos Williams, W. B. Yeats and others. Within this 'school' of poetry the emergence of a persona as the voice in the poem meant that a poem could blend the voice of the poet with a character or speaker. This might be seen as similar to the way in which some fiction writers adapt or merge characters from real life and give them a new framework or mask as a character within the story. So, too, in poems of the twentieth century to the present, where a speaker, as in John Stammers' poem 'Funeral', smokes 'an ugly brown cigarello' at a funeral:

> its liverous grey wisps swell the nose.
> We shall float up, a grey twist
> of smoke

and the reader is unable to say for sure if the person smoking the cigarello is the poet himself or a character/persona invented by Stammers for the purposes of the poem. Is the 'We' *floating up* (like smoke) the funeral attendees? Or that more amorphous collective, the readers of this poem?

People who want to write poems might consider that there is a psychology of voice in poetry, particularly in the use of the second and third person, which function differently than the first person, 'I' voice. Poets have long written odes to objects, creatures, seasons and of course to those whom the poet loves. And they often use the second person, 'you', to extol the virtues of the subject of the poem, for example 'Thou still unravish'd bride of quietness' is addressed to 'thou' (that is, 'you') – *the Grecian urn* in John Keats' famous ode. And D. H. Lawrence observes and reports in 'Baby Tortoise' on the

> Voiceless little bird,
> Resting your head half out of your wimple
> In the slow dignity of your eternal pause

The titles of Keats' and Lawrence's poems make it clear to whom or what the speaker is addressing by using 'you' in the second person. There is clearly an 'I' and a 'you'. However, one of the shifts which might be described as part of a postmodern reconsideration of the use of voice in a poem is the emergence of a different approach to, or use of, the second-person point of view (and the resulting imperative tone) in a poem. How-to books on writing often advise against using the second person, either in prose or in poetry, and it is by no means a common phenomenon. Nevertheless, the use of 'you', and the imperative tone most often associated with the second person, has altered the landscape of expression within poetry.

'You has no borders' says Martin Buber in '*I and Thou*'. It is not now so easy to identify this *you* speaking to us from the poem; the poet will likely be considering the *you* as either a direct address to the reader and/or, perhaps less often, a reflexive *you* commenting on the self in the poem. In Katha Pollit's 'From a Notebook' this reflexive you is evident in the voice:

> ... even today
> at the last possible moment
> you can walk away, as out of a cheap hotel,
> leaving ten dollars under the key on the bureau.

We can be fairly confident that the speaker is trying to convince herself – is there really anyone else to talk like this to? – to leave whatever unnamed situation she finds herself in, to face the uncertainty of life outside the 'cheap hotel', because she wants to believe 'you're not your life', and we understand this feeling and this need; it's there for us in the *you*. So, if handled well, an unqualified 'you' in a poem can be a powerful tool in the voice 'box', with its illusion of address and complicated self-reflection.

The third person, using 'he', 'she' or 'they', is the historically dominant mode in poetry and this point of view can, as with prose, suggest an omniscient narrator or an objective detached voice telling a story or offering a lyrical observation of an object or situation – for example, in 'Bestiary for the Fingers of My Right Hand', Charles Simic appears to observe his own thumb as a character in its own right:

> Horn of a devil. Fat worm
> They have attached to my flesh
> At the time of my birth.
> It takes four to hold him down,
> Bend him in half, until the bone
> Begins to whimper ...

The tone of voice in this poem is affected by the characterization, the personification and the conceit driving the poem. Voice needs careful consideration when writing a poem and it is a good idea for beginning poets to practise changing the point of view of any finished poem, particularly if written in the first person, to see what happens when it appears in second or third person. So, a line such as 'I walk with my sister to the rope of trees / and we tell the truth of step and say' would become: 'She walks with her sister to the rope of trees / and they tell the truth of step and say'. Or, in second person: 'You walk with your sister to the rope of trees / and you tell the truth of step and say'. Each of these three 'voices' takes a position with regard to the subject and brings a new or different way for the reader to understand and (hopefully) connect with the speaker. It's worth noting that, in the latter, the second person *you* makes it less clear who is telling 'the truth of step and say'. But this obfuscation can be deliberate in its effect.

On a critical level, we may understand the use of voice in a poem as characterizing 'the tonal qualities, attitudes, or even the entire personality of this speaker as it reveals itself directly or indirectly (through sound, choice of diction, and other stylistic devices) ... [voice] reminds us that a human being is behind the words of a poem'.[1]

Since every human being is different, it is inevitable that each poet will, intentionally or not, present a distinct voice (that is, 'the entire personality of this speaker') even when addressing the same theme. But the consideration of voice usually goes beyond where the poet is from and how they talk 'in real life', to a choice he or she makes in communicating the idea or conceit of each poem. Some poets use the voice of 'everyday' speech – this is often but not exclusively associated with a writing style often called *reportage* – and this everyday voice can make a poem clear, direct and accessible. However it can also be so informal and casual that it risks losing a broader poetic quality and turning into unruly prose on short lines. There is a balance to be made in avoiding 'pretentious' or self-consciously poetic diction but also presenting a voice which does more than simply chat to us over line breaks.

We can observe the range of voices possible for a poet to employ. It is a great bag of tricks; from children's playground chants to hip-hop raps – both of which often embrace playfulness in voice that could also be employed in what Sylvia Plath called, 'garden-variety poems', that is, straightforward lyrical poems[2] – an individual tells a tale or narrates a scene using their voice as the sole technique to express themselves. Without the literary techniques of the written word it is tone of voice, along with rhythm (and sometimes rhyme), in the recitation which is crucial in order to present a memorable oral piece of work. It serves the poet well to have a broad vocabulary and a love of language.

There's no doubt that *Beowulf*, as a story, survived orally before its eighth-century transcription, not just because it is a memorable tale but because there were storytellers with strong voices recounting the epic tale to generations of eager listeners. But a strong voice doesn't always have to be loud.

Of course, voice in a piece of writing is not simply about intonation in oral recitation; for poets today the way they engage with 'voice' is usually seen as being as important as the way they engage with form, and that voice may not simply be their own. Carolyn Forché's long poem, 'The Angel of History', is described as 'giving voice to the unutterable' by which we understand the poem uses language and personae – disparate voices to conjure other forgotten voices. Forché the poet becomes Forché the speaker, but not just as herself; the voice is polyphonic:

In the night-vaulted corridors of the Hôtel-Dieu, a
sleepless woman pushes her stretcher
    along the corridors of the past. *Bonjour, Madame.*
Je m'appelle Ellie.

And, later, the speaker and 'Ellie' – the two voices – may be seen to become one voice; for example:

And the fields? Aren't the fields changed by what happened?
The dead aren't like us.
How can the fields continue as simple fields?

Voice in poetry is as simple and direct or as complex and obtuse as the poem requires; in a good poem it is unlikely to be unconsidered. Anyone wishing to write a poem will want to consider the way the voice they use affects the poem – most obviously with regard to tone and diction. But ultimately, without a convincing voice, a poem is just an idea or an image in short lines.

Bibliography

Bishop, Elizabeth (1983) *The Complete Poems* (New York: Farrar Straus Giroux)

Browning, Robert (1994) *The Poems of Robert Browning* (Ware: Wordsworth Editions)

Forché, Carolyn (1994) *The Angel of History* (Tarset: Bloodaxe Books)

Keats, John (1994) *The Complete Poems* (New York: Random House)

Lawrence, D. H. (2008) *Selected Poems* (London: Penguin)

Plath, Sylvia (1977) *Johnny Panic & The Bible of Dreams* (London: Faber & Faber)

Pollit, Katha (2012) *The Mind-Body Problem* (Bridgend: Seren)

Preminger, Alex (ed.) (1965) *Princeton Encyclopedia of Poetry and Poetics* (Princeton, NJ: Princeton University Press)

Simic, Charles (1999) *Selected Early Poems* (New York: George Braziller)

Stammers, John (2010) *Interior Night* (London: Picador)

Whitman, Walt (2006) *Leaves of Grass* (New York: Simon & Schuster)

24
The Singing Within

Ann Drysdale

De la musique avant toute chose

Paul Verlaine[1]

As it happens, this is not about the music that Verlaine advocated – which was more a sort of floating inaccuracy that partially obscured the subject, like the nipples of Salome between veils. It is about the choices that determine the diction of a poem: the echoes in the head; the music in the mouth.

Emily Dickinson said it better:[2]

Split the Lark – and you'll find the Music—
Bulb after Bulb, in Silver rolled—
Scantily dealt to the Summer Morning
Saved for your Ear when Lutes be old.

Music is what makes a poem memorable; it is why we want to remember it at all. Music is what crystallizes the meaning and fast-tracks it to the heart. Without it a poem is prose.

It captivates us as toddlers, the nursery rhyme and the nonsense that tempts us to say it aloud.

Baa Baa Black Sheep[3]
    Have you any wool?
    Yes, sir. Yes, sir.
    Three bags full...

We can say the little tune of it:

Da-da Da-da
Diddle-diddle Dum
Da-da Da-da
Dum Dum Dum

And we are beginning to see what is meant by meter. When we learn to read for ourselves and find a voice of our own we look for verse to speak aloud. One of my own favourites was G. K. Chesterton's 'Lepanto',[4] with lines such as:

> Dim drums throbbing, in the hills half heard,
> Where only on a nameless throne a crownless prince has stirred,
> Where, risen from a doubtful seat and half attainted stall,
> The last knight of Europe takes weapons from the wall,
> The last and lingering troubadour to whom the bird has sung,
> That once went singing southward when all the world was young.

Now, let's split the lark and see what makes it sing. Well, in this case there's *rhyme*; here it is at the end of each pair of lines: 'heard', 'stirred', 'sung', 'young' and so on. Then there's alliteration, the use of the same letter at the beginnings of words: 'dim drums', 'hills half heard' and 'weapons from the wall', which occurs in different places within the lines.

More subtle (because they occur within the words), but equally powerful, are the twin tricks of assonance and consonance. Assonance is the repetition of vowel sounds in words that are close to each other – 'only', 'throne', 'crown-'. Like alliteration, it is the sound rather than the letter used that is important. Consonance is characterized by the repetition of the same consonant sound within a group of words: 'nameless', 'crownless prince'.

In Welsh language poetry there is a name for the music – *cynghanedd* (pronounced *kung-haneth*),[5] which means 'harmony' and refers to the sound arrangement within a single line using strict and specialized variants of the tools above. Cynghanedd is still used today by many poets writing in Welsh and several poets have experimented with it in English, for instance Gerard Manley Hopkins and Dylan Thomas. Seek them out, though they may persuade you that overuse of the mechanics can sound a bit self-conscious.

In the bailiwick of free verse the music is even more essential because that's all there is. With no end-rhyme and no meter to hold the frame together the integrity of it depends on the endings of the lines and the singing within them. For example:

After the Sea Ship[6]

> After the sea-ship, after the whistling winds,
> After the white-gray sails taut to their spars and ropes,
> Below, a myriad myriad waves hastening, lifting up their necks,
> Tending in ceaseless flow toward the track of the ship,
> Waves of the ocean bubbling and gurgling, blithely prying,

Waves, undulating waves, liquid, uneven, emulous waves,
Toward that whirling current, laughing and buoyant, with curves,
Where the great vessel sailing and tacking displaced the surface,
Larger and smaller waves in the spread of the ocean yearnfully flowing,
The wake of the sea-ship after she passes, flashing and frolicsome under the sun,
A motley procession with many a fleck of foam and many fragments,
Following the stately and rapid ship, in the wake following.

Walt Whitman

I find it interesting to note that Whitman observes the convention of beginning each line with a capital letter and uses commas at the ends of them, indicating that each is a subordinate clause in the whole poem-sentence. Here, he tells us, is where you must breathe. Can you split the lark of this one and find the musical devices in Whitman's work?

Some points to think about. Does the search for music inhibit freedom of expression? A reader might think so but many practising poets would agree with W. H. Auden that attention to craft disciplines the mind and allows the underlying thought to be expressed with greater clarity – or at least with more satisfying fidelity to the poet's original idea.

W. B. Yeats wrote in his poem 'Adam's Curse':[7]

   ... A line will take us hours maybe;
   Yet if it does not seem a moment's thought,
   Our stitching and unstitching has been naught.

Wordsworth unstitched as he went along, as his notebooks demonstrate.[8] His sonnet 'Composed Upon Westminster Bridge' varies at first between 'Earth hath (not anything to show more fair)' in many editions and online quotations and 'Earth has...' which is what he originally wrote. Can you hear why? Put both phrases in your mouth and speak them – 'earth hath' sounds (and feels) as if you've got a hair on your tongue.

Sometimes, when they have been practising their craft for a long time the head-song falls straight onto the page and takes the poet by surprise. Trust me, the achievement of this occasional effortless success is well worth the apprenticeship of the drafting and grafting, for when the singing is in place, all the components of the poem – the rhyme, meter, sound, diction, grammar and content – will all fit together in such a way that there could be no other way.

'This poem is my song and within it I have hidden the seeds of the tune to which you should sing it.' Listen – can you hear it?

Bibliography

Cooper, Mary (ed.) (1744) *Tommy Thumb's Pretty Song Book Voll. [sic] II*, (London)

Dickinson, Emily (1924) *Complete Poems* (Boston: Little, Brown and Company)

Methuen, Algernon (ed.) (1923) *An Anthology of Modern Verse* (London: Methuen's English Classics)

Preminger, Alex, Terry V. F. Brogan and Frank J. Warnke (eds) (1993) *Princeton Encyclopedia of Poetry and Poetics* (Princeton, NJ: Princeton University Press)

Verlaine, Paul (1884) *Jadis et naguère* (Paris: L Vanier)

Whitman, Walt (1961) *Leaves of Grass* (New York: Penguin Classics)

Wordsworth, William, British Library ADD MS 47864

Yeats, W. B. (1989) *The Collected Poems* (New York: Macmillan)

PART III:
POETICS & PRACTICE

25

Gerard Manley Hopkins: Sprung Rhythm, Inscape and Instress

Nigel McLoughlin

When students are first confronted by the work of Hopkins, there is inevitably much discussion about *sprung rhythm, inscape* and *instress*. These discussions tend to be about defining the terms and showing examples which may be conveniently quoted in essays and so on. In this chapter I look at what each of these actually means in practical terms and what use they are to the modern poet writing today and the apprentice poet learning his or her trade in particular.

Sprung rhythm

In his preface to his poems Hopkins gives the following detailed definition of sprung rhythm:

> Sprung Rhythm, as used in this book, is measured by feet of from one to four syllables, regularly, and for particular effects any number of weak or slack syllables may be used. It has one stress, which falls on the only syllable, if there is only one, or, if there are more, then scanning as above, on the first and so gives rise to four sorts of feet, a monosyllable and the so-called accentual Trochee, Dactyl, and the First Paeon.[1]

This quote shows that sprung rhythm, as Hopkins envisaged it, was made up of a mixture of four metric feet. These can occur in any order and for the purposes of defining the rhythm it is unimportant how many slack or unstressed syllables occur within the line; what matters is the number of stressed syllables. In this it bears a striking resemblance to the base meter of music where what is important is the number of beats to the bar rather than the number of grace notes included.

In order to get a handle on how Hopkins thought of the rhythm of poetry, it might be best to start with that analogy. The line of verse is equivalent to the musical bar. The number of stressed syllables within the line form the number of beats to the bar – the time signature of the bar. Depending on the type of foot used, there can be a variety of effects on the music of the poem. If one uses mainly monosyllables (one stressed syllable) and trochaic feet (one stressed syllable followed by one unstressed syllable), the line will be short and staccato as in the following lines from *Pied Beauty*:

> **Whatev**er is **fickle**, **freckled** (**who** knows **how?**)
> With **swift, slow; sweet, sour;** adazzle **dim;**[2]

If one tends to use more *dactyls* (a stressed syllable followed by two unstressed syllables) or *first paeons* (a stressed syllable followed by three unstressed syllables) the line will feel rushed and elided due to the large number of unstressed syllables to be covered in the same 'time signature' – the musical equivalent of having lots of grace notes as in the following section from 'The Windhover':

> As a **skate's** heel **sweeps** smooth on a **bow**-bend: the **hurl** and **glid**ing
> Re**buff**ed the **big** wind. My **heart** in **hid**ing
> **Stir**red for a **bird**, - the a**chieve** of, the **mast**ery of the **thing!**[3]

These effects can be used to add great life and energy to the line of poetry – they force the line to verge on song. This in itself is not surprising. Hopkins certainly recognized that sprung rhythm was a 'logaoedic' or mixed one.[4] Logaoedic rhythm was considered by the ancient Greeks to lie on the boundary between speech and song.

Hopkins was Professor of Rhetoric at Roehampton, and as such was academically interested in the tropes and devices that poetry used to achieve its effects as well as being interested from a poetic point of view. One particular piece of information which is included in the Preface is telling. It deals with Hopkins' theory that sprung rhythm naturally arises:

> nursery rhymes, weather saws ... once made in running rhythm, the terminations having dropped off by the change of language, the stresses come together and so the rhythm is sprung.[5]

There is no doubt that English was once a much more inflected language than it is now, and that these usually unstressed inflections have been lost. The effect would tend to bring stressed syllables together and disrupt regular rhythm (Hopkins called this *running rhythm* – iambic pentameter is an example). What is telling about it is its subtext; the effect arises through the flux generated by the change in language. Languages today find themselves in similar states of flux; consider the energy and staccato rhythms of rap and how much of that can be said to be generated by the leaving out or eliding of unnecessary usually unstressed words such as 'the', 'a', 'it', 'of', 'in', and so on.

Hopkins said that the lines within a stanza should

> be *rove over*, that is for the scanning of each line immediately to take up that of the one before, so that if the first has one or more syllables at its end the other must have so many less at its beginning; and in fact the scanning runs on without break from the beginning, say, of a stanza to the end and all the stanza is one long strain, though written in lines asunder.[6]

This effect occurs in running rhythm also, where it is referred to as compensation. The difference, however, is that Hopkins' system is more flexible in that compensations within running rhythm usually only apply to one unstressed syllable – Hopkins seems willing to allow one, two or three unstressed syllables and treats the stanza as the base unit of coherence. The latter end of that quotation is particularly interesting – 'the stanza is one long strain'. The word 'strain' here implies music and speaks to Hopkins' equation of musical integrity and coherence in poetry, but it also implies pressure and force, which will become very pertinent later when we come to discuss inscape and instress.

Hopkins allowed a number of licences in his description of sprung rhythm, the most important of these are what he called *hangers* or *outrides*. These consisted of 'one, two or three slack syllables added to a foot and not counting in the nominal scanning.'[7] They were extra-metrical in a further sense also. Hopkins said of them that they 'seem to hang below the line or ride forward or backward from it in another dimension than the line itself'.[8] The last part of that quotation is intriguing. What does Hopkins mean by 'in another dimension than the line itself'? Hopkins' notation for them (a loop underneath them) may prove helpful. The notation implies a musical 'tie', where different notes are blurred into one another. In writing this may be achieved by glossing over or eliding unstressed syllables into one another. Consider the following 'hangers or outrides' from 'Spelt from Sibyl's Leaves':

> **Fíre féa**turing **heaven**. For **earth** | her **being** has un**bound**, her **dapple** is at an end, as-
> tray or a**swarm**, all **through**ther, in **throngs**; | self **ín** self **steepèd** and **pásh**ed – **qúite**
> disre**mem**bering, **dísmém**bering | **áll** now. **Heart**, you **round** me right[9]

Note how the use of a series of unstressed syllables towards the end of the first line allows it to tail off musically before the powerful rhythm reasserts itself at the beginning of the following line. This is a good example of how outrides operate. It allows the rhythm of the poem to tail off, making its reassertion all the more dramatic and noticeable – in this sense, although it is an extra-metrical effect it does add another dimension to the verse in that it contributes an additional musical effect outside the normal meter through its disruption and restoration. The second effect I would draw the reader's attention to is the effect of the hangers at the beginning of the third line above. Here two unstressed syllables begin the line. Clearly Hopkins intended the stress to fall as disreMEMbering as he indicates through his use of symbols that the following very similar word is to be pronounced more unusually as DIS-MEMbering. These hanging syllables allow Hopkins to counterpoint the rhythm of the two words as well as juxtaposing them. This effect heightens the sense of the symbolic disintegrations, both physical and mental, which the words describe and enacts a musical disintegration which in itself becomes a musical metaphor of what is being verbally described. This adds an extra dimension to the poem above and beyond the metrical effect and the verbal effect since it is an interaction between the two.

Hopkins also points out that sprung rhythm naturally allows the equivalent licence to musical rests. These tend to occur where a stressed syllable is omitted and replaced with silence. This occurs in poems in running rhythm also where the effect is referred to as caesura, and is commonly said to occur where the sense breaks halfway through a line of verse (after a full stop or a semicolon for instance). The classical guidance has always been to 'include an extra comma's worth of pause' – however, to my knowledge, no one has yet come up with a definitive definition of exactly how much pause that is.

Hopkins used a series of musical allusions to the effects he wanted in his poems and included a series of symbols which were designed to show that he wanted certain effects at certain places. He had loops which signified 'slurs'. These were syllables which were tied musically 'into the time of one'.[10] He had pauses signified by a semicircle above a full stop to show that a syllable should be dwelt on and twirls to show that the rhythm is reversed or counterpointed. Counterpointed rhythm was also adapted from the musical term and applied to the notion that the new rhythm was mounted upon the old, since the ear would be expecting one rhythm (the base rhythm which the rest of the poem followed) and receiving another (the new counterpointed rhythm).[11]

It is also telling that Hopkins believed that the key to the sonnet was not length but proportion. He envisaged a system whereby the ratio 8:6, or more accurately 4:3, was the important thing rather than the actual number of lines. Sprung rhythm gave him the flexibility to exploit this in his curtal sonnets, *Pied Beauty* being a classic example where the structure of the sonnet is 6 lines to 4.5 lines. That is exactly in ratio 4:3 and it acts like a sonnet; it has a volta or classic turn but it feels short and sharp and the last line is a compelling, abrupt conclusion.

Exercise

Try writing half a page in prose about a scene from nature. Be descriptive. Seek out the unusual or surprising image. Change viewpoint and look at it again. Write a second prose piece from this other viewpoint, again about half a page.

Now go through both pieces and remove all the articles ('a' and 'the').

Read the pieces again out loud. Do you detect any discernible effect on the rhythm?

Now go through again and remove all the unstressed pronouns, that is, those which are not emphasized.

Read the pieces out loud again – some of it might no longer make sense. That's OK; at this stage, you are reading for rhythm.

Now go through again and make changes either cutting prepositions or adding stressed words to fill the gaps in sense left by the removal of the unstressed pronouns.

Now read the pieces out loud again. You should now have at least some passages in sprung rhythm.

Hold on to this; we will be reworking it later.

Inscape and instress

In dealing with these two terms we need to consider two ideas. The first is the Platonic idea, which Hopkins may well have developed from his reading of Duns Scotus, that everything has an essence which makes it that thing. This is sometimes referred to rather inexactly as its 'thinginess'. In representing something, or in observing something, the mind receives and expresses a representation of the thing not the thing itself. Poets, Hopkins felt, strove to get to 'the thing itself' to represent the 'thing' in all its 'thinginess', to capture its essence.

Let's take an example. Take a bird (such as 'The Windhover', for example). When you see the bird, what you actually see is the mind's representation of the bird, not the actual bird. When you paint a picture of a bird, you don't have the bird, but a painting of the bird. All representation is at least one remove from the object itself. All reality, therefore, exists only as far as our perception of it exists. Clearly the bird exists whether we look at it or draw it or not, and it is that essence of bird-ness, the part that is lost in representing it, that Hopkins described as inscape: the internal essence of the thing itself. Hopkins believed that you must use all the sensual and emotive effects evoked by poetry to get at the inscape of things. What you got from this was the heightened awareness of the nature of the thing, a glimpse of its inscape. This, for Hopkins, had particularly religious overtones. It became almost a way of using poetry to glimpse the divine in the ordinary things of the world.

Closely related to the notion of inscape was the notion of instress. Instress was the internal energy possessed by the thing which allowed it to exist and to transfer its inscape onto the world, and by extension to communicate the inscape to the poet. Hopkins tends to use electrical imagery in order to get at it – flashes and charges feature prominently in his imagery, as though something was sparking across the void between the observer and the observed. That is instress. Again, this carried religious overtones for Hopkins, since this energy was for him the divine essence, the God within all things.

Earlier in the chapter we remarked on the significance of the word 'strain'. This is where it comes into its own. Each stanza is a strain, not only in the musical sense, but a straining towards the expression of the inscape of the thing being observed. It is put under strain by the need to receive the inscape by acting as a conductor for instress and transmitting the instress and the inscape to the reader. The electrical tension that this requires places strain on the verse which tautens it into poetry. This required of Hopkins the use of sprung rhythm – which itself implies the storage and release of potential energy. It required the subversion of nouns into verbs, the invention of words and the making of compound words. It required the juxtaposition of conflicting and unusual images. All in all, there is a feeling of a poet under extreme strain, the feeling of pressure to express. These are elements which all poets should aspire to and employ in their own work.

Exercise

Go back to your draft from the earlier exercise on sprung rhythm. Go through the passages and try out the effect of changing the nouns to verbs. Not all of the nouns will change happily, others will not add anything new through the change, but one or two probably will. Add in any new ideas that are stimulated by this process. What is the effect of these changes on the rhythm and energy of the language?

Go through again and pick out several images you are proud of. Are there any which can be directly juxtaposed? What is the effect of this? These juxtapositions may well stimulate more images. Work these into your descriptions.

Go through one last time; try and identify the patterns emerging in the imagery. Can you add to or develop these into a multidimensional portrait? How close are you to getting at the thing itself?

At this stage you may want to begin shaping the material into a poem using a particular form or in free verse – what shape does the poem want to take? What rhythms does the language establish?

Bibliography

Hopkins, Gerard Manley (1994) *The Works of Gerard Manley Hopkins* (Ware: The Wordsworth Poetry Library)

26

Towards a Reading of 'The Mountain' by Robert Frost

Siobhan Campbell

Like many of Robert Frost's poems on a first reading, 'The Mountain' appears to be deceptively simple. We could be forgiven for doubting whether an encounter between a narrator and an old man and their conversation about the mountain behind them could yield more than some remarks on how a mainly blank verse poem of over 100 lines seems quick to read and ends in a way which sends you back to the beginning.

But it is that apparent simplicity of purpose which does send us back to reread this poem and it is only on several readings that we can begin to address what may be afoot.

'The Mountain' is from Frost's second book, *North of Boston*, where it appears alongside several other pieces in blank verse, including 'Mending Wall' and 'The Death of the Hired Man'. Blank verse uses an unrhymed iambic line with 10 stresses and 5 beats. The easiest way to hear this is to say a line aloud such as 'I saw so much before I slept there once' while tapping out the rhythm of Da-**Dum**, Da-**Dum**, Da-**Dum**, Da-**Dum**, Da-**Dum**, with emphasis on the words *saw, much, -fore, slept* and *once*. If you continue through the poem, you will notice that, as with other works he writes in blank verse, Frost can vary the 10-stress/5-beat dictum at will and indeed the first line has an extra stress – 'The mountain held the town as in a shadow' – which may foretell that this 'shadow' will be important to the symbolic register of the piece.

Blank verse, familiar to most of us from reading Shakespeare, is close to human speech in its rhythms and thus can appear at first to be less stylized than it actually is. Because it is unrhymed, the blank verse line lends itself to enjambment (where the sense of one line carries over into the next) and we will see that this can allow for a line to be read in more than one way which suits Frost's purpose perfectly.

How do we begin making a 'reading' of a poem like 'The Mountain'? It may be helpful to break down the approach to the poem into a series of questions. Useful questions in addressing any poem include: how many characters are in the poem and what are their characteristics? How would I describe any ambiguities or anomalies in the poem? After answering these, the best action is nearly always to read the poem again.

What characters appear in 'The Mountain'?

The first person we meet is the narrator, the 'I' of the poem, who is characterized as a traveller visiting the area. The opening stanza seems to imply that he arrived at night and due to the presence of the mountain in the dark noticed that he 'missed stars in the west'. The overbearing presence of the mountain at night is mitigated somewhat by his early morning walk when he finds perhaps more fields and more land than he expected between his temporary abode and the mountain, as well as finding the river that he has to cross.

> Near me it seemed: I felt it like a wall
> Behind which I was sheltered from a wind.
> And yet between the town and it I found,
> When I walked forth at dawn to see new things,
> Were fields, a river, and beyond, more fields.

It may be important to note that in New England (USA), land is divided into 'towns' which are not urban areas necessarily but rather a combination of 'villages' which make up a kind of townland. This makes sense of what the narrator is told by the 'man who moved so slow' – that the mountain means there can be no real village in their 'town', as it 'takes all the room!'

Our narrator knows a bit about farming it seems. He notices that the river has gullied out good grassland and left driftwood and sand in the grass. Could it be that the constancy of the mountain is here contrasted with the seasonal moods of the river?

Once he meets the man with 'oxen in a heavy cart' and stops him without much effort, our narrator proceeds to ask a total of ten questions of his new acquaintance, ostensibly in an attempt to gather information and assuage his curiosity. From 'What town is this?' to 'You've lived here all your life?' we notice a progression as the traveller tries to establish some details about climbing the mountain and about the spring that may be up there. We notice, too, that he does not mind asking for further corroboration by putting questions in the negative: 'You've never climbed it?'; 'You never saw it?'

As we read his questioning, our curiosity as readers is piqued. Why should this mountain exert such fascination to a person only in the area for perhaps a day or two? Why, after all the talk of the possible climb and of the 'fellow' mentioned as having made some of it, does our narrator then ask 'Can one walk around it? Would it be too far?' Could it be that since the old man has never climbed the mountain, and since the 'fellow' didn't get 'high enough to see', the idea of the climb has lost its appeal to our narrator? Or is it that the mountain itself acquires a symbolic significance, one that renders climbing it almost irrelevant since its power is now seen as embodied in the imagination and in the poem?

The second character is the man with the oxen, the 'man who moved so slow' whose efforts seem to be focused on interesting the traveller in climbing the mountain to see the fabled brook, 'cold in summer, warm in winter'. This man becomes most animated when describing the great sight of this stream, 'steaming in winter like an ox's breath'. When our narrator speculates that there might be a view worth seeing from the summit, the old man brings him back to the notion of the spring, 'right on the top, tip-top', saying, 'that ought to be worth seeing'. Do we detect a note of reprimand in his repetition of what should be seen on the mountain and how do we feel about this admonishment when we recall that he has not climbed it himself? His explanation for why he has not climbed it is interesting: 'It doesn't seem so much to climb a mountain / You've worked around the foot of all your life.' We might speculate that there is a sense the climb might disappoint, for how could it live up to the beauty he has imagined for it? He implies as much in saying, "Twouldn't seem real to climb for climbing it.', which may be a way of Frost reminding us that this is a mountain in a poem and therefore not 'real' but yet really there in the imagination of the reader.

The third person is someone we just hear about. He is the fellow mentioned by the old man as having been on the climb. It is worth looking at this reported exchange closely, since the very strange answer given to our narrator is: 'He said there was a lake / Somewhere in Ireland on a mountain top.' – a reply requiring a large associative leap of imagination. In a reverse action to that described above, it is now the narrator's turn to steer the conversation back to the spring. All this toing and froing leads the reader to conclude that the spring is intended to gather symbolic resonance as the poem continues, even if the conversational tone and use of blank verse seems at first to work against a feeling of portent.

But what of 'Hor' itself? Perhaps we could argue that the other 'character' here, and the only one with many described characteristics, is the mountain. As our narrator is told:

The boundary lines keep in so close to it.
Hor is the township, and the township's Hor –

By now, alert to that word 'boundary', the reader may feel the import of it could relate to boundaries between truth and invention, between reality and imagination. The mountain may be named for a mountain in

New England or perhaps for the Old Testament mountain where Aaron is taken to die. In this poem, however, it is both real and unreal. As a reader, it would be a good exercise to list all the characteristics attributed to this mountain before attempting to say what its function actually is. Frost's genius is that each of our answers will say a lot about how we make our own 'reading' of this work, and in so doing, we are also forced to characterize our own poetics.

How would I describe ambiguity and anomaly in the poem?

Many initial statements are subsequently revised or undermined within this piece. The first line, 'The mountain held the town as in a shadow', is revised by the speaker when he realises that the town he slept in is not after all the town of the mountain: 'Then I was wrong'.

We continue to encounter things that are not as they seem at first. There's something that 'looks like a path' but the old man discounts this as the place from which to start the climb. Indeed, he speaks so knowledgeably about aspects of that climb that it is a surprise to hear he has never been up to see the things he describes. And when he says of the spring, 'I guess there's no doubt about it being there', he immediately undermines this by 'I never saw it.' and 'It may not be right on the top.'

If you take a highlighter pen and mark every time a statement is revised or modified, you will find that almost the entire poem declares itself as ambiguous and full of anomaly. The most obvious pointer of this is the stream, as we know it is cold in summer and warm in winter. But here, the old man seems to draw on science as a counterpoint to his observation, raising the issue of comparative temperature:

> You and I know enough to know it's warm
> Compared with cold, and cold compared with warm.

However, as is his wont, he trumps this with 'But all the fun's in how you say a thing.' – perhaps a coda for the poem. The poet may be reminding us that we are encountering a work of art here, one that takes delight in pointing out that 'creation' happens within the mind and that we inhabit a world as much imagined as empirically observed.

Could 'the mountain' actually be a symbol for the power of imagined reality? Could it in fact be standing in for poetry itself? The final words of the man to the narrator's question 'You've lived here all your life?' are cut off:

> 'Ever since Hor'
> Was no bigger than a—' What, I did not hear.

But the implication is that the mountain has 'grown' and this may be true of something that grows in the imagination, acquiring significance as a symbol which speaks back to life. Frost appears to be saying that we make up the world we live within, partly by powerful acts of imaginative storytelling.

Read the poem again

We noticed that 'The Mountain' is a poem which sends you back to the beginning. This is due in part to the many ambiguities, to the oddity of the characters and their strangely underdescribed motives, and to the nature of the decasyllabic line itself which seems to be able to convey more of the mysterious to our 'inward ear' than it appears to when first read. But our real impulse in reading the poem again is to remind ourselves how this all began:

> The mountain held the town as in a shadow
> I saw so much before I slept there once:

And there it is. We see now that the 'shadow' is not a literal but a metaphoric one. We notice that the mountain is doing the holding and therefore is an active participant. Frost has ensured that the reader is drawn into this 'shadow' by the mountain. The 'as in' implies simile, something we were not attuned to on our first reading and a pointer to the reader to be aware that the poem has designs on us. And then we unpick the enjambment and realise that the second line can be read to imply that our narrator has visited before or that he has encountered such a shadow in his life before he 'sees' this one, *or* that he saw the shadow 'so much' before this encounter but has now been changed by the latter. Frost is the master of the blank verse line that allows for ambiguity and a multi-layered set of readings to develop. You will enjoy looking out for this trait in other poems by him. For now, let's imagine what he might say to us as we begin our second 'reading' of the poem. Perhaps, knowing him, 'I don't advise your trying from this side.'

Bibliography

Frost, Robert (1975) *The Poetry of Robert Frost: The Collected Poems* ed. by Edward Connery Lathem (New York: Henry Holt and Company)
Lewis Tuten, Nancy and John Zubizarreta (2001) *The Robert Frost Encyclopedia* (Westport, CT: Greenwood Press)

27
Amy Lowell: Common-Sense Readings

Ashley Lister

Lowell argues, 'No art has suffered so much from printing as has poetry.'[1] She elaborates on this point by adding:

> Poetry is as much an art to be heard as is music, if we could only get people to understand the fact. To read it off the printed page without pronouncing it is to get only a portion of its beauty, and yet it is just this that most people do.[2]

In her essay, *Poetry as a Spoken Art*, Lowell discusses the advantages she perceives of the spoken word over the written word and the differences between the good traditions and bad traditions of reading poetry, and suggests a common-sense approach to reading for performance. Below we shall look at how these opinions might be interpreted today and some of the ways they can influence our approaches to the contemporary production and performance of poetry.

Heard, not seen

Few would argue with Lowell's assertion that poetry has a musical quality that requires some degree of performance.[3] She points out that, like sheet music, the marks on the page are representations of what is intended to be heard rather than what is meant to be read. Unlike sheet music, the marks on the page of a piece of poetry don't require the reader to possess the specialist knowledge or training of a musical education for interpretation or comprehension. The alphanumeric characters within a piece of poetry require little knowledge beyond basic literacy and a comprehension of the vocabulary used by the poet. Lowell insists, 'Poetry and oratorical prose have this in common, that they are both primarily intended to be heard, not seen.'[4]

It is worth noting here that Lowell identified herself as part of the imagist school of poetry. Aside from writing alongside peers such as Ezra Pound, H. D. (Hilda Dolittle) and D. H. Lawrence, she edited anthologies of imagist poetry including the 1915 collection *Some Imagist Poets: An Anthology*. In the preface to this collection Lowell defines the principles of the imagist poets. It is somewhat telling that the first principle in the preface insists poets '... use the language of common speech, but to employ always the *exact* word, not the nearly-exact, nor the merely decorative word'.[5]

This sentiment is echoed in her essay on poetry as a spoken art, where she reiterates the audible relationship between music and poetry and emphasizes the need to use an accessible vocabulary. 'Everybody uses words, and uses them all the time,' Lowell explains. 'The most uneducated peasant talks. Words are the birthright of humanity.'[6]

Exercise

Take an unfamiliar poem and read it silently. Make notes on your responses to this work. Was it evocative? Was it rhythmical? Did the cadence match the mood you expected to experience from the piece?

Read the same poem a second time – but this time read it aloud. Again, make notes on your responses to the piece. Did the rhythm seem more obvious when the poem was spoken aloud? Did reading aloud draw attention to any word choices which seemed unusual or striking? Did some words or phrases demand a particularly emotive phrasing? Was this need for an emotive phrasing more obvious when the poem was articulated?

Keep notes of your responses to these two manners of reading. Be aware of the differences (if any) of your response to the same poem during those two different readings.

The good tradition vs. bad traditions

It is because we so seldom hear poetry adequately rendered that the art has for so long lapsed in popular favour.[7]

Lowell alludes to a good tradition of reading poetry and 'ninety and nine' bad traditions. She cites examples of the good tradition as being those where the reader puts feeling into the voice, but then warns against the trap of the bad tradition where a reader tries to achieve the same effect by employing a tone of artificial sentimentality. She notes a bad tradition of sing-song readings with exaggerated rhythm, and also cautions against the opposite extreme of flat and monotone prose-like readings.

In her essay, Lowell explicitly identifies many of the pitfalls and bad traditions of reading poetry which include mispronounced words, a tendency to over-accent rhythm and the habit of following punctuation marks rather than the swing of the poem's meter. It is worth examining some of the issues she raises.

On the subject of mispronouncing words, Lowell cites examples of the word *wind* (with a short *i*, /'wɪnd/ to rhyme with sinned/tinned, and so on) being pronounced as *winde* (with a long *i*, /waɪnd/ to rhyme with bind/find, and so on). According to Lowell, common mispronunciations such as this have come about through a combination of taught errors, misunderstandings of the laws of English prosody and contemporary desires to force audible rhymes where only eye-rhymes were intended by the author. She summarizes these thoughts by declaring:

> An important rule for the reading of poetry is never to mispronounce words. Give them the sound they have in everyday speech, and let the blunder of a false rhyme, if there be one, rest on the author.[8]

Lowell also reminds the reader that poetry is not prose and, to that end, should not be read as prose. Again, she calls for a common sense balance in the reading of poetry, arguing that the rhythm of a piece should be neither under-accented nor over-accented. She asserts that a good tradition of poetry reading would strike a happy mean between the exaggeration of sing-song readings and the monotony of understated performances.

Exercise

Take an emotive poem – either one of your own or a piece from a favourite poet – and prepare to follow this three-step exercise.

1. Read the poem in a flat monotone without any emotion. Make notes about whether or not this reading honestly conveys the emotional content of the poem.
2. Read the poem with a theatrical show of excessive emotion. Make notes about whether or not this reading honestly conveys the emotional content of the poem.
3. Read the poem with the emotional content pitched somewhere between the previous two styles – aiming for a balance between the extremes.

Note that this is a three-part exercise and completing the first two parts can be helpful in finding the correct balance for that all-important third reading. There are some emotive phrases that are almost impossible to read in the emotionless monotone required for the first part of this exercise. There are some phrases that sound ludicrous being overdone in the excess of the second part of this exercise. By acknowledging the absurdity of those extremes and pitching a reading between their excesses, it is easier to find the balance for how a poem should be read. As Lowell observed:

> The few people who attempt to read [poetry] aloud are handicapped by the realization of the unusual quality of their task, and lose their sense of proportion and simplicity in the welter of artistic theories of expression which have gradually come into being.[9]

Embrace the task of reading poetry and all the challenges it incorporates. Always remember that the main focus of any reading is to ensure an audience is moved by the poem whilst remaining all but oblivious to the person reading the poem.

Common-sense readings

> In reading [...] the audience must see nothing with its eyes which detracts from its mental vision. It must be made to imagine so vividly that it forgets the reader in the thing read. The dramatic quality of the piece must be given just in so far as it stimulates imagination, but never so far as to call attention to the reader as an actual personality.[10]

Lowell had a distinct vision of how poetry should be performed before an audience. Her desire to see poetry being properly presented to audiences resulted in her saying: 'Poetry will come into its Paradise when carefully trained speakers make a business of interpreting it to the world.'[11] It is arguable that, in our contemporary world of iPods and MP3/4 players, coupled with the instantaneous availability of professionally performed poetry, we have already achieved this nirvana that she predicted. However, whilst it would be tempting to rely on the skills of professional readers, as poets it behoves us to be able to perform any poetry that we produce to the best of our ability. Audiences often attend poetry performances to hear the author's interpretation of a specific piece. Whether the author's interpretation is perceived as definitive or merely indicative of an interpretation, the author's rendering of the poem should never be anything less than professional.

> If the modern movement in poetry could be defined in a sentence, the truest thing which could be said of it, and which would include all its variations, would be that it is a movement to restore the audible quality to poetry, to insist upon it as a spoken art.[12]

Exercise

> Where stanzas are printed in an even pattern of metrical lines, some
> sense of rhythm can be gained by the eye. Where they are not, as
> in *vers libre*, the reading aloud becomes an absolute condition of
> comprehension.[13]

To test Lowell's assertion that the reading aloud is essential for the comprehension of vers libre, read silently through the text below, the final stanza
from Lowell's *Lilacs*, then read it aloud. As with the previous exercise, make
notes as to whether or not there is a difference in your response to the
silent reading and the audible reading.

> Lilacs,
> False blue,
> White,
> Purple,
> Color of lilac.
> Heart-leaves of lilac all over New England,
> Roots of lilac under all the soil of New England,
> Lilac in me because I am New England,
> Because my roots are in it,
> Because my leaves are of it,
> Because my flowers are for it,
> Because it is my country
> And I speak to it of itself
> And sing of it with my own voice
> Since certainly it is mine.[14]

Are devices such as repetition made more obvious by reading aloud?
Whilst reading aloud, is there more focus drawn to the structural parallel-
ism of such lines as: 'Because my roots are in it, / Because my leaves are of
it, / Because my flowers are for it?'

Conclusion

But, it may be asked, how is one to know when a rhythm is to be merely
indicated, and when it is to be actively stressed? I can only reply that
much experience is required to know this. But experience is a sure guide.
Knowledge of an author's methods, sympathy with the aim of the poem,
a realization that certain meters require certain renderings, all these things
tell the reader what to do.[15]

As Lowell says, the only way to develop the experience and skills of poetry reading comes through practice. Contemporary poets, whenever possible, should attend poetry presentations, listen to professional readings and participate in open-mic events. At each of these events, poets should be aware of how poetry is being presented to an audience and how judiciously they interpret it when it is being presented most effectively with a common-sense reading. As Lowell observed:

> In the last analysis it is common sense, and nowhere is common sense more needed than in the reading of poetry.[16]

Bibliography

Lowell, Amy (1915) *Some Imagist Poets: An Anthology* (New York: Houghton Mifflin)

Lowell, Amy (1925) *What's O'Clock* (New York: Houghton Mifflin)

Lowell, Amy (1971) *Poetry and Poets: Essays* (New York: Biblo and Tannen)

28
Eliot and Pound: The Better Makers

Todd Swift

Ezra Pound and T. S. Eliot are linked in terms of their poetic creations and careers, but one poet has fared far better in the public imagination. Eliot's *The Waste Land* is the best-known English language poem of the twentieth century and in the twenty-first century is one of the most celebrated 'poetry apps' as well. Further, Eliot's poems 'The Love Song of J. Alfred Prufrock' and 'Ash Wednesday', as well as his long sequence, *The Four Quartets*, are also held in enduring esteem, both for their style and the manner in which ideas and beliefs are combined with other texts and poems, intertextuality avant la lettre.

Though Pound, another American poet who had moved to London, edited *The Waste Land* ruthlessly, in the process inventing 'the modern poem' as we know it today, his reputation has become troubling. This is because during the Second World War he made radio broadcasts from fascist Italy, sent to Americans, expressing anti-Jewish sentiments and attacking the banking system as he then saw it. For Pound, usury (*usura*) was a terrible evil and Jews were at the heart of this problem, which was essentially the taking of interest for lending money, something Christians were for centuries forbidden to do (see *The Merchant of Venice* for an intriguing and also controversial take on this aspect of Western culture). Pound's major work, a very long poem, or series of poetic fragments, *The Cantos*, seems obsessed with usury.

Eliot, too, expressed anti-Semitic views, but these were less dramatically shared with the world, and so, unlike his friend, he was not tried for treason, nor did he have his sentence commuted on the grounds of insanity (Pound spent years in Washington, D.C. in a mental asylum); instead, Eliot became a successful banker, critic, poet, editor and publisher and eventually won the Nobel Prize for Literature. At the end of his long life, Pound, meanwhile, was awarded the prestigious American Bollingen Prize, a sign of his increasing significance for many writers and poets, despite his earlier rantings and sinister political leanings. In the second half of the twentieth century, many avant-garde poets in Britain, Canada and America saw Pound as the way forward and Eliot as a conservative traditionalist who had blemished his record with books such as *The Idea of a Christian Society*.

Still, it is nearly impossible to have an intelligent conversation about poetry, even today, without being acquainted with several key ideas and essays written by these two poets, who began making a mark around a hundred years ago; and for anyone who has seen the musical *Cats*, based on some of Eliot's poems, his work feels fresh even now. Unlike many other poet-critics, their writing on poetry is just as often about how to write better poetry as it is about evaluating already written poems. In this, they were both somewhat radical, as well as in their eccentric desire to rediscover and reclaim many obscure and out-of-print poets from past centuries – particularly the so-called metaphysicals such as John Donne, and on Pound's part, poets from China, as well as the troubadours.

This imaginative interest in the present and the past of poetry – what was to come, what had been – led to many translations, manifestos and critical essays, as Pound and Eliot, linked by friendship and a drive to 'make things new', sought to locate the deepest sources for poetic fertility in a debased mechanical age prone to warfare and secularism. They were experimental, but at times, also elitist and traditional – if only in the sense that they sought to redefine the 'canon' of what was to be read as a great poem or play, to make it relevant to the complexity of the age they lived in as they understood it.

Eliot's most famous critical essay, 'Tradition and The Individual Talent', includes a number of inventive analogies and critical perspectives with which to read poetry and literature, and you should go read it as soon as possible because it still has useful things to think and say about poetry.

What is important for us is that this is one of the first times that a poet asserts the importance of criticism as writing in its own right (a view perhaps borrowed from Pater or Wilde). For Eliot, 'criticism is as inevitable as breathing'. The Signal idea here is that poets are most original when they are aware of the literary past: 'with a feeling that the whole of the literature of Europe from Homer and within it the whole of the literature of his own country has a simultaneous existence and composes a simultaneous order.'

This is a hugely prescient concept. For anyone who has a Spotify account now knows, it is possible to create playlists that combine the best tracks of the week, with classics from the earliest recordings; but in Eliot's time there was no simple way to digitally 'surf' all that had been created and written or 'mash it up', so that is what he sought to do himself in his own poems.

Vitally, the 'existing monuments' (classic texts) 'form an ideal order among themselves, which is modified by the introduction of the new (the really new) work of art among them'. In short, the 'whole existing order' is 'slightly, altered' by new work. With this exciting idea, Eliot proposed how and why new poetry could continue – arguably forever – to remain important and original – by being both aware of all that had gone before and, in doing something a little bit different, changing everything about a little by altering the context in which all previous work was to be read.

The new shed new light on the old. To again use the idea of the Spotify playlist – by adding the Beatles, David Bowie, Radiohead and Aretha Franklin to your playlist alongside Adele, Amy Winehouse, Lorde and Lana Del Rey – you can begin to hear similarities and differences in themes, styles, forms and creative strategies in the song-writing of the past 50 or 60 years. Listening to these great new and old tracks, one can begin to imagine new ways forward. In this idea of Eliot's lies a recipe for endless poetic innovation and a role for the poet as second to none in studying and transforming Western Culture. It is a high calling, but one any individual poet with talent can take upon themselves.

However, this individual person must not think that their chief poetic goal is to, like the Romantic poets, 'express themselves'. Not at all. Again, Eliot is startling in his scientific tones and arguments here (the mind of the poet as a shred of platinum) when he calls for poetic objectivity: 'the progress of an artist is a continual self-sacrifice, a continual extinction of personality.' It is in this way, with this 'depersonalization' that 'art may be said to approach the condition of science'. This is an outrageous aim that Eliot never managed to achieve in his own work, which has precious little to say about science (compared to, say, William Empson, Auden or Lynette Roberts); but more to the point, especially given the burgeoning science of psychology, it is a curious act of repression, or projection perhaps, for Eliot's own poetry is riddled with many veiled references to his own personality and personal life, with its many crises (a failed marriage, a nervous breakdown, a crisis of faith, and so on).

Eliot is a most anxious poet, but the complex surface of his poems appears mandarin and masterful – but never entirely depersonalized. For our purposes, though, it is handy to see how, by trying harder to conceal and complicate his self (or selves), Eliot's poetic texts managed to take on many personae, as did Pound's. In this, they are more classical than romantic. Eliot also argues here for the 'intensity' of the artistic process – a fusion of elements under much pressure: 'Poetry is not a turning loose of emotion, but an escape from emotion.' Readers can judge for themselves how much or little emotion there is in 'Prufrock'.

Eliot, however, was not entirely opposed to the strategic use of emotion in the writing of great works of art – just the uncontrolled or excessive use. In another of his classic essays, 'Hamlet and His Problems', he notes that *Hamlet*, the play, far from being Shakespeare's masterpiece, is 'a failure'. This was likely a clever rhetorical strategy for waking every reader up – since it is in some ways a manifestly unjust claim.

Eliot does have a reason for making this impressive evaluation though: he feels that the source of Hamlet's emotional content is not properly handled or even expressed. As he writes: 'the intense feeling, ecstatic or otherwise, without an object or exceeding its object, is something which every person of sensibility has known; it is doubtless a study to pathologists. It often occurs in adolescence.' In short, why does Hamlet go mad (if he does)? Actors often want to know what their 'motivation' is – in this drama, that may not be clear, for Hamlet's 'disgust' with his mother, for instance, 'envelops and exceeds her'. We don't have enough facts to warrant the monstrous size of Hamlet's suffering, ravings and astonishing self-inflicted dilemmas.

Eliot, I think, is wrong here – the point of the Hamlet character, and his greatness, is that he opens up a personal self and reveals a universal problem: being itself (or not being). What is key to us is how Eliot develops the concept of the *objective correlative* here – the need for the emotions evoked in the reader by the poet to correspond to an objectively apprehensible 'set of objects, a situation, a chain of events which shall be the formula of that *particular* emotion' – so-called 'external facts'.

How this is important to poets studying creative writing is that sometimes our poems baffle other readers because they cannot locate the source of the meaning or the reason why the poem 'matters'. In a workshop I ran in Maida Vale, Emily Berry, a young British poet published by Faber & Faber used to call this the 'So What Test'. Why does the poem matter to us? What is its objective correlative? A policeman shooting an innocent person? A long-desired kiss? A deleted Facebook account? A new Olympic record? A rainstorm? A bout of the flu? A particularly good spag bol? Each event, object or occasion can be what another poet, Richard Hugo, has called a 'trigger' – the occasion for the poem. But without a sense of what is out there for the poem's emotions to speak to, the poem and readers flail about.

Ezra Pound, too, has written important essays, perhaps most famously his *Poetry* magazine article, 'Some Don'ts By An Imagiste', which introduced, aphoristically, a caustic, cantankerous and certain new voice in poetry criticism. It was as if Moses had dropped some new tablets down for us, so immediate was the impact on the galvanized world of contemporary poetry.

The online link to the article can be accessed at: www.poetryfoundation. org/poetrymagazine/article/335. You can read it in five minutes and reflect upon it for the rest of your life as a poet. Here are a few of the most vital quotes, a little cut away from the whole:

- 'An "Image" is that which presents an intellectual and emotional complex in an instant of time.'
- 'It is better to present one Image in a lifetime than to produce voluminous works.'
- 'Use no superfluous word, no adjective, which does not reveal something. Don't use such an expression as "dim lands *of peace*." It

dulls the image. It mixes an abstraction with the concrete. It comes from the writer's not realizing that the natural object is always the *adequate* symbol.'

- 'Go in fear of abstractions. Don't retell in mediocre verse what has already been done in good prose.'
- 'Don't imagine that the art of poetry is any simpler than the art of music, or that you can please the expert before you have spent at least as much effort on the art of verse as the average piano teacher spends on the art of music.'
- 'Use either no ornament or good ornament.'
- 'Don't imagine that a thing will "go" in verse just because it's too dull to go in prose.'
- 'Don't be "viewy"—leave that to the writers of pretty little philosophic essays. Don't be descriptive; remember that the painter can describe a landscape much better than you can, and that he has to know a deal more about it.'
- 'That part of your poetry which strikes upon the imaginative *eye* of the reader will lose nothing by translation into a foreign tongue; that which appeals to the ear can reach only those who take it in the original.'
- 'Good prose will do you no harm, and there is good discipline to be had by trying to write it.'
- 'If you are using a symmetrical form, don't put in what you want to say and then fill up the remaining vacuums with slush.'

This is mostly good advice, and in fact, about 50 per cent of all poetry workshop comments are *still* to this day derived, directly or indirectly, explicitly or implicitly, from a handful of essays, squibs and manifestos that Ezra Pound published between 1909 and 1965. His advice has the force of conviction, and also of cutting away a lot of dead wood. Remember, Pound's poetic enemy was the poetry of his immediate predecessors (the Edwardians and the Victorians) – poetry that was poorly written, didactic, emotive, sentimental and often lazy. It was, from his perspective (and Eliot's), the low point of poetry in English.

Pound's famous 'make it new!' project was mainly a blasting away of what was weakest in the generations just prior to his coming on the scene, and a bit of canny hucksterism was involved too. But there is a lot in this advice that is still useful – primarily because so many poets now write in some form of open or free verse or with a light use of iambic pentameter.

So, the ability to see poetry in terms of prose is both a challenge and a warning: poets need to write clearly, to write well and to not overstuff their poems with unnecessary imagery or dead ideas simply to appear poetic. As well, the turn to forms (sonnets, villanelles, sestinas) was much down to Pound's rediscovery of these forms and the idea that poets should do their homework – he had himself worked with Yeats to learn his craft and in the process aided Yeats in finding his modern later style.

What we can say today is this: Pound and Eliot remain the best (albeit a bit scary) older brothers young poets of today could ever hope to have because they wrote down almost all the advice they assumed any poet who followed after them would ever need. Remarkably, as shown above, little of their advice has failed to stand the test of time and most of it has simply become absorbed into how everyone now reads, writes and teaches poetry a hundred years later. An immediate way to get a step on one's competitors and to really hit the ground running, as a new poet, is to get your hands on their early essays and read them in a few weeks. They will surely be dizzyingly, thrillingly, informative, maddening, inspiring and just a little bit intimidating. These are seriously well-read guys – as smart as any poets have ever been. But they were also passionate, fallible, a bit crazy and, at times, funny. And, the best news is, their work is very easy to find online, in libraries and in bookshops.

Bibliography

Altieri, Charles (2006) *The Art of Twentieth-Century American Poetry: Modernism and After* (Malden: Blackwell Publishing)

Baldick, Chris (2004) *1910–1940: The Modern Movement*, The Oxford English Literary History, 13 vols (Oxford: Oxford University Press), x

Beasley, Rebecca (2007) *Theorists of Modernist Poetry: T.S. Eliot, T.E. Hulme, Ezra Pound* (Abingdon: Routledge)

Cook, Jon (ed.) (2004) *Poetry in Theory: An Anthology 1900–2000* (Oxford: Blackwell Publishing)

Davie, Donald (1988) *With the Grain: Essays on Thomas Hardy and Modern British Poetry* (Manchester: Carcanet)

Davie, Donald (1989) *Under Briggflatts: A History of Poetry in Great Britain 1960–1988* (Manchester: Carcanet)

Davie, Donald (2004) *Modernist Essays: Yeats, Pound, Eliot*, ed. by Clive Wilmer (Manchester: Carcanet)

Davie, Donald (2006) *Purity of Diction in English Verse and Articulate Energy*, 2nd edn (Manchester: Carcanet)

Eliot, T. S. (1953) *Selected Prose*, ed. by John Hayward (London: Penguin Books)

Eliot, T. S. (1960; repr. 1964) *The Sacred Wood: Essays on Poetry and Criticism* (London: Methuen University Paperbacks)

Eliot, T. S. (1970) *For Lancelot Andrewes: Essays on style and order* (London: Faber & Faber)

Eliot, T. S. (1979) *On Poetry and Poets*, 6th edn (London: Faber & Faber)

Eliot, T. S. (1980) *The Use of Poetry and the Use of Criticism: Studies in the Relation of Criticism to Poetry in England*, 5th edn (London: Faber & Faber)

Eliot, T. S. (1993) *The Varieties of Metaphysical Poetry*, ed. by Ronald Schuchard (New York: Harcourt Brace & Company)

Goldman, Jane (2004) *Modernism, 1910–1945: Image to Apocalypse* (Basingstoke: Palgrave Macmillan)

Hulme, T. E. (1960) *Speculations: Essays on Humanism and the Philosophy of Art*, ed. by Herbert Read (London: Routledge & Kegan Paul)

Mellors, Anthony (2005) *Late Modernist Poetics: From Pound to Prynne* (Manchester: Manchester University Press)

29

William Empson: The Meaning of Meaning

Claire Crowther

When William Empson wrote *Seven Types of Ambiguity* in 1927, it was generally assumed that a poem was given one meaning by the poet and that meaning should be obvious. But in 1920 Hope Mirrlees had published the modernist masterpiece, *Paris*; the equally riddling *The Waste Land* followed three years later – both in a way reflecting that physics was currently coming to terms with there being no absolute cause of the universe. Of course, poets, like philosophers and linguists, were not strangers to ambiguity. Critic Philip Hobsbaum describes the line 'they flee from me who sometime did me seek' from the well-known sixteenth-century poem by Thomas Wyatt:

> The details that flesh out this inclusive concept, 'they', suggest nothing central to the experience. Rather they have a tentative, hesitating quality, like movements seen out of the corner of one's eye. ... But at no point do they commit the poem or the reader to an explicit statement of fact.

This effect, frequent in English poetry, is called 'ambiguity'. The word *ambiguity* is itself ambiguous: does it mean 'several meanings' or 'undecided meaning' or 'two meanings'? Empson suggests not worrying too much about that. The important thing for practising poets is that ambiguity is a tool. It allows meanings to be created by the reader. It suggests human complexity. It does not dictate and it exists because there are no final answers to the questions poems, or any other texts, pose. Ambiguity is impossible to avoid even with the most strenuous efforts to limit meaning.

This is obvious in a poem such as William Blake's 'Tiger': 'Tiger tiger burning bright / in the forests of the night.' These lines must be imagined as much as visualized – both ways of clarifying a poem. How do you imagine these lines as you read them? What you may mean by 'tiger' is not what I or William Blake mean. Readers are as separate in their readings as poets are in their writing. I can enjoy trying to work out what Blake means and thus understand my difference to him. That is one way of reading poetry. But I will also have my own reaction to his lines and that personal experience, even if other readers class it as 'wrong', will haunt my mind as I read the poem.

Bearing in mind that, as Empson says, any prose statement could be called ambiguous once looked at in depth, it is not surprising that he demonstrates triumphantly that ambiguity is part of the normal structure of a poem. Graham Hough has said that the usual contemporary critical assumption that 'a literary text is a complex entity composed of different meanings, presented not as alternatives and not successively, but mutually interacting and simultaneous', is due to Empson's pioneering work.

WARNING: this has its dangers for new poets. A poem must be ambiguous in some way, but to embrace ambiguity and try to produce it as an effect could produce blurry work. The poem while it is being written wants to make things clear: you, the poet, must allow it to aim at clarity.

Empson defined ambiguity as 'any verbal nuance, however slight, which gives room for alternative reactions to the same piece of language'.[1] He delineated seven types of logical (as opposed to psychological) ambiguity but these are not exhaustive and, he says himself, not even precise. He refers to them as inconclusive or vague or limited, implying at times that the seven distinctions are confusing. However, it is worth listing them as a starting point not so much for understanding as for helping you to deal with ambiguity in your own poetry:

TYPE 1: A word or grammatical structure is effective in several ways at once due to metaphor being at the roots of language. All the 'ways' combine to give the line its beauty and 'there is a sort of ambiguity in not knowing which of them to hold most clearly in the mind'.[2] Empson points out that 'the process of becoming accustomed to a new author is very much that of learning what to exclude'.[3] This can also work in the other direction: we can learn what to include in a set of poems to enrich the individual poems. You will be familiar with the practice of reading a poet who becomes either less or more 'deep' as you read and reread. I have experienced this as a poet being read. Nathan Thompson reviewed my first collection and then re-reviewed it a year later. He said he had not understood it the first time round and now was more satisfied with the work. One reason he gave was that: 'however clear the mode of expression, that which is expressed remains just out of reach, giving the reader his or her own space in which to reflect or contribute'. It may be that in poems which use ambiguity, the reader has more work to do in this first Empsonian sense – learning just what to leave out and how to take their own sense of space in the poem.

Exercise

Take a collection of poems that you have read previously and found obscure in some way. Reread the collection several times and write a short 're-review'; it may be more or less positive but allow yourself to inhabit the poet's ambiguities in your own way. Make 're-reviewing' collections a normal part of your practice as a working poet.

TYPE 2: Two or more meanings are resolved into one. This simple ambiguity can be caused by punctuation, where, for example, a comma allows the reader to join phrases in different ways. Rhetorical balance is also a source of ambiguity. Most of the lines of Shakespeare's sonnet LXXXI can be read differently when coupled with either the following or preceding line:

> Your name from hence immortall life shall have
> Though I (once gone) to all the world must dye,
> The earth can yield me but a common grave,
> When you entombed in men's eyes shall lye

TYPE 3: Two ideas are fused into one word. Empson says this is, in itself, an inferior kind of ambiguity and needs a wider frame of reference – though that is the fifth ambiguity! The third ambiguity focuses on the pun and allegory, though the normal use of allegory is not to be ambiguous but to show one real concealed meaning. In a later edition of the book, Empson defends himself for including allegory: '[it] has to be considered because it can be used for effects which are undoubtedly ambiguous.'[4] This is the more important point: it is the consequences of the device, not its use as such, that defines ambiguity. His example from George Herbert's 'Pilgrimage' shows allegory as ambiguity, as well as punning language:

> That led me to the wild of Passion, which
>   Some called the wold:
> A wasted place, but sometimes rich.
> Here was I robbed of all my gold,
> Save one good Angel, which a friend had tied
>   Close to my side.

Note that 'wild' and 'wold' would have suggested 'willed' and 'would' to Herbert's contemporaries. An angel was also a coin and perhaps a wife. The whole verse can be read two ways: about a secular ambitious life or about a spiritual quest. Bringing qualities together, says Empson, is a main part of the value of a poem because 'they are so hard to bring together in life'.[5]

TYPES 4–6: The fourth, fifth and sixth ambiguities are acknowledged by Empson to be vague. The fourth occurs where two or more meanings of a statement don't agree but combine to clarify the writer's state of mind. This, says Empson, is a 'vague enough definition' to cover 'much of the third type and almost everything in the types that follow'.[6] The fifth happens when the writer discovers their idea in the act of writing; they will make a simile that lies halfway between two things and doesn't apply to either. The sixth allows that a statement may say nothing because it is tautologous or contradictory or irrelevant. Then the reader is forced to invent her own, probably contradictory, statements.

TYPE 7: Empson's seventh ambiguity is 'the most ambiguous that can be conceived' and less logical than psychological: two meanings of a word are the two opposite meanings defined by the context showing a fundamental division in the writer's mind.

> Keats often used ambiguities of this type to convey a dissolution of normal experience into intensity of sensation. This need not be concentrated into an ambiguity. 'Let the rich wine within the goblet boil / Cold as a bubbling well' is an example of what I mean; and the contrast between cold weather and the heat of passion which is never forgotten throughout *St Agnes' Eve*.[7]

Note Empson's ambiguous position toward the example he has chosen, not unusual in this scrupulously honest account of one man's examination of meaning. 'A contradiction of this kind may be meaningless, but can never be a blank. ... it is at once an indecision and a structure, like the symbol of the Cross.'[8] The identity of opposites is a good place to start as well as to finish when exploring ambiguity. This seventh ambiguity allows Empson to make a rollercoaster tour of conflict, alternative and opposition.

The value of Empson's book is not so much classification as the many pages of careful and good-natured dissection of poems. This is close reading and, after Empson published *Seven Types of Ambiguity*, it became very popular. He claimed to have derived it from Robert Graves and Laura Riding's monograph, *A Survey of Modernist Poetry*. Riding and Graves understood that ambiguity, or the possibility of meaning in a poem, is managed by more than one sort of poetic form. They defined modern poetry as far from ambiguous, as very precise in fact, in rendering experience and, in using any syntactic, grammatical or verbal means, freer than previous poetries. e. e. cummings, they suggest, used any such means as well as line length to make clear his meanings but his poems were still found obscure. Do you find the following lines from his poem 'because', about a train ride in Italy, confusing or clarifying?

> There is nothing left of the world but
> into this noth

ing il treno per
Roma si-gnori?
jerk.
ilyr, ushes

Note that clarity and ambiguity are not necessarily opposites though clarity and obscurity might be. Riding and Graves wrote:

> the quarrel now is between the reading public and the modernist poet over the definition of clearness. Both agree that perfect clearness is the end of poetry but the reading public insists that no poetry is clear except what it can understand at a glance; the modernist poet insists that the clearness of which the poetic mind is capable demands thought and language of a far greater sensitiveness and complexity than the enlarged reading public will permit it to use.

Exercise

Here are some devices which make ambiguity possible in a poem: homonymous or portmanteau words, unconventional syntax or punctuation, and allusion; tautology or vague vocabulary are others. List reasons why it is often assumed that the first list is acceptable if used well and the second is unacceptable in any circumstances. List any of these devices in a poem of your own. Then evaluate the contribution each makes to ambiguity within the poem. Was this ambiguity designed? Does this matter? If you have found unexpected ambiguity, is this a strength or a weakness? Do the extra meanings clash or add depth? Now replace two or three words with portmanteau words which carry extra meanings than your original word, for example. Or change the syntax in a part of your poem to a construction the reader will not be expecting. When you feel your chosen device works, interrogate the new poem: has the decision to complicate the poem added depth as well as complexity? Are there meanings you had not originally intended?

Through the twentieth century, support for ambiguity came and went. Critics such as Marjorie Perloff point out we have lived through a society hallmarked by indeterminacy and an ambiguous literature reflects that. Others, such as Winifred Nowottny, have delighted in ambiguity as a literary strength, coining new names such as Nowottny's 'extralocution'. Today, traditional readers, and a sector of British poets, demand complete transparency and a leading meaning laid down by the poet. It is what Veronica Forrest-Thomson warned against back in 1978. She called it 'Naturalization', a 'tendency to convert all verbal organisation into extended meaning, to transform pattern into theme'. This may not ignore the riches of language, nuances of culture and pleasure to be derived in discovering more and more within a poem as you read it several times, but it does dismiss the satisfactions of other language-aware approaches that foreground ambiguity.

Bibliography

Empson, William (1995) *Seven Types of Ambiguity* (London: Penguin)

Forrest-Thompson, Veronica (1978) *Poetic Artifice* (Manchester: Manchester University Press)

Graves, Robert and Laura Riding (2002) *A Survey of Modernist Poetry and a Pamphlet against Anthologies,* ed. Charles Mundye and Patrick McGuinness (Manchester: Carcanet)

Hobsbaum, Philip (1993) *Essentials of Literary Criticism* (London: Thames and Hudson)

Nowottny, Winifred (1975) *The Language Poets Use* (London: The Athlone Press)

Perloff, Marjorie (1996) *Wittgenstein's Ladder: Poetic Language and the Strangeness of the Ordinary* (Chicago: University of Chicago Press)

Thompson, Nathan *Searching for Closure: A Re-Review* in *Gists & Piths* online review 23 September 2008

30
Gertrude Stein: Poetry and Grammar

J. T. Welsch

Modernism and philosophy

It's exciting to see the art and artists of the early twentieth century as pioneers of a new era. The period we still refer to as modernism, beginning more or less with the century itself and declining gradually between the wars, is often depicted as a radical break with the past, in which artists and writers led the way in casting off Victorian shackles, embracing new technologies and new social orders, and heeding Ezra Pound's call to 'make it new!' as they changed art and the world forever. But it's a funny thing: the further we get from modernism, the more likely we are to sentimentalize its revolution. How long can we hold up Eliot's *The Waste Land* or Joyce's *Ulysses*, both of which have just turned 90, as pinnacles of what we think of as modern literature? More to the point: what does modernism have to do with us, writing here and now?

The problem isn't modernism, but the idea of a clean break with the past. There's no such thing – not for the writers of that period (no matter how much they insisted) and not for us, if we imagine our own breakthrough depends on escaping or exceeding our history. The real revolution of modernism, and what it offers us by example, is in the radical ways its writers came to terms with their own history, adapting some of humanity's most enduring ideas and questions to their strange new century, as we might do with ours.

Among these children of the nineteenth century, Gertrude Stein did more than perhaps any other writer in English to re-examine and challenge our approach to language – the medium of the writer's art. Rather than see language as merely a vehicle for meaning, the words themselves are foregrounded in Stein's work, becoming as physical and immediate as the paint in her good friend Picasso's paintings. Although you may have heard her identified with certain avant-garde schools, her ideas about language in her many essays and lectures address issues that are absolutely fundamental to any style and any form of writing. As she acknowledges in her lecture on *Poetry and Grammar*, these ideas comprise a radical intervention for both poetry and prose. However, part of what is so exciting about Stein's discussion of language is how it engages with an older philosophical discussion with much wider implications.

For Stein, as for many other modernist writers, poetry and experimentation with language isn't an end in itself: it says something and actually *does* something about our relationship with the world. The pragmatist William James was Stein's tutor when she was studying philosophy at university, and we can trace a fairly direct line in her thinking from James, through Ralph Waldo Emerson's transcendentalism, Samuel Taylor Coleridge's romanticism, all the way back to the idealism of Immanuel Kant. Within this metaphysical tradition, Stein's writing is obsessively concerned with the interaction between *consciousness* and *things* – objects, reality itself – and the question of whether language stands between these internal and external realms, either as a barrier or as a means of reconciling them.

Grammar

Bearing all of this in mind, you'll notice that the main lesson of *Poetry and Grammar* is also quite simple: you must pay attention to grammar and punctuation. It is more complex and more important that you think. Be self-conscious about it. 'Worry' about it, as Stein advises and admits to doing. But I've included the background above partly to suggest what's at stake here – and it's more than a school teacher's red ink beside your malformed sentences. The implication throughout the lecture is that the structure of syntax, and especially the naming function of language, has something much more profound to do with the interaction between conscious experience and objects, thinking and being. Stein refers to her own *Tender Buttons* repeatedly as a book where she manipulated grammar in an attempt to bridge that gap. If you haven't read it, you can see the ideas from *Poetry and Grammar* in action in this series of prose-poems giving intense and playful attention to single objects: eggs, milk, a grey hat and so on.

Again, unlike that school teacher, Stein's lecture is emphatically not about the rules of grammar, or even rules for using grammar in poetry. Because of her reputation at this point, Stein had been invited to return from Paris, where she had been living for many years, to give a lecture tour across the United States in 1934. But rather than assume a position of authority, Stein levels with the university students and other members of the public in her audience: 'There is no use in telling more than you know, no not even if you do not know it.' Instead of putting forward a certain theory of language, she offers a series of 'things to think about' or 'things that are very interesting to know'. In this regard, Stein's lecture style also provides a model of open-mindedness toward the possibility that one's ideas about writing will have changed over time and will likely continue to change – a thing sometimes difficult for poets to admit.

So then, what are these 'interesting' things to know about grammar? Well, for starters, if you're going to take your medium more seriously by getting serious about grammar, you're going to need to know the basic parts of speech. Sadly, Stein's assumption, 80 years ago, of her audience's education in grammar can't be taken for granted today. 'I suppose other things may be more exciting to others when they are at school,' she tells us near the start of the lecture,

> but to me undoubtedly when I was at school the really completely exciting thing was diagramming sentences and that has been to me ever since the one thing that has been completely exciting and completely completing. I like the feeling the everlasting feeling of sentences as they diagram themselves.[1]

Exercise: diagramming sentences

When was the last time you diagrammed a sentence? Do it now. Take a sentence or two from a piece of writing you love and get down to the level of these nuts and bolts. Embrace that childhood sense of discovery or 'the everlasting feeling of sentences as they diagram themselves'. Use different coloured highlighters if it helps. Don't get too fancy, but don't leave it until every word is marked as either a noun, pronoun, verb, adjective, adverb, conjunction, preposition or article. Look them up if you need to refresh your memory. Then work out the bigger structures: what are the subject and predicate? Does the sentence have multiple clauses? Which are dependent (or subordinate) clauses and couldn't stand on their own?

Naming

Okay, now that we're all up to speed with our parts of speech, whatever decade of ancient memory that required tapping, let's see what Stein has to say about each part. She starts with **nouns** and returns to them several times throughout the lecture. Stein hates nouns. Or she's not sure about nouns. The big problem with nouns is the bigger problem with names. She explains:

> A noun is a name of anything, why after a thing is named write about it. A name is adequate or it is not. If it is adequate then why go on calling it, if it is not then calling it by its name does no good.[2]

This is another of those old philosophical dilemmas, maybe as old as philosophy itself: the name is never quite the thing it points to. There's always a kind of hollowness in the pointing itself, where you're meant to fill in the concept. Which concept? The one you've learned from someone else. So, someone else's name for what you can only assume but never know is the thing itself, the thing you experience. For Stein – and for other modernist poets concerned with this problem of words and objects, such as William Carlos Williams, Wallace Stevens, Louis Zukofsky – nouns are where language is at its least useful, because it's where it is least itself. It's a kind of paradox: In its desperation to conjure some *thing* outside language, the noun-name neglects its own 'thingness' as a word, thus perpetuating the apparent division between words and things. Get it? By being purely referential, by presenting itself as a mere mental placeholder for some 'real' thing it can never really take the place of, the noun reinforces the division (Cartesian division, if we're being fancy) between consciousness and reality.

Although Stein says early in the lecture that 'one does not use nouns', she later admits that 'as the names of anything of course one has had to use them'.[3] This is one of the moments where she admits a change in thinking. 'Something happened', she says,

> and I began to discover the names of things, that is not discover the names but discover the things the things to see the things to look at and in so doing I had of course to name them not to give them new names but to see that I could find out how to know that they were there by their names or by replacing their names.[4]

What does she mean by 'replacing their names'? If she seems vague on this point, it's due to the difficulty of expressing certain problems of language in language. In other ways though, she is quite specific about what she wants, explaining that at some point in 'the English nineteenth century' poetry had reached a dead end with naming, or was caught invoking the same old names in the same old way, with everyone assuming everyone else meant and felt or imagined whatever they were meant to. 'Inevitably', she says, a poet like Walt Whitman came along and found ways 'to express the thing' itself, beyond its name. She herself had 'struggled with the ridding myself of nouns', trying desperately to 'realize the thing' or 'recreate that thing', before realizing that 'the name of a thing might be something in itself'.[5]

In other words, she would embrace the paradox that nouns embody. Play with it. Make it the basis for all poetry. I know this is confusing in the lecture itself, since she makes her points all out of order, but if you flip back, about halfway through, she spells it out:

Poetry is concerned with using with abusing, with losing with wanting, with denying with avoiding with adoring with replacing the noun. It is doing that always doing that, doing that and doing nothing but that. Poetry is doing nothing but using losing refusing and pleasing and betraying and caressing nouns. This is what poetry does, that is what poetry has to do no matter what kind of poetry it is.[6]

A succinct example is her own (in)famous line, 'A rose is a rose is a rose'. 'In that line', she told a crowd on the same lecture tour, 'the rose is red for the first time in English poetry for a hundred years'.[7] By calling attention to the naming process, by recreating that thrilling, childlike 'discovery' of the name, the noun-name is brought back into service, as it were, as a real object in itself, invoking the 'thingness' of the rose more readily by its own 'thingness'. As she says, 'the name was not new but the thing being alive was always new'.[8] The trick is to perpetuate that newness in the words.

The rest of language

The repercussions for the other parts of speech are straightforward enough. **Adjectives** are always attached to and do similar work to nouns, and therefore are 'not really and truly interesting' in themselves. '**Verbs** and **adverbs** are more interesting', because they can be 'mistaken' for other parts of speech, thus holding up the reader and calling attention to themselves. **Prepositions** are often 'nothing but mistaken', which 'makes them irritating if you feel that way about mistakes but certainly something that you can be continuously using and everlastingly enjoying'. '**Articles** are interesting', precisely because nouns aren't – articles are the physical remainder of the naming process. '**Conjunctions** have made themselves live by their work.' 'You see why I like to write with prepositions and conjunctions and articles and verbs and adverbs but not with nouns and adjectives', she finally explains. 'If you read my writing you will you do [*sic*.] see what I mean.'[9]

If her lecture leaves you with more questions about language than answers, Stein would be most pleased to hear it. As you'll have seen from any of these quotations or the text itself, she likes to catch you up, making you recreate the logic of the sentence as you read. There's another whole section on her use of punctuation, which you may have noticed is rather spare.[10] As with grammar, though, the rationale is that poetry is a language game – or, more specifically, a game of language calling attention to itself as language, as this paradoxical thing which points outwards just as it points to itself. Whatever sort of poetry you're interested in reading or writing, this ducking and diving and circling and avoiding will lie behind whatever strategies you find for bringing language out of its modes of practical meaning and into the realm of art.

Bibliography

Stein, Gertrude (2004) 'Poetry and Grammar', in *Look At Me Now and Here I Am: Selected Works, 1909–45* (London: Peter Owen), pp. 123–45

31

Charles Olson's Projective Verse: The Breath and the Line

Kate North

What is it?

'Projective Verse' is an essay written by Charles Olson, an American poet, in 1950.[1] It was seen as an important reference point for American and British poets alike throughout the 1960s and 1970s. In 'Projective Verse' Olson asserts a new direction for poetry, one that prioritizes the syllable and the line over the image or the symbol. Olson called the type of poetry that he proposes in the essay 'field composition',[2] now more commonly referred to as 'free verse'.

Olson became rector at Black Mountain College in North Carolina in 1951. In his time there Black Mountain became a point of focus for many poets, often termed after Olson's essay as The Projectivists, such as Robert Creeley. Although Black Mountain College was only open for 23 years, its innovative liberal arts curriculum arguably helped give birth to a wave of avant-garde and postmodern artists and writers in 1960s America.

How does it work?

Free verse, or 'field composition', allows the content of the poem (the themes, the subject matter, the sounds of the words) to dictate what the poem looks like on the page. Unlike poetic forms that have strict rules, such as the sonnet or the villanelle, the poet allows the sound and meaning of the poem to suggest and form its layout.

The kinetics

In his essay, Olson explained that a writer of 'field composition', or free verse as we now more commonly call it, must be aware of three essential elements, the first being 'the kinetics of the thing'. Here Olson uses the language of physics to explain the desired effect of a poem. The word kinetics comes from the Greek *kinesis* meaning 'movement' or 'to move'. In physics, more specifically, kinetics is the study of motion, or movement, and its causes.

Olson stated that 'the poem itself must be a high energy-construct and, at all points, an energy-discharge'.[3] Olson was explaining that a poem is a creation into which the poet inserts kinetic energy. The poet's job is to construct a poem in such a way that when it is read the energy is delivered or discharged to the reader. Let's look at an example from Walt Whitman's seminal *Leaves of Grass* published in 1855. This extract is taken from 'Song of Myself':

> I celebrate myself, and sing myself,
> And what I assume you shall assume,
> For every atom belonging to me as good belongs to you.[4]

On initial inspection the use of 'I' and 'you' makes it feel like we are being directly addressed as readers. However, 'what I assume you shall assume' connects the voice of the speaker with the reader.

Now, try reading the Whitman extract aloud. How does this feel? Has the meaning changed? As poetry is both a written and a spoken form it is possible for the reader to take on the voice of the poem when reading it aloud. In doing so, the reader is singing his or herself along with the voice of the poem. Whitman was interested in representing a new, independent yet collective voice, which he understood to be emerging in America at the time. This new and energetic voice was one of a young nation that had recently gained independence from British rule in the late eighteenth century. It could be argued that Whitman's use of 'I' and 'you' charged the poem with a kinetic energy that is imparted to the reader. This energy could be said to represent a recently emerged independent American voice.

The principle

The second element outlined by Olson was 'the principle'.[5] Olson declared the principle, with some help from Robert Creeley, as thus: 'Form is never more than an extension of content.' You can understand content as the poem's meaning or subject. Form can be understood as the appearance of the poem, the physicality and the layout of it.

In closed forms, such as the sonnet, the sestina or the villanelle, the poem's construction and layout is orchestrated by a set number of syllables and lines. However, field composition or free verse does not adhere to these strict rules. Instead, as Olson believed, free verse has its form dictated by the content of the poem. Let's look at an example. Below is a poem from my collection, *Bistro*:

The Birth of Venus

A dart is flying down the M4 this evening.
when she hits home
she'll take the wind out of everyone's sails.
But as she's stripping off, she's growing.

With a smile like a canoe that's announcing,
all sorts of baggage resting in the boot,
she walks through the front door and declares;

I'm growing my hair.
I'm heading to Llangrannog.
I'm going to that little cave where I sat with you.
    I'll count all the pearls of the coast,
            trying to keep them here
                in my lap.

Today I made myself a necklace of pearls.
Significant rounds, sea sliding across my neck.
Give me more for my arms and my legs,
    let them be painted,
        I want to glow in the dark.[6]

In this poem the speaker is attempting to assert her relationship with the landscape and her own physicality. The poem follows the speaker's journey across Wales from east to west. In the first two stanzas I've attempted to represent the movement of a vehicle travelling along a motorway through the block shaped layout. I've also made use of punctuation to control the delivery.

In the opening stanza the use of full stops aid in creating a declarative and assertive tone. The speaker is both initiating a journey and setting out an agenda. In the second stanza, the use of commas is aimed at merging notions of travel, over the landscape and the body. The idea is to suggest their correlation, to assert the interconnectedness of interior and exterior journeys. If I had used full stops at the end of each line I feel I would have separated these ideas. Or, if I had totally removed punctuation from the second stanza we would be left with an unwieldy and difficult stanza to speak aloud.

In the third stanza the layout changes significantly. Here I have tried to mimic the motion of the sea with line breaks and to use punctuation in order to suggest a feeling of movement. In the last four lines of the stanza I have also aimed to specifically represent the cove that is Llangrannog Beach in terms of layout. I have used the words 'you', 'coast', 'here' and 'in my lap' to form the shape of a small cove, with the intention of associating this with the image of the speaker cupping pearls in her lap.

The final stanza continues to replicate the motion of the sea in terms of the indented layout. The idea behind this being that the forward pushing motion represents the future of the speaker, again, inherently linked to the landscape that she inhabits.

To summarize, I've attempted to allow the content of the poem (the speaker, the landscape and their interdependence) to dictate the form (the staggered line breaks reminiscent of the tide, the punctuation suggesting pauses in between motion).

Exercise

Read the poem aloud. Note where you took a breath. Did you breathe at the point of a line break, a semi-colon or a comma? Try to read the extract in one breath. Does this change the meaning of what is spoken? Is it harder to understand?

The process

The third element of a poem is described by Olson as 'the process of the thing' in which 'one perception must immediately and directly lead to a further perception'.[7] So, we can understand a poem as something that supplies multiple perceptions to the reader, one after another.

Taking another look at *The Birth of Venus* we can see what Olson means. In the first two stanzas we are introduced to the subject, the setting and also the activity taking place in the setting by the subject. The third and fourth stanzas represent the impact of the subject upon the setting. As Olson states, 'get on with it, keep moving'. The poem is not a static entity, if it were the reader would fall asleep. This process could be compared to mining. Drilling deeper and deeper, discovering new layers and gemstones as we do so, moving onward.

The syllable and the line

So, how is a poet to balance the kinetics, the principle and the process without a strict meter or form to aid in the structure of a poem? Or, put simply, how does one organize the poem's layout without any strict 'rules' as are found in meter and form?

Olson suggests two areas of attention for the writer of free verse. He states: verse will only do in which a poet manages to register both the acquisitions of his ear *and* the pressures of his breath.[8]

Here Olson is associating the written form with the aural and the spoken. The poet needs to pay attention to the sound of the writing, how it is heard and understood as well as how it is spoken.

When thinking about the sounds of words it is possible to break them down into units, or syllables. Olson suggested that the syllable was of primary importance. He described it as 'the king and pin of versification' meaning that it has authority over the poem, working technically to hold it together.[9] Given that all words are constructed from syllables, this idea makes sense. This is true of all languages and so the syllable is a universal idea capable of carrying a weight of meaning. As Olson points out, syllables bear many connections across languages such as 'not' in English and 'na' in Sanskrit.

Olson is not the first American poet to have written with attention to the spoken idiom. Here is another example from Walt Whitman:

I sing the body electric;
The armies of those I love engirth me, and I engirth them;
They will not let me off till I go with them, respond to them,
And discorrupt them, and charge them full with the charge of the soul.[10]

Notice the primacy of the first-person pronoun and how it locates the experience through the poet. The unabashed 'I' is both declarative and repetitious dictating the subject, tone and the rhythm of the poem. The layout is manipulated according to the sound of what is spoken, in turn enabling the reader to embody the voice themselves as they read along or to take the address almost as if at an audience with the speaker.

Whitman is considered a departure for American poetry. At the time of its publication many viewed Whitman's lack of form along with his focus on physical pleasure and experience of the natural world as obscene. Previous European traditions of poetry concentrated on spiritual and religious subjects or used allegory and symbols to represent subject matter. Whitman dispensed with these traditions and attempted to mediate experience directly. At a time of burgeoning national identity and separation from British convention and rule, it makes sense that new ways of writing poetry were beginning to emerge.

As well as the syllable, Olson suggested that the line was of particular importance to the poet. He said that 'together, these two, the syllable *and* the line, they make a poem'.[11] Whereas the syllable is linked to sound in terms of meaning, Olson believed that the line is linked to breath. So, as a result, the poet should organize their lines in accordance with breath. A line is thus dictated by its ability to be spoken.

Again, looking at the Whitman extract it is possible to understand each line as if spoken in a single breath. From here it is possible to discern how a line becomes a unit of meaning in itself, as well as conveying sense as part of the poem's process as a whole. Let's look again at the first two lines of the Whitman poem:

> I sing the body electric;
> The armies of those I love engirth me, and I engirth them;[12]

The first line can be read as an announcement of intent for the poem. It can be understood as imparting the theme or subject of the poem. It is descriptive, outlining and declaring the purpose of the poetic voice. The purpose of the poem/poetic voice in this instance is to 'sing the body electric'. It is for the reader to understand what the 'body electric' means or represents.

Note the punctuation at the end of the first line. The semi-colon enables the first line to be read independently, as a unit of meaning in itself, as outlined above. However, the semi-colon also enables the first line to be read in conjunction with the second line. It acts as a bridge between two independent statements that can each stand alone, but that can also be understood in relation to one another. With this in mind it is now possible to read the 'armies of those I love' as part of the previously stated 'body electric'. So, Whitman's 'body electric' is the voice of the poem, the subject of the poem and a description of the people who contribute to the voice and subject. Put simply, the 'body electric' can be understood as both the individual voice of the speaker and as a larger collective voice. This larger collective voice has been understood by critics as representing the emergent American idiom of the time, a new mode of speech departing from the earlier European literary traditions that America inherited before independence.

How can I use it?

Use the concept of 'field composition' when you don't want to be restricted by form. Use this approach when you want the poem's layout to be influenced by the meaning and sound of the writing. Use this when you feel that other forms would change the meaning of what you are trying to say.

Exercise

Describe an action from the point of view of an observer. For example, describe someone chopping wood, throwing a ball, or washing a car. Try to incorporate all five senses into your description: taste, sound, smell, touch and sight. Do this for ten minutes.

Now, go through what you have written and remove any unnecessary articles ('a', 'an' and 'the'). Then remove all of the third-person pronouns ('he', 'she' and 'they'). Replace them with 'I' or 'my' and adjust the grammar to make sense accordingly.

Next, read through for any repetitions in language. Unless they are connected to the action itself (he raised the axe and swung the blade down towards the log, then he raised the axe again) remove the repetitions.

Read aloud what you have left. Make a note of where you pause for breath and insert a line break here. What effect does this have on the writing? Is it starting to look like a poem yet?

Now organize the lines into stanzas and add or remove punctuation to aid expression.

Bibliography

North, Kate (2012) *Bistro* (Blaenau Ffestiniog: Cinnamon Press)

Olson, Charles (2004) 'Projective Verse' In Jon Cook (ed.) *Poetry In Theory* (London: Blackwell)

Whitman, Walt (1995) *The Complete Poems of Walt Whitman* (Hertfordshire: Wordsworth Editions)

32

Frank O'Hara: Personism

Barbara Smith

On 3 September 1959, Frank O'Hara put the finishing touches to a short piece supposedly explaining his own style of poetry. First published in *Yugen 7*, a journal, in 1961, 'Personism: A Manifesto' was very provocative, with O'Hara's trademark cheeky charm, compressed ideas and multiple references. He began with his own work, saying that 'Everything is in the poems', but that he was writing because one of his 'fellow poets thinks that a poem of mine can't be got at one reading'. He added that he doesn't use 'elaborately sounded structures'; that he hates Vachel Lindsey (died 1931, an American 'bard' poet who sang his work); and doesn't like 'rhythm, assonance, all that stuff'. In the first short paragraph of his manifesto, O'Hara has put to one side all the technical apparatus of poetry as most people might know it. But what O'Hara doesn't really do is to explain what he really means by 'Personism'.

O'Hara moves on to the reception of his work, using amusing analogies. For him, it doesn't matter whether people get it or that it 'improves them. Improves them for what? ... Too many poets act like a middle-aged mother trying to get her kids to eat too much cooked meat, and potatoes with drippings (tears)'. We are not so far removed from the 1950s/1960s to recognize O'Hara's analogy as representing the argument that poetry might have become stodgy and unhealthy. So what is 'Personism'? In order to answer this, a quick look at the time O'Hara lives in is in order.

'Personism' challenged the notion of T. S. Eliot and James Joyce of depersonalization, as O'Hara expresses it: that there had to be 'abstract removal' between the poet and the audience. O'Hara was also swiping at the academic style of poetry of the time, as well as advocating a personal directness in poetry. His own poetry shows a direct engagement with popular culture and diverse influences during the fifties and early sixties – when the majority of his work was written – as well as a disregard for the conventions of the time with regard to poetic form, style and content, combined with his determined use of the 'I'.

Born in 1926, O'Hara grew up in Massachusetts, studied music and then served in the Navy in the Pacific during the Second World War. After the war he studied at Harvard College, where he began writing poetry and met John Ashbery. Although music was his major, he switched and left in 1950 with a degree in English. The 1950s in the United States were a period of huge post-war economic development: popular culture, television, consumerism and all sorts of technological innovations were all beginning to take flight and nowhere in this country might have seemed more exciting than New York. Abstract modernism in art, new developments in theatre, film and literature were all flourishing and contributing to a growing sense of confident exuberance. It was against this backdrop that O'Hara moved to New York, began working in the Museum of Modern Art and wrote his poetry.

O'Hara's poetry is distinguishable from any other by its immediacy and intimacy. It is of and about the moment, reading almost as though it is addressed to one person: you, the reader. His oeuvre came to be regarded as part of an antithesis to New Criticism. New Criticism developed from how reviewers analysed literature during the 1920s and 1930s and was at its peak in the 1940s and 1950s, being named after John Crowe Ransom's book *The New Criticism* published in 1941. New Critics tried to focus on the text alone, examining how structure and syntax informed content, while trying to disregard all outside factors, such as historical and cultural context, author intention or reader response. It became an overtly academic approach to poetry, a regard for formal technicality and literary tradition. As David Lehman highlights in *The Last Avant-Garde*, New Criticism regarded the poetry of the metaphysics, Donne, Marvell and Herbert as being 'interpretatively richer' than the poetry that came after because it was seen as a combination of formal technique and content – a point that O'Hara wittily refers to in 'Personism: A Manifesto':

> As for measure and other technical apparatus, that's just common sense: if you're going to buy a pair of pants you want them to be tight enough so everyone will want to go to bed with you. There's nothing metaphysical about it.

Two volumes of poetry that illustrated the contrast between New Criticism and O'Hara's preferred relaxed vernacular style were published towards the end of the 1950s. The first, *The New Poets of England and America* co-edited by Donald Hall, Robert Pack and Louis Simpson in 1957, was the New Critical approach, with an introduction by Robert Frost. Among poets included were Donald Davie, Thom Gunn, Geoffrey Hill and Philip Larkin from Britain, and Anthony Hecht, Donald Justice, Robert Lowell, James Merrill, W. S. Merwin, Howard Nemerov, Adrienne Rich, May Swenson, Richard Wilbur and James Wright from the United States. Form, technique and literary wit were foregrounded in this overtly academic anthology.

The second contrasting volume followed in 1960. Donald Allen edited *The New American Poetry*, which included five 'schools' of American poetry: the Beats (Allen Ginsberg, Gregory Corso, Jack Kerouac), the Black Mountain poets (Olson, Robert Duncan, Robert Creeley, Denise Levertov), the San Franciscan Renaissance poets (Lawrence Ferlinghetti, Philip Lamartia) and the New York poets (John Ashbery, Kenneth Koch, Frank O'Hara, James Schuyler, Barbara Guest), as well as others not easily categorized (LeRoi Jones (now known as Amiri Baraka), Gary Snyder, Philip Whalen, John Wieners). These poems did not rhyme or scan, and rather than build on literary tradition, they borrowed from popular culture: blues, jazz, Eastern mysticism, French surrealism – many diverse influences. Allen argued that these poets were more like Ezra Pound and William Carlos Williams, creating poetry that captured a real American oral idiom: poetry that didn't need academic training to be understood.

This is the poetic and critical background that Frank O'Hara may best be appreciated against. His 1959 manifesto urges that 'you just go on your nerve' rather than worry about stylistic devices: spontaneity, colloquialisms, the personal – these elements are what his poetry consists of. In the poem 'Getting Up Ahead of Someone' he calls his work his '"I do this I do that" poems'. O'Hara's poems are the opposite of Wordsworth's 'emotion recollected in tranquillity'. They are busy poems, recording what he does and sees in his lunchtimes, with an overlay of fleeting thoughts and impressions.

'Personal Poem', to take one example, describes one of his lunchtimes, where he begins with a walk 'through the luminous humidity' of New York, 'passing the House of Seagram with its wet / and its loungers and the construction to / the left that closed the sidewalk'. That immediacy of detail has us seeing what O'Hara sees. He waits to meet his friend LeRoi Jones, possibly in a bar or restaurant, and overhears chit-chat about 'who wants to be a mover and / shaker' and other people talking about batting averages. Now it reads as though we are eavesdropping on O'Hara's surroundings.

LeRoi joins O'Hara and tells him that 'Miles Davis was clubbed 12 / times last night outside BIRDLAND by a cop'. To the reader this is shocking news, with the benefit of cultural hindsight, but the two move on swiftly to discuss their literary interests: 'we don't like' Lionel Trilling (a literary critic) 'we like' Don(ald) Allen (mentioned above), 'we don't like Henry James so much' (realist novel writer, then deceased about 40 years) and 'we like' Herman Melville (author of *Moby Dick*). This is followed by a reference to a possible San Francisco poetry 'walk' that they don't want to take part in, but they do 'want to be rich / and walk on girders in our silver hats', perhaps a camp reference to the construction work going on around them. The poem then moves off as O'Hara parts company with his friend thinking whether 'one person out of the 8,000,000' (presumably the then population of the city) 'is thinking of me' while he is buying 'a strap for my wristwatch' and goes back to work, 'happy at the thought possibly so'.

There is no regularity to the meter, no discernible rhythm, little poetic language ('luminous humidity' might just qualify here) and little in the way of punctuation either. The line lengths read as though they could well have been governed by the width of the page he wrote on. There are impressions, thoughts, images and activity all compressed into the poem. The overall effect is one of someone maximizing the time they have during lunchtime, as well as someone who has some intellectual nous. A lack of cynicism is also evident, in that the poem ends on a positive note.

But O'Hara's poems are more than just a record of the moment. As O'Hara shows in 'Personism', he realized one day that he could 'use the telephone instead of writing the poem'. He wanted to place the poem 'squarely between the poet and the person [...] without the intermediary of critical perception or any other distractions. He was arguing, like each poetry generation has done before it, for personal clarity in poetic expression, for change, for something that could be 'new'. But O'Hara also thought that it was 'too new, too vital a movement to promise everything' that was expected from it, and that 'propagandists for technique on one hand, and for content on the other, had better watch out'. The new versus the old, once again.

Exercise

If you work in a city, or large town, try writing your own 'lunchtime' poem. The point about picking this particular time is that the time is normally your own: you have been released from the constraints of your work both physically and mentally, and may go out to buy a sandwich or meet someone for lunch. If you stay at your desk and read personal emails or use social networking media, eat lunch and chat to your colleagues; try and get out and do something different.

Pay particular attention to what is going on around you: construction that may be taking place or conversely shops or businesses that may be closing. Eavesdrop on other conversations – don't be afraid to use gossip, whether local or national. Buy a newspaper or at least browse in a newsagents looking at the major headlines – these could be used. Major news stories can also help to specify the time and date for you, which become important after time has passed. Social networking sites might also prove a useful accessory to your work here: trending topics may lend themselves to use.

Try to work in humour and wit and don't be afraid to include other interests you might have. O'Hara was fond of including his poetry friends, as well as artists, musicians and actors. His one big love, among many interests, was the movies: many of his poems include film references, or actors. His paean to the movies 'Ave Maria' – 'Mothers of America / let your kids go to the movies!' demonstrates his cultural understanding of the escapism that films offer, as well as the culture around movie-going, and is well worth reading.

Use your actual journey from the office, whether you walk or drive, and make sure that you record all the thoughts and impressions you have, but avoid making qualified judgements in your piece of writing. When writing this piece, don't worry about shape or lines – let the paper size dictate line length. What you are aiming for is immediacy and record. Other times to try this sort of writing are on holidays or when you are doing something out of the ordinary. Try not to be too 'poetic' in the language you employ either. Put this draft to one side and let it lie for a few days, even a few weeks, and let it go stone cold. When you come back to it, see if it really records what you saw and thought that day.

For a real touch of O'Hara, try writing a series of these types of poems across a month – it may prove to be a valuable haul of material for other poems you might want to work on.

Bibliography

Allen, Donald (ed.) (1960) *The New American Poetry 1945–1960* (New York: Grove Press)

Hall, Donald, Robert Pack and Louis Simpson (eds) (1957) *The New Poets of England and America* (New York: Meridian Books)

Lehman, David (1998) *The Last Avant Garde: The Making of the New York School of Poets* (New York: Doubleday)

O'Hara, Frank (2015) *Personism: A Manifesto.* [Online] Available at: www.poetspath.com/transmissions/messages/ohara.html, accessed 30 May 2015

Ransom, John Crowe (1979) *The New Criticism (essays)* (Westport, CT: Greenwood Press)

33
William Carlos Williams: Music and Machines

Susan Millar DuMars

William Carlos Williams was a doctor who lived, practised and died in New Jersey (1883–1963). He worked in obstetrics, delivering more than three thousand babies into the world during his long career. One of the most significant, and productive, of twentieth-century poets, he also delivered hundreds of poems into existence. (There are 248 poems in his *Complete Collected Poems, 1906–1938*.) He is perhaps best known for his work of the 1930s, including his well-known poem 'This is Just To Say' – a poem so accessible in terms of vocabulary and message that generations of schoolchildren have responded to it by raising their eyebrows suspiciously and asking, 'Is this *really* a poem?' It is; in its brevity, wit, colloquial language and direct appeal to the reader's senses, it was in its time a groundbreaking poem. In our time, its playful yet exacting style is a challenge and invitation to modern poets to write tight, well-crafted verse relevant to their own everyday lives.

Williams also wrote a great deal about the process of writing poetry. His essays, taken together, form a bridge between the work of the Imagists (first described by Ezra Pound in 1912) and the Beat Poets (specifically, the writings of Allen Ginsberg in the mid 1950s). Williams' own best poetry exemplifies both the embrace of the vernacular, which was a tenet of the Beats, and the muscular, meticulous approach of the Imagists. It's these two ingredients of Williams' work I focus on in this chapter.

The music of everyday language

Williams wrote the introduction to the first edition of Ginsberg's seminal work, *Howl* (1956), which is dedicated to Carl Solomon.

> Literally he has, from all the evidence, been through hell. On the way he met a man named Carl Solomon with whom he shared among the teeth and excrement of this life something that cannot be described but in the words he has used to describe it.[1]

213

Here is laid out one of Williams' greatest gifts to modern poets – the advice to use one's own vocabulary and syntax when writing poems. To, in fact, let the music and movement of the poem be shaped by the character of one's own speech. With this edict, Williams attempts to move poetry from the airless institutions of culture and learning and return it to the sun, wind and clamour of ordinary streets, full of ordinary people – potential poets, all. In an introduction to his own poetry, written in 1944, Williams wrote:

> When a man makes a poem, makes it, mind you, he takes words as he finds them interrelated about him and composes them – without distortion which would mar their exact significances – into an intense expression of his perceptions and ardors that they may constitute a revelation in the speech that he uses.[2]

The Beats, a small but highly influential group of American post-war writers, were happy to run with this idea. The Beats were disturbed by the consumer culture of the United States in the 1950s, as well as what they saw as the prudish attitudes of the previous generation, including its artists. In their writing they eagerly employed colloquial phrases, slang and expletives to fashion writing of tremendous expressive power. Not all of their work has stood up well to the tests of time; the best of it, however, continues to inspire. It may be missing the point to argue the merits of the Beat canon, anyway. The Beats helped make the arts subversive again. That is perhaps their greatest gift to those of us who came after.

In the poem 'Late for Summer Weather' (1935), Williams describes a couple in faded, dirty clothes wandering aimlessly 'through / the upper town they kick / their way through / heaps of / fallen maple leaves / still green – and / crisp as dollar bills / Nothing to do. Hot cha!'[3] In brief lines he sketches a scene that could appear in an Edward Hopper painting. A man and woman who, like their country, have seen better days are looking for diversion on a sunny afternoon. They scuffle through leaves. The 'hot cha!' at the end can be read either as the mocking call of the jazz-age city that surrounds them, making promises of plenty it can't possibly keep, or as the couple's own defiant cry of pleasure despite their make-do circumstances. Either way, the exclamation and the reference to dollars place our twosome irrefutably in a context of time and place. More importantly, the tension between, on the one hand, the image of crisp currency and sound of modern, frivolous dance music, and on the other, the couple's deprived circumstances, gives the poem its poignancy.

Jump forward 21 years: Ginsberg, in *Howl*, delivers the ugly-beautiful world of subway cars and juke boxes, Benzedrine and the Brooklyn Bridge, in a poem of hypnotic excess that has the capability to move us because it, too, employs tension between these modern elements and timeless, tragic human experience – persecution, isolation, thoughts glimpsed under a night sky which may be philosophy or may be madness. Ginsberg's 'angelheaded hipsters' are the clear descendants of Williams' hard-luck lovers. Both wander an up-to-the-minute urban landscape, tantalized and excluded by its fast-paced glitter. Both are rendered in up-to-the-minute language and thus have a freshness that makes them relatable and all the more vulnerable.

> ... each speech having its own character, the poetry it engenders will be peculiar to that speech also in its own intrinsic form. The effect is beauty ...[4]

Exercise one

List words, phrases and brand names you associate with modern, fast-paced, consumer society (for example, cappuccino, iPads, city breaks, *lol*). Now use some or all of these vocabulary words in a poem that depicts an opposite world, an inner terrain of loneliness, entrapment, struggle or boredom. Exploit the tension between your glitzy jargon and sombre theme.

A machine made of words

In 'Notes for *Howl* and Other Poems', Ginsberg credits Williams' influence on his own poetic evolution:

> By 1955, I wrote poetry adapted from prose seeds, journals, scratchings, arranged by phrasing or breath groups into little short-line patterns according to ideas of measure of American speech I'd picked up from W.C. Williams' imagist preoccupations.[5]

Imagism is a school of poetry founded by American poet Ezra Pound in 1912. Pound, H. D. (the writing name of Hilda Dolittle) and Richard Aldington agreed on a set of three principles for Imagist writing:

1. Direct treatment of the 'thing' whether subjective or objective.
2. To use absolutely no word that does not contribute to the presentation.
3. As regarding rhythm, to compose in the sequence of the musical phrase, not in sequence of a metronome.[6]

In the same essay in which he enumerates these guidelines, Pound lists one of Williams' early works as an example of 'beautiful' poetry.

Williams also wrote about this approach to poetry, in particular the idea of leaving out unneeded words (and defining 'unneeded' quite strictly). In doing so he created a useful and eloquent metaphor: the poem as machine.

> To make two bald statements: There's nothing sentimental about a machine, and: A poem is a small (or large) machine made of words. When I say there's nothing sentimental about a poem I mean that there can be no part, as in any other machine, that is redundant.[7]

He could hardly have made it more clear, through his imagery, that this is a modern, practical approach to writing. Imagism is, of course, the offspring of older poetic forms, most obviously the Japanese haiku. A haiku is a very short (usually three-line) poem containing two images juxtaposed to evoke a sensation. There are no abstractions – there's no room for them – and this is true of Imagist poetry as well. Like most 'new' poetic forms, Imagism's creation was one part invention and one part appropriation. But it did challenge ideas about poetry popular at the time and, in Pound and Williams, Imagism had two forceful, iconoclastic spokesmen.

Here is an extract from Williams' poem, 'Between Walls' (1938):

> in which shine
> the broken
>
> pieces of a green
> bottle[8]

The poem follows the rules of Imagism. The subject is treated directly (the bottle isn't likened to anything else); there are no unneeded words (one could argue to drop the 'the' before 'broken', but this would allow the possibility of *theoretical* pieces of bottle as opposed to *the* pieces that Williams has definitely seen and identified); and the poem has a rhythm dictated not by metrical rules but by the subject matter. The subject is a broken bottle and the halting, fragmented lines echo, both visually and aurally, the bottle itself. There is also an aesthetic spark created by juxtaposing, in haiku manner, two distinct images. The first is an ash-strewn, barren bit of overlooked land; the second, bits of green glass that 'shine'. The tension between these two images allows us to see the glass as unexpectedly vibrant. Perhaps even beautiful.

There is a story, often repeated, that William's later poems are so short because their first drafts were composed on the backs of prescription tablets the busy Dr. Williams had to hand. I don't know whether this is true. It seems, from Williams' essays on poetry, that his authorial choices were made more deliberately than the anecdote implies. However, the image of Dr. Williams pausing on his way into hospital to jot down a few lines on his prescription pad about the broken bottle he'd just stepped around is so endearing, I'm reluctant to dismiss it entirely. And the image leads us neatly into Exercise two.

Exercise two

Try writing a poem on an index card or a post-it or on the back of a receipt. Let the surface's dimensions dictate the length of the poem and of its lines. Leave out every word that is not absolutely necessary for your meaning to be clear.

Exercise three

Look for two images that present side by side but between which there is tension (if not opposition). One example would be a flower growing in a landfill. Another would be a person in worn, tattered clothes standing in a queue in an exclusive department store. Write a poem describing the two images – as simply as possible.

Williams' approach to poetry was both rigorous and democratic. His work celebrates the music of ordinary speech. The shape and rhythm of his poems is determined not by the rules of formal verse but by each poem's subject. He insisted that every word in a poem must earn its keep. Williams' longevity as an artist allowed him to act as a bridge between the theories of the precise Imagists and the anarchic Beats; his restless intellect and generosity as an artist allowed him to champion both movements. There is much instruction and inspiration to be taken from Williams' work by the poets of today.

Bibliography

Ginsberg, Allen (1960) 'Notes for *Howl* and Other Poems', *The New American Poetry*, ed. by Donald Allen (Berkeley: University of California Press)

Pound, Ezra (1968) *A Retrospect, Selected Prose, 1909–1965* (New York: New Directions)

Williams, William Carlos (1954) *Selected Essays* (New York: Random House)

Williams, William Carlos (1956) 'Introduction' *Howl and Other Poems* by Allen Ginsberg (San Francisco: City Lights Books)

Williams, William Carlos (1985) *William Carlos Williams, Selected Poems*, ed. by Charles Tomlinson (New York: New Directions)

Williams, William Carlos (1991) *Collected Poems I,* eds A. Walton Litz and Christopher MacGowan (New York: New Directions)

34
Maurice Scully and the Avant-Garde

Paul Perry

Maurice Scully has been working outside the Irish lyric tradition for nearly 30 years now. His latest full-length book of new work since *Things That Happen (1981–2006)* is *Humming,*[1] a body of poems which immerse themselves in the daring process of notating the mind at work, at play, and registering the idle moments of consciousness and of being in the world. He is a good example of a contemporary avant-garde poet at work.

The avant-garde has variously been used as a catch-all term for artistic work that is both innovative and experimental. In poetry it can be seen as poetic utterance which opposes mainstream poetic norms, for example, the saturation of the short first-person lyric seen in today's poetry journals or for example a rhyming 14-line sonnet. Jorie Graham in her introduction to *The Best American Poetry 1990* writes that the poetry she has selected 'breaks the fluid progress of the poem, that destabilize the reader's relationship to the illusion of the poem as text spoken by a single speaker in deep thought, aroused contemplation or recollection'.[2] This is one of the things avant-garde poetry does. The avant-garde poem, in William Carlos Williams' words, is a 'field of action', then, a contested space, and Maurice Scully in Ireland explores this space with his own avant-garde poetics.

The poems in *Humming* act, on one level, as a deep-image sound-scape, the leitmotif of 'humming' ringing throughout:

Teach is *teach* in Irish
& Irish is an adjective (too) in English
in whose house the messenger
arrives to say: (drop)
it's summer: wake up.
Flood cells with brood-food
or lose all the larvae now!
The messenger is here. A dish of syrup.
Múin é. No í.[3]

—'Song'

A regulated meter is jettisoned for a varying cadenced register of notes. It's not so much Williams' 'variable foot' as Scully's 'wrack-line', as I would put it, when poetry has reached the end of its own line, the end of its tether even. Its anchors, or the conventional ones anyway, have given way, or been dismantled, or ignored and the line becomes unhinged and therefore open to all manner of new discoveries and revelations:

> But wait! It's the middle of the night & time to wake up
> I mean the middle of yr life & further along the ledge
> past the diggers & set foundations parent birds attack.
> You will discover starfish ingesting molluscs & ugly
> dishonesties between people. You will have been a poet. Why?[4]

—'Ballad'

The line is a questioned entity in all avant-garde poetry and in Scully's work in particular; it is in other words a suspicious and interrogated unit in the make-up of a poem. In this sense, Scully displays what the American poet Tony Hoagland has described, with a new wave of US poets in mind, as a 'pervasive sense of the inadequacy or exhaustion of all modes other than the associative'.[5]

In unison, or 'uni-song', with this sometimes rhapsodic, Beckettian, obsessive music, the poems work on another level, a typographical one, where the poem itself becomes an object, made up of brush strokes on the canvas of the page. There are ellipses, dashes, numbers, spaces, shapes, italics, indentations, all collaborating on creating a visual artefact as well as an aural one. Sometimes the words on the page sit side by side inviting a simultaneous reading. On the first page of the collection, for example, in 'Sonnet Song' we are told: '(one little thought experiment deserves another).'[6] It's a characteristic and playful parenthetical interjection.

When I read Scully's work, I think of Jackson Pollock's painting process. When Pollock talked about his painting not coming from the easel and preferring to tack the unstretched canvas to the hard wall or the floor because he needed 'the resistance of a hard surface', I think, too, of Scully's sonnets which are a mischievous evolution and avant-garde of the traditional form:

> some paper   space   time's table dissolved
> snow melting from an eave   can that be birdsong?
>
> hum of a small plane in the distance   hum of my pen
> moving   hum of my half-mind following   hum of
> the beginning etc[7]

—'Sonnet'

As Jackson Pollock tacks the canvas to the hard wall, Maurice Scully tacks the poem to the hard surface of the *wor(l)d*. Pollock said: 'On the floor I am more at ease. I feel nearer, more part of the painting, since this way I can walk around it, work from the four sides and literally be in the painting.'[8] This is what an avant-garde or Maurice Scully poem is like and you as the reader can walk 'around it' and literally 'be in,' the poem. The poem's borders are permeable in other words; its stanzas are not secure walls, but wracked buildings where we can come and go. While Imagist poets like Williams once announced that anything was available for the subject of the poem, Scully turns the paradigm on its head. The poem becomes less about subject matter, or what the poem is 'about', and more an occasion or experience in itself:

> change gear &]
> > hum numbers to the edge out
> the impossible, but don't forget: you're next.
> Goodnight.[9]

—'Song'

Maurice Scully's avant-garde poetry is playful, irreverent, skittish, rhapsodic and paratactic all at the same time. The modernist tag Scully has been given along the way seems a little outdated and out-modish even. At least that's how it feels now. Better the elliptical description of Hoagland's, where narrative is eschewed for real cultural reasons, an aversion to authoritarianism, closure, progress even, and demonstrating a poetry equal to the 'speed and disruption' within culture. While at one moment, in Scully's *Humming*, the Arts Council is derided in 'Ballad', in another moment a 'Neanderthal burial site' is found, 60,000 years old, where 'flowers are known to have been used in a funeral ceremony' for the first time.

This then is avant-garde poetry not 'modernist'. Scully as a proponent of avant-garde poetry can also be seen in *A Tour of the Lattice*,[10] a reconfiguration of his eight-book project *Things That Happen*. The poet takes *Things That Happen* as raw material and reshapes it to make a new work and, by implication, shows that several new works are possible to derive from the mother project. This process is different from that which results in a 'selected poems'. Scully is an Irish poet. His first work was published by the renegade Raven Arts Press, whose editor Dermot Bolger, a poet himself in the 1970s and 1980s, was publishing Paul Durcan, Anthony Cronin and Frances Stuart, amongst others. There was always a sense that Raven was doing something outside the mainstream, publishing riskier authors, authors who fell outside the fabricated image of an official Ireland. Nothing the tourist board may have sanctioned. That may sound flippant, but it's not supposed to be: there are still living Irish authors who experienced the penalties of the Irish Censorship Board. While there may not be a culture of official censorship now in Irish poetry, there are still dismissive announcements made by a rather entrenched establishment. In a recent appearance at the Dublin Writers' Festival, the beloved Michael Longley fobbed off the efforts of writers who scatter words about the page. Scully is a profligate 'scatterer' of words and has gone on to publish regularly with a number of different publishers in Ireland and the United Kingdom over the years.

If Tony Harrison's heart beats iambically, as he once admitted, then Maurice Scully's skips and jitters in avant-garde fervour. But he doesn't just write with the heart, but with the attentive élan of someone willing to trace each thought, sometimes whimsical, sometimes factual, sometimes peripheral. In other words, there's a striking fluidity of form in *Lattice*, a playful jouissance in the possibilities and contradictions of formal patterns. I love the both casual and poignant musicality of chance and possibility Scully effects by allowing language to tumble about the page and suggest its own connotative directions and connections.

The poem *Prior* opens the book with the 'sweatshop rag' and 'whisper-movement of the grass' where everything is 'mistaken for everything else'.[11] This 'mistakening' is not 'the associative necessity that determines metaphor' as C. K. Williams writes in 'Poetry and Consciousness', but 'the ability of the poet to *dissociate*'.[12] In one of many unconventional 'sonnets', Scully writes of that kind of process taking place:

ripple-zeros on a roadside pool. crescent of shell in the sand.
they have to keep naming these places.
if.

    yes yes (cloud the mirror) then inside the
    world's space
    hang on   this hat's too tight.

        pinecone in dogshit on path.

           to make a table
           you need a gun
           filled with rhetoric.

                so you're another – what?
                storyteller twiddling dice
                in a game called Risk? two parts

                    confection, one part grit.[13]

Scully's sonnets in other words are not 14-liners and, like Gerald Stern and others, Scully is reclaiming the sonnet back to its original meaning as 'a little song'. And why not? 'The Gap In Your Understanding' is a line from another Scully sonnet which ends with the mischievously: 'in detail in impotence under / the table where I tell you / this.'[14]

C. K. Williams makes a convincing case for the 'nondetermined, apparently arbitrary phenomena generated by the mind' as 'the foundation of the imagination'.[15] The 'universe of possibility' that a poetry which traces its makers consciousness can very well be 'arbitrary, unpredictable, and undetermined'.[16] The disruption and dissociation I am talking about here lends itself to another striking characteristic of Scully's work and that is humour. Humour is not always something associated with the avant-garde, but like the American poet John Ashbery, Maurice Scully's avant-garde poetry is peppered with wry and humorous 'wrack-lines'. Again and again, Scully's work swings its way back and forth from whimsy to wryness and back again. Here is something from Part II of the section *Bread*, to give you a taste:

> happy art fluid art
> who are so
> serious
>
> happy art a cow
> in experience
> daisies
>
> buttercup grass happy
> art a vow
> to experience[17]

I wondered in my discussion to *Humming* how it was possible to gauge the development of the poet's work, but reading *Lattice* I think the answer is there because the development of the work is a reflection of the mind's own progress through time. In 'Poem', Scully writes:

> I was a boy once, then a young man; now in middle age, both;
>   (the edge of the allegory twining the spine of the rentbook).
> To fool a trout, Blue Lulu. To fool me, a peck of honesty.[18]

A Tour of the Lattice, and *Humming*, is a criss-crossing avant-garde pleasure of ellipses, dashes, numbers, spaces, shapes, italics, indentations, all collaborating to create a visual and aural poetic canvas. The poems contain 'wrack-lines', prose and other 'scatterings', suggesting that avant-garde poetry is a poetry that takes place in 'real' time and reflects the mind's own machinations in time, rather than a conventional product-based poetics of established orders and inherited forms. In this sense, Maurice Scully's poetry is a fabulously rich and unflinching avant-garde achievement.

Exercise

Take an older poem of yours and revise it with the avant-garde 'wrack line' in mind. Unhinge lines at unusual and pivotal points in the poem. Look for what linguists might call 'syntactic deviance' or what Charles Bernstein calls 'syntactic scissoring'. Consider the following in your revision:

- Don't think of the line as a measure of breath, but a measure of the mind thinking.
- Spread the poem about the page. Think of the unit of the poem not as the line, but the page.
- Compare the new version of the original and discuss with a group/ workshop.

Bibliography

Scully, Maurice (2009) *Humming* (Bristol: Shearsman Press)
Scully, Maurice (2011) *A Tour of Lattice* (London: Veer)
Williams, C. K. (1998) *Poetry and Consciousness* (Ann Arbor: University of Michigan Press)

Websites

Poets.org
www.poets.org/viewmedia.php prmMID/16612, accessed 30 November 2012.

Guggenhein.org
www.guggenheim.org/new-york/collections/collection-online/show-full/ piece/?search=Alchemy&page=&f=Title&object=76.2553.150, accessed 30 November 2012.

35
When is a Riddle Not a Riddle?

Helen Ivory

Unrest Field is Vasko Popa's second collection, and it is reasonable to suggest that the title is a direct reference to this Serbian riddle, which Popa included in *The Golden Apple*:

The dead carries the living over a field of unrest.[1]

The answer to the riddle is 'boat'. 'The dead' is a metaphor for the boat – which when alive was a tree. 'The living' in this relationship are people (maybe animals, too) and the 'field of unrest' is a metaphor for choppy water, most likely the sea. Describing water as a 'field' makes it reckonable and containable, yet it is affected by the word 'unrest' which is the most mysterious word in this sentence. It leads one to make jumps into the dark in order to fathom out what it could be. It is difficult not to think of a battlefield, with the dead being at such close quarters to the living, but then the 'field of unrest' might also be a more general description of what life is; liable to change, like water.

Aristotle describes this wordplay in his *Poetics*: 'The essence of a riddle is to express facts by combining them in an impossible way; this cannot be done by the mere arrangement of words but requires the use of metaphor.' In Popa's *The Golden Apple*, he has made the answer to the riddle the title, so it is no longer a puzzle. By this he aims at 're-establishing for the reader the natural movement of the creative process'.[2] We start with boat, and then we find the metaphor to carry it and to talk about something bigger – as Elias Lonnrot who compiled a collection of Finnish riddles in 1844 said, a riddle 'exercise[s] the mind to understand the unknown, starting with known conditions'.[3] The riddle also strips the everyday of its familiarity and presents it in an almost unrecognizable state. This 'making strange' or to use the Russian Formalist term *ostranenie*, is a way of reanimating commonplace things that have become invisible through familiarity. So, not only is the commonplace made strange, an attempt is being made to explore the unknown through the familiar.

The riddle is an ancient form of wordplay and recognizes that there is more to meaning than literalism. In this metaphorical world of boat, people, water – life and death occupy the same plain. 'The dead' has an impact on 'the living', and without 'the living', 'the dead' would have no purpose in life. Without the 'field of unrest' 'the living' would not need 'the dead'. To unpack the riddle one must follow its logic and rules. Perhaps the act of the dead carrying the living is a protective one, perhaps it says something about how the dead affect and drive the living, and that the 'field of unrest' is water of the dead's making. The riddle, says Charles Simic 'comes out of the recognition of the double nature of language. Language is both contract (naming what is there) and an option (inventing what is there)'[4] there is a gap between these two, which is the space for dialogue. This ties in with what Blake called 'double vision'[5] whereby seeing the world *with* the eye results in a two-dimensional literal interpretation of what is there, but seeing *through* the eye one is able to see beyond the literal into a metaphorical world and the world of the imagination. The way that riddles work is the stuff of poetry – it is the reinvention of the world through words, designed to surprise the reader into seeing things afresh.

In his first collection *Bark*, which in Serbian means both the bark of a tree and the crust of bread, Popa wrote his own riddles in a sequence called 'List' exploring the gap Simic describes. Here is the first poem in the sequence:

Duck

She waddles through the dust
In which no fish are smiling
Within her sides she carries
The restlessness of water

Clumsy
She waddles slowly
The thinking reed
Will catch her anyway

Never
Never was she able
To walk
As she was able
To plough the mirrors

On a very basic level, we see a duck looking uncomfortable on land, remembering her own fluency in water for which she has become a metaphorical vessel. That the duck is 'she' not 'it' makes her seem human, and therefore the experience of displacement and dispossession more universal. The landscape around her is animated and where, previously, fish would be 'smiling' like happy food might, now the reed, which is there to trick her, is 'thinking'. The 'dust', through which she now waddles, is barren in comparison with the mirrors she was once able to 'plough', which sees her as a former farmer. Mirrors here could be a symbol for truth and imagination as well as a visual representation of a lake. The duck has been forced from an environment of plenty – an Eden, a womb – to waddle artlessly through a barren land forever, as the last stanza suggests.

This intimate relationship between personal and collective fate is often found in folk tales. So the answer to the riddle 'when is a duck not a duck?' would be, 'when it is mankind's struggle with existence on earth'. As the Serbian proverb goes: 'His mind is wandering through the world, but the axe is at his neck.'[6]

With *Bark*, Vasko Popa set out one of the main themes that were to appear in future collections, namely, man's struggle to live in the world in which he finds himself, which is essentially evil and inhumane. He does this through metaphor and symbol, building his own austere version of the universe. The first sequence in *Unrest Field* is called 'Games' and further surveys the bleakness of existence. Here, human actions are pared down to a series of functions, which read like instructions for a very unpleasant set of games the reader is invited to play. Here is one:

Hide-and-Seek

Someone hides from someone
Hides under his tongue
He looks for him under the earth

He looks in his forehead
He looks for him in the sky

He hides in his forgetting
He looks for him in the grass

Looks for him looks
Where he doesn't look for him
And looking for him loses himself.

The wordplay here helps with the hiding. How many 'someone's do you see? Are they the same 'someone' in the first line or are they two? Is he hiding from himself or are there two people involved in this game? Despite the simplicity of Popa's word choice, or perhaps because of it, there is plenty of room for manoeuvre when trying to pin down exactly what you are looking at. Perhaps the idea is that we see one in the many and many in the one, but whichever way you look at it, neither the hider nor the seeker has a chance of winning this game. The seeker is always looking outside, whereas the hiding happens internally.

The poem appears to be the image of a man's head, super-imposed on the image of a landscape. For example, *tongue* and *earth* are ghosted upon one another. With the word 'tongue' comes language, and if somebody hides under his own tongue, this could mean a silencing, imposed or otherwise. With 'earth' it is impossible not to think of a burial or grave, especially if a person is 'under the earth'. The forehead and the sky are in the same place in this image, and there is a compulsion here, to use the jargon phrase 'blue-sky thinking'. And when we want to forget something we metaphorically 'kick it into the long grass', the sentiment of which is echoed in the imagery of the third stanza.

The last stanza tangles itself up in looking. Again we question how many people are involved in this game – if you think you can only see one 'him', look again and next time there will be two. Look again, and maybe there is ultimately just an empty landscape. The trick is not to fix it; allow it to shift around in your head and try not to let it worry you. The shifting is part of what poetry is about and is a specific function of this particular poem.

One of the most immediately obvious things about Popa's poetry is that he does not use punctuation – just the occasional apostrophe for clarification sometimes and capital letters at the start of each line. This means that the line breaks and stanza breaks take on the whole task of adding silence and breath to the poems.

The Nail

One be the nail another the pincers
The others are workmen

The pincers grip the nail by the head
Grip him with their teeth with their hands
And tug him tug him

To get him out of the floor
Usually they only pull his head off
It's hard to get a nail out of the floor

Then the workmen say
The pincers are no good
They smash their jaws and break their arms
And throw them out of the window

> After that someone else be the pincers
> Someone else the nail
> The others are workmen

It seems here that the roles are interchangeable and that once the pincers have been defenestrated (a bad workman always blaming his tools) it can be just as easy for any of the nameless mass to take on the role of the pincers, and another to ready themselves to be a decapitated nail, for it seems also that this process is perpetual. Here, the lack of punctuation adds urgency and tightness to phrases like: 'Grip him with their teeth with their hands / And tug him tug him'.

Some of the body parts in this poem are more readily associated with DIY terms, such as the nail's head, and the jaws and teeth of the pincers. But in the second stanza the pincers have grown hands, and then arms in the penultimate stanza, which is a more unusual morphing and builds up more evidence that these objects are actually people. The struggle is bloodless, yet violent, which is more chilling for that. Again, the juxtaposition of seemingly unrelated, but not unconnected things allows a conversation between ideas to take place, drawing a picture. Here is another Serbian riddle which has the same pact with language: 'Saw: Wooden body, iron teeth, gnaws through stone.'[7]

In *Words Words Words*, linguist David Crystal writes about how we play games with words on a day-to-day basis. He talks about what he calls 'ping-pong punning', where people take great delight in trying to outdo each other with worse and worse puns and so on. He says that 'Everybody plays with language. Everybody.'[8] And goes on to say that writing poetry is a more sophisticated version of this, where 'the ludic motivation is replaced by the aesthetic'.[9] It would be advisable to keep the ludic motivation about your person in the early stages of a poem, though, before the serious play begins.

Exercise one

Here are some more examples of Serbian riddles from *The Golden Apple*:

> SUN: One plate serves the whole world.
> EYESIGHT: I stretched a gold thread through the wide world and wound it up in a nut shell
> CAULDRON: Black dog hanging from the sky
> BRIDGE OVER WATER: God's creation, man's making, a saddled serpent.

Use a similar type of logic to write some riddle images of your own. The trick is to keep the image and functions of the riddle's subject in your mind's eye, while in your other mind's eye find a direct comparison. This could be a visual image – like the cauldron here, or both a visual and functional comparison, like the sun riddle. Like when you are writing a poem, you need to meet the reader halfway – do not totally mystify your reader with an unguessable puzzle.

Now take the one that surprises you the most and use it as a starting point for a poem.

Exercise two

Write your own directions for a game, or maybe instructions on how to put something together, or perhaps a recipe. Think of how this might be a metaphor for something else – like when writing a riddle. Try to see two things at once using both of your mind's eyes. Look at the spare way Popa uses language and try to borrow something of his chilling instructional tone.

Bibliography

Crystal, David (2006) *Words Words Words* (Oxford: Oxford University Press)

Maranda, Elli Köngäs (1976) 'Riddles and Riddling: An Introduction', *The Journal of American Folklore*, vol. 89, no. 352, pp. 127–37.

Popa, Vasko (1980) *The Golden Apple*, trans. by Andrew Harvey and Anne Pennington (London: Anvil Press Poetry)

Popa, Vasko (1987) *Homage to the Lone Wolf: Vasko Popa Selected Poems*, trans. and introduced by Charles Simic (Oberlin, OH: Oberlin College Press)

36
Muriel Rukeyser: The Social Role of Poetry

Claire Crowther

Never mind the contemporary dominance of the personal lyric written by a lone voice, poetry has always demanded a social role. Muriel Rukeyser's *The Life of Poetry* (1949) is a classic contribution to the theory of a poet's political task. She lived from 1913 to 1980 and from the beginning of her writing career she expected a public life for her poetry with the full personal commitment of both poet and reader. She engaged with politics as a practising poet: at 19, she went to help the Spanish Civil War in Barcelona; in 1975, she visited Vietnam with Denise Levertov. Her political work gave her the material of poems.

Found material

An extended poem, *The Book of the Dead*, written in 1938 when Rukeyser was 25, uses researched material (legal documents, journalism and interviews) arising from a scandal over the deaths of workers during the construction of Gauley Tunnel in West Virginia. Thus, the poem's formal structure derives from community texts. Found or quoted text is blended subtly with abstract and lyrical reflection:

> No plane can ever lift us high enough
> to see forgetful countries underneath
> but always now the map and Xray seem
> resemblent pictures of one living breath
> one country marked by error
> and one air.

> It sets up a gradual scar formation;
> this increases, blocking all drainage from the lung,
> eventually scars, blocking the blood supply,

and then they block the air passageways.
Shortness of breath,
pains around the chest,
he notices lack of vigor.[1]

While epics such as *The Book of the Dead* and, on the other hand, celebratory poems for public figures are just two of the sorts of community-focused poems English poetry has relegated to minor status nowadays, poetry will nevertheless try to reflect and address the culture its makers belong to.

Persuasion, though, is a word debased by spin in every era. But it can be defined as having a moral force. Shelley, despite his Victorian need to represent 'the more select classes of poetical readers with beautiful idealisms',[2] nevertheless argued for poetry as 'an intense and impassioned power of communicating intense and impassioned impressions respecting man and nature' and held that the business of this communication was 'the production of beneficial change'. This is the passionate exchange between poet and 'witness' (reader) that Muriel Rukeyser called for.

In a 'Note From the Author' introducing *The Life of Poetry*, Rukeyser says: 'poetry ... is an art that lives in time, expressing and evoking the moving relationship between the individual consciousness and the world'. That, in itself, precisely captures the always shifting nature of poetry. But Rukeyser went further: she believed that 'the work that a poem does is a transfer of human energy and I think human energy may be defined as consciousness, the capacity to make change in existing conditions'. This Shelleyan idea gave her a positive approach to a state and an era whose politics could have depressed her: she was watched by the FBI, as a supposed Communist sympathizer, for 40 years.

Energy as metaphor

Thomas Hardy summed up that positive energy in an image brilliantly lost in the middle of his famous poem 'In Time of "The Breaking of Nations"', showing how ordinary human activities carry on through periods of international drama. Many readers will recall the 'man harrowing clods' of the first verse and the 'maid and her wight' of the third; but who notices the 'thin smoke without flame / From the heaps of couch-grass' in the central stanza? This is not even humanized as the other verses are, yet we sense human agency in an enabling metaphor. Organic life both represents us and is affected by us and the life of a pile of couch-grass, that unkillable weed, is signified by the smoke rising from it. This is energy and more powerful than dynasties.

Rukeyser's definition of poetry at work appeals because it equates empowerment with awareness. Changes in society need a previous siren call. Thus, Rukeyser claims, a poem is real work. Something is done when a poem is written and read. Rukeyser was not the first to say this. The preface to *An Anthology of Revolutionary Poetry* (1929) says:

> If there be any among the radical movement who ignore the poet as a practical factor in the fight for freedom, let such recall the lives of Milton, Byron, and Shelley, not to mention the successful influence of Thomas Hood and George Crabbe in mitigating the cruel laws of great Britain.

This could not be further from W. H. Auden's nostrum that 'poetry makes nothing happen'.

Rukeyser's 'Poem' describes the experience of living morally in a military context:

> I lived in the first century of world wars.
> Most mornings I would be more or less insane,
> …
> In the day I would be reminded of those men and women
> Brave, setting up signals across vast distances
> Considering a nameless way of living, of almost unimagined values.[3]

Rukeyser believed that society had rejected poetry but could be saved by it, that poetry's sort of information is a weapon of humanity against war. This is a grand claim that many poets now are loath to make. But individualist poets could gain from experimenting with public commitment.

Exercise

Take any poem you have written that has already been shared with a reader or listener – in a publication, at a reading or workshop, or between friends. Think about how the audience reacted and how your sense of the audience affected your reading. Perhaps you chose this audience because you thought the poem would suit them. Now revise it with that same audience in mind. What changes would you be willing to make to help the audience? What resistance do you put up as a poet to rewriting for an audience? How do you feel about changing a poem that has been recognized publicly in a certain form? What anxieties do you have about your poem being porous to influence, not being a solid object?

Now imagine you have been commissioned to provide a version of the same poem for a special occasion which will have a very different audience.

Perhaps you are not told who the audience is – it becomes what Rukeyser calls, the 'unknown witness' of your poem. You will be well paid AND/OR you will be honoured for your contribution. This is a commission you are pleased to be given and you are excited to rewrite the poem. Stick to your (imagined) brief and rewrite the poem. Compare the three versions.

This business of redrafting for an audience triggers great anxiety in some poets but must be acknowledged by those who offer poems to a public forum. A sense of audience is important for socially engaged poetry but it does not mean the poet will offer less than a truthful account of their experience. The poem, as Rukeyser says, is a truth-creating system:

> The giving and taking of a poem is, then, a triadic relation. It can never be reduced to a pair; we are always confronted by the poet, the poem, and the audience ... I should like to use another word: 'audience' or 'reader' or 'listener' seems inadequate. I suggest the old word 'witness' which includes the act of seeing or knowing by personal experience, as well as the act of giving evidence.[4]

Shelley thought similarly that poetry is 'an intense and impassioned power of communicating intense and impassioned impressions'.

Jeffrey Wainwright said of this statement that implicit in it is 'a conception of language as vehicular, of communicating impressions by means of power over and so through words'. This is exactly what Rukeyser describes in *The Life of Poetry*. Adrienne Rich made similar statements in her poem 'Implosion': 'I wanted to choose words that even you / would have to be changed by.' Rich suggests in these lines that her choice of words is moderated by whoever 'even you' is.

The Life of Poetry is a book of poetics not social theory so Rukeyser deals with the social problems of poetry itself. Poetry is discounted like 'the Negroes, the Reds, the Jews' and it is resisted. Poetry is, of all arts, the 'least acceptable. Anyone dealing with poetry and the love of poetry must first deal, then, with the hatred of poetry'. Rukeyser suggests that this is due to fear of the total emotional response poetry demands: 'The angry things that have been said about our poetry have also been said about our time. They are both "confused" "chaotic" "violent" "obscure".'[5]

It is poetry itself that relates the poet to her time. Wallace Stevens writes in his poem *Modern Poetry*:

> It has to be living, to learn the speech of the place.
> It has to face the men of the time and to meet
> The women of the time. It has to think about war.

Since poetry is about relationship, this means more than poet and reader, but reaches back and forth in time. Rukeyser gives an impassioned description of lost poetry, folksong, poets whose worth was not recognized and suggests it is a cultural task to resurrect this buried life. Some of her most accomplished poems are specifically concerned with those she does not know:

> Battles whose names I do not know
> Weapons whose wish they dare not teach
> Wars whose need they will not show
> Tear us tear us each from each ...
>
> Looking[6]

This statement is developed into story, as in *Don Baty, the draft resister*:

> I Muriel stood at the altar-table
> The young man Don Baty stood with us
> I Muriel fell away in me
> in dread but in a welcoming ...[7]

In a book largely composed of praises, perhaps the heart of *The Life of Poetry* is praise 'for the untold'. She analyses silence – in the theatre, in society, in history. While she acknowledges that as poets it is 'language and the relations of language with which we deal', throughout this book, those outside accepted language, those to whom the poet gives a voice, are at the heart of poetics:

> I wish to defend the wordless – the mute act, which proves itself without speech, which declares and insinuates in silence, and is stamped on memory. Even in concern for poetry, we realise the life of the unspoken. It appears today as a look from one; the slow turning of the body of another, filled with recognition; the stroke of the club, brought down on the head of the man in the subway...[8]

There is a sense through the book that a poet needs to find this wordless place or place of words which have been lost or are unacknowledged, and work from that point. In this way, poetry is a public work. Contemporary poets such as Juliana Spahr, for example in her poem *Gentle Now, Don't Add to Heartache* write public poetry of this sort, tracing in words the connections between collectivities, as Kimberly Lamm has put it:

> We came into the world at the edge of a stream.
> The stream had no name, but it began from a spring and flowed down a hill into the Scioto that then flowed into the Ohio that then flowed into the Mississippi that then flowed into the Gulf of Mexico.

The stream was a part of us and we were a part of the stream and we were
thus part of the rivers and thus part of the gulfs and the oceans.
And we began to learn the stream.

Note how 'I' is a collective pronoun. Spahr's lines are biblical in proportion,
made of strings of clauses. The stringing together of words, phrases, clauses,
and lines is enhanced by the repeated words 'and', 'that then' and 'thus'.
Can you hear the biblical construction 'begat ... begat' in the background?
All of this delivers a message of responsibility. Like Rukeyser, Spahr's poem
builds a clear picture of a landscape, full of other collectivities than the
human, contaminated and neglected by humans.

Poem as film

The idea of relationship, the heart of Rukeyser's poetics, is played out in
popular culture, particularly in Rukeyser's era, in film. She compares the
process of film editing to that of redrafting a poem:

> sequences are thrown into relation with each other to make a movie.
> The selection and ordering are a work of preparation and equilibrium,
> of the breaking of the balance and the further growth. The single image,
> which arrives with its own speed, takes its place in a sequence which
> reinforces that image. This happens most recognizably in films and in
> poetry. If you isolate certain moments in Hitchcock films, you have the
> illustration of the reinforced image that is used in poetry constantly.[9]

Rukeyser realized that an unwilling reader could find pleasure in 'the
assembling' of images presented by filmmakers and poets – like seeing the
possibilities of a new toy. This is because we are 'animals who take pleasure
in relating'.[10] (Not that she was naive about the economic imperatives dictating to screenwriters. She worked in the film world for years.) Rukeyser
imagines 'the function of the person who works with the sound of a film as
a "writer-musician"'. The creative use of sound used as directors work with
the composition and 'framing' of scenes, the use of words, music, noise
and silence as part of the dramatic unity of the film, would make language,
says Rukeyser, part of the soundtrack and also of the image track.

Exercise

Take any short silent film or film section on YouTube or simply a film with
the sound turned down and add a language soundtrack, including sound
syllables as well as words, but no music. When you have completed this,

redraft it as a long poem without accompanying film. How has the origin of the piece affected its structure? Which piece do you prefer? How can you further draft the piece to bring out what has been lost with the film?

The Life of Poetry begins with a description of the Spanish Civil War and ends with a call for peace. It is an impassioned plea for poetics, not a treatise. It delivers the idea of form as a strategy which it follows itself, building arguments piecemeal, growing the conception of dynamic poetry organically rather than logically. If it also argues its claims and stands its grounds against expected criticism, it does so with spirit and emotion. Yet where you expect distancing from a scientific anti-emotional age, Rukeyser embraces science, likening its process to poetry. Where you might think she would dismiss a contemporary cinema she describes as verbally unrealized, she paints a glorious picture of a coming age of poets as sound directors of film.

It is a book of poetics to argue about, be astonished by, and no doubt, in parts, reject. Like her poems, this is written by a poet who has learned how to be honest and wants readers and writers to benefit from her practice.

Bibliography

Graham, Marcus (ed.) (1929) *An Anthology of Revolutionary Poetry* (New York: Active Press)

Hardy, Thomas (2001) *The Complete Poems*, ed. by James Gibson (Basingstoke: Palgrave Macmillan)

Orr, David (2008), 'The Politics of Poetry' *Poetry* (July/August 2008)

Rich, Adrienne (2002) *The Fact of a Doorframe: Poems 1950–2001* (New York: W. W. Norton)

Rukeyser, Muriel (1973) *Breaking Open* (New York: Random House)

Rukeyser, Muriel (1994) *A Muriel Rukeyser Reader*, ed. by Jan Heller Levi (New York: W. W. Norton)

Rukeyser, Muriel (1996) *The Life of Poetry* (Ashfield, MA: Paris Press)

Spahr, Juliana (2007) 'Gentle Now, Don't Add to Heartache', in Claudia Rankine and Lisa Sewell (eds) *American Poets in the 21st Century* (Middletown, CT: Wesleyan University Press), p. 124

Stevens, Wallace (1990) *The Collected Poems* (New York: Vintage Books)

Notes

Chapter 3

1 Annie Finch and Marie-Elizabeth Mali (eds) (2012) *Villanelles: Everyman's Library Pocket Poets* (London: Alfred A. Knopf), p. 22; Amanda French (2004) 'Refrain, Again: The Return of the Villanelle', Ph.D. thesis (University of Virginia), p. 22.
2 Martha Collins, *The Catastrophe of Rainbows* (Cleveland: Cleveland State University Press, 1985), p. 11.

Chapter 4

1 Francis J. Child, *The English and Scottish Popular Ballads* (Houghton, Mifflin & Co. 1882–1898), p. 44.
2 Child, p. 39.
3 Child, p. 42.
4 Child, p. 10.
5 Child, p. 12.

Chapter 5

1 Barbara Smythe, *Trobador Poets: Selections from the Poems of Eight Trobadors*, Old Occitan Series, Cambridge, Ontario, 2000, www.yorku.ca/inpar/trobador_smythe.pdf.
2 Poetry London, Issue 58, Autumn 2007, www.poetrylondon.co.uk/magazines/58/poem/seven-weeks.

Chapter 8

1 Whilst acknowledging the inherent sexism in the terminology of prosody, that masculine is strong and feminine weak, it is nevertheless important to know how these widely used terms are defined.

Chapter 10

1 In 'The Prose Poem in Great Britain', *Sentence: A Journal of Prose Poetics* 3 (2005), p. 58.
2 Some of this section appeared in similar form in my essay, 'Poetry in the Prose: Getting to Know the Prose Poem', *Poetry Review* 102.2 (Summer 2012): 69–71.

Chapter 11

1 See Charles Olson, 'from "Projective Verse"', in W. N. Herbert and Matthew Hollis (eds.), *Strong Words: Modern Poets on Modern Poetry* (Tarset: Bloodaxe, 2000).
2 Harriet Tarlo (ed.), *The Ground Aslant: An Anthology of Radical Landscape Poetry* (Exeter: Shearsman Books, 2011).
3 Derek Attridge, *The Singularity of Literature* (London and New York: Routledge, 2004), p. 113.

4   Bob Cobbing and Bill Griffiths (eds), *Verbi Visi Voco* (London: Writers Forum, 1992).
5   See his *Uncreative Writing* (New York: Columbia University Press, 2011) and his Ubuweb website at www.ubu.com, which is a resource for all kinds of avant-garde forms.
6   See Marjorie Perloff's *Radical Artifice* and *Unoriginal Genius: Poetry by Other Means in the New Century* (Chicago and London: Chicago University Press, 2010).
7   Bob Cobbing, [1965] *ABC in Sound* (London: Veer, 2015).
8   Parts D, P and T may be heard at www.ubu.com/sound/cobbing.html. A group reading of the text at The Other Room, Manchester, in 2012 may be watched at http://vimeo.com/52068018. The CD is Bob Cobbing (2007), British Library CD: *The Spoken Word: Bob Cobbing* (NSACD 42).
9   The best introduction is W. F. Motte, Jnr. (ed.) *Oulipo: A Primer of Potential Literature* (Lincoln and London: University of Nebraska Press, 1986).
10   The poem is in Mathews' *A Mid-Season Sky: Poems 1954–1991* (Manchester: Carcanet, 1992), pp. 61–83.
11   Philip Terry, *Shakespeare's Sonnets* (Manchester: Carcanet, 2010).
12   See www.bevrowe.info/Queneau/QueneauHome_v2.html. They may be found in the original French at www.growndodo.com/wordplay/oulipo/10%5E14 sonnets.html, accessed 11 September 2012.
13   Jeff Hilson (ed.) *The Reality Street Book of Sonnets* (Hastings: Reality Street, 2008). Of poets mentioned in this chapter, it contains the work of Bob Cobbing, Bernadette Mayer, David Miller and myself.
14   See Goldsmith, *Uncreative Writing*.
15   Kenneth Goldsmith, *Day* (Great Barrington, MA: The Figures, 2003).
16   Craig Dworkin and Kenneth Goldsmith (eds) *Against Expression: An Anthology of Conceptual Writing* (Evanston: Northwestern University Press, 2011).
17   Robert Sheppard (2015) 'How to Produce Conceptual Writing' at www.robertsheppard.blogspot.co.uk/2015/06/robert-sheppard-how-to-produce. html, accessed 14 June 2015.
18   See 'Feverish Propositions', in her *Curves to the Apple* (New York: New Directions, 2006), pp. 13–16. This piece is also anthologized in Jerome Rothenberg and Pierre Joris (eds.) *Poems for the Millennium: Volume Two* (Berkeley: University of California Press, 1998), pp. 568–9. It contains work by Silliman, Cobbing and Bernstein.
19   Ron Silliman, *Tjanting* (Cambridge: Salt Publishing, 2002).
20   Keith Waldrop and Rosmarie Waldrop. *Ceci n'est pas Keith/Ceci n'est pas Rosmarie* (Providence: Burning Deck, 2002), p. 91.
21   See Charles Bernstein (1996–2014), 'Experiments',   http://writing.upenn.edu/ bernstein/experiments.html, accessed 11 June 2015.
22   David Miller (ed.) *The Alchemist's Mind: a book of narrative prose by poets* (Hastings: Reality Street, 2012). Of poets mentioned in this chapter it contains work by Miller, Bernadette Mayer and Rosmarie Waldrop, as well as myself.

Chapter 12

1   My sense of *spatial form* is distinct from (and was arrived at independently of) Joseph Frank's theoretical term describing how certain modern literary works are designed to be read and understood 'spatially' (that is, in a moment, as a unitary pattern of internal textual references) rather than as a linear/narrative sequence of meanings.

Chapter 14

1   Ruth Padel, *The Poem and the Journey* (London: Vintage, 2008), p. 26.
2   http://media.podcasts.ox.ac.uk/kebl/general/2011-11-30_geoffrey_hill_poetry.
    mp3.
3   Quoted in *The Poetry Show 2*, ed. David Orme and James Sale (Macmillan, 1987), p. 31.
4   'The Sonnet-Ballad'.
5   'Two for Dad' *The Fiddle* (Stride 1999), reprinted in *Letting Go* (Mother's Milk
    Books, 2013).
6   'Them And [Uz]' poem.

Chapter 16

1   Chris Baldick (ed.), *The Concise Oxford Dictionary of Literary Terms* (Oxford: Oxford
    University Press, 1990), p. 134.
2   George Lakoff, 'The contemporary theory of metaphor', in Andrew Ortony (ed.)
    Metaphor and Thought 2nd edn (Cambridge: Cambridge University Press, 1993), pp.
    202–51.
3   George Lakoff and Mark Johnson, *Metaphors We Live By* (Chicago: University of
    Chicago Press, 1980).
4   Many of the types which follow can also be found listed in such websites as: http://
    changingminds.org/techniques/language/metaphor/metaphor.htm www.cod.edu/
    people/faculty/bobtam/website/metaphor.htm,   http://grammar.about.com/od/
    rhetoricstyle/a/13metaphors.htm or in books such as Joseph T. Shipley (ed.),
    Dictionary of World Literary Terms (London: George Allen & Unwin, 1970); for 'meta-
    phor' see pp. 197–8.
5   Daniel Chandler, *Semiotics: The Basics* (London: Routledge, 2007), p. 127.
6   Emily Dickinson, *Poems* selected by Ted Hughes (London: Faber & Faber, 2001),
    p. 3.
7   Quoted in James Scully (ed.) *Modern Poets on Modern Poetry* (London: Fontana,
    1970), p. 158.

Chapter 17

1   Marina Warner, *From The Beast to the Blonde* (Vintage 1995).
2   Bruno Bettelheim, *The Uses of Enchantment* (Penguin 1999).

Chapter 18

1   Neil Astley (ed.) *Staying Alive: Real Poems for Unreal Times* (Tarset: Bloodaxe, 2002).
2   Sophie Hannah, *Pessimism for Beginners* (Manchester: Carcanet, 2007).
3   Peter Reading, *Collected Poems: 1970–84* (Tarset: Bloodaxe, 1995).
4   Pulp. 1995. 'I Spy' *Different Class*, Polygram / Island Records.
5   Nick Cohen, *What's Left* (London: Fourth Estate, 2007).

Chapter 21

1   Philip Sidney, *Apology for Poetry*, (1595).
2   *English Essays: Sidney to Macaulay*. Vol. XXVII. The Harvard Classics. (New York:
    P.F. Collier & Son, 1909–14; Bartleby.com, 2001).
3   Viktor Shklovsky, 'Art as Technique' In Lee T Lemon and Marion J Reis, *Russian
    Formalist Criticism: Four Essays* (Nebraska: University of Nebraska Press, 1965).

Chapter 22

1   Carl Jung, *Four Archetypes*, 3rd edn (Abingdon: Routledge, 1999), p. 65.
2   Peter Stitt, *Excerpts from Interviews with John Berryman*, www.english.illinois.edu/maps/poets/a_f/berryman/interviews.htm, accessed 12 August 2012.
3   M. Ferguson, M. J. Salter and J. Stallworthy (eds) *The Norton Anthology of Poetry* 5th edn (New York: W. W. Norton, 2005), p. 870.
4   M. R. Peacocke, *Selves* (Calstock: Peterloo Poets, 1995), p. 21.
5   W. H. Auden, *Another Time* (London: Random House, 1940), p. 83.
6   W. B. Yeats, *Early Poems* (Mineola, N.Y.: Dover Publications, 1993), p. 29.
7   M. Ferguson, M. J. Salter and J. Stallworthy (eds) *The Norton Anthology of Poetry* 5th edn (New York: W. W. Norton, 2005), p. 1533.
8   Ibid., p. 1221.
9   Ibid., p. 1237.
10   Ibid., p. 1750.
11   Ibid., p. 2007.
12   Ibid., p. 1791.

Chapter 23

1   Alex Preminger (ed.) *Princeton Encyclopedia of Poetry and Poetics* (Princeton, NJ: Princeton University Press, 1965).
2   Sylvia Plath, 'A Comparison' [1960] *Johnny Panic & The Bible of Dreams* (London: Faber & Faber, 1977).

Chapter 24

1   Paul Verlaine, *Jadis et naguère* (Paris: L Vanier, 1884).
2   Emily Dickinson, *Complete Poems* (Boston: Little, Brown and Company, 1924).
3   Mary Cooper (ed.) *Tommy Thumb's Pretty Song Book Voll.* [sic] *II*, (London, 1744).
4   Algernon Methuen (ed.) *An Anthology of Modern Verse* (London: Methuen's English Classics, 1923).
5   Alex Preminger, Terry V. F. Brogan and Frank J. Warnke (eds) *Princeton Encyclopedia of Poetry and Poetics* (Princeton, NJ: Princeton University Press, 1993).
6   Walt Whitman, *Leaves of Grass* (New York: Penguin Classics, 1961).
7   W. B. Yeats, *The Collected Poems* (London: Macmillan, 1989).
8   William Wordsworth, British Library Shelfmark ADD MS 47864.

Chapter 25

1   Gerard Manley Hopkins, *The Works of Gerard Manley Hopkins* (Ware: The Wordsworth Poetry Library, 1994), pp. 3–4.
2   Ibid., p. 30.
3   Ibid., p. 29.
4   Ibid., p. 4.
5   Ibid., p. 5.
6   Ibid., p. 4.
7   Ibid., pp. 4–5.
8   Ibid., p. 5.
9   Ibid., p. 51.
10   Ibid., p. 5.
11   Ibid., p. 3.

Chapter 27

1 Amy Lowell, *Poetry and Poets: Essays* (New York: Biblo and Tannen, 1971), p. 11.
2 Ibid., pp., 12–13.
3 Admittedly there is a caveat here in that the performance aspect to which Lowell refers only applies to those poems that were intended to be spoken, and doesn't include concrete poetry or any other form of poetry that is intended solely for visual consumption.
4 Ibid., p. 10.
5 Amy Lowell, *Some Imagist Poets: An Anthology* (New York: Houghton Mifflin, 1915), p. vii.
6 Amy Lowell, *Poetry and Poets: Essays* (New York: Biblo and Tannen, 1971) p. 13.
7 Ibid., p. 15.
8 Ibid., p. 20.
9 Ibid., p. 15.
10 Ibid., p. 17.
11 Ibid., p. 13.
12 Ibid., p. 23.
13 Ibid.
14 Amy Lowell, *What's O'Clock* (New York: Houghton Mifflin Co., 1925).
15 Amy Lowell, *Poetry and Poets: Essays* (New York: Biblo and Tannen, 1971), pp. 21–2.
16 Ibid.

Chapter 29

1 William Empson, *Seven Types of Ambiguity* (London: Penguin, 1995), p. 19.
2 Ibid., p. 21.
3 Ibid., p. 23.
4 Ibid., p. 155.
5 Ibid., p. 140.
6 Ibid., p. 160.
7 Ibid., p. 249.
8 Ibid., pp. 225–6.

Chapter 30

1 Gertrude Stein, 'Poetry and Grammar', in *Look At Me Now and Here I Am: Selected Works, 1909–45* (London: Peter Owen, 2004), p. 124.
2 Ibid., p. 123.
3 Ibid., pp. 124, 134.
4 Ibid., p. 138.
5 Ibid., pp. 140, 142.
6 Ibid., p. 136.
7 Ibid., p. 7.
8 Ibid., p. 139.
9 Ibid., p. 125. Emphasis added.
10 Ibid., pp. 126–30.

Chapter 31

1 Charles Olson (1950) 'Projective Verse', in Jon Cook (ed.), *Poetry In Theory* (London: Blackwell, 2004), pp. 289–98.

2   Ibid.
3   Ibid., p. 289.
4   Walt Whitman, *The Complete Poems of Walt Whitman* (Hertfordshire: Wordsworth Editions, 1995), p. 24.
5   Olson in Cook, p. 289.
6   Kate North, *Bistro* (Blaenau Ffestiniog: Cinnamon Press, 2012), p. 37.
7   Olson in Cook, p. 289.
8   Ibid., p. 290.
9   Ibid.
10   Whitman, p. 72.
11   Olson in Cook, pp. 290–1.
12   Whitman, p. 64.

Chapter 33

1   William Carlos Williams, 'Introduction' *Howl and Other Poems* by Allen Ginsberg (San Francisco: City Lights Books, 1956).
2   William Carlos Williams, *Selected Essays* (New York: Random House, 1954), p. 257.
3   Williams, *Collected Poems I*, p. 384.
4   Williams, *Selected Essays*, p. 256.
5   Allen Ginsberg, 'Notes for *Howl* and Other Poems', *The New American Poetry*, ed. Donald Allen (Berkeley: University of California Press, 1960), p. 414.
6   Ezra Pound, *A Retrospect, Selected Prose, 1909–1965* (New York: New Directions, 1968), p. 3.
7   Williams, *Selected Essays*, p. 256.
8   Williams, *William Carlos Williams, Selected Poems I*, p. 453.

Chapter 34

1   Maurice Scully, *Humming* (Bristol: Shearsman Press, 2009).
2   Available at www.poets.org/viewmedia.php/prmMID/16612, accessed 30 November 2012.
3   Scully, p. 16.
4   Ibid., p. 35.
5   Available at www.poetryfoundation.org/poetrymagazine/article/177773, accessed 30 November 2012.
6   Scully, p. 11.
7   Ibid., p. 27.
8   Available at www.guggenheim.org/new-york/collections/collection-online/show-full/piece/?search=Alchemy&page=&f=Title&object=76.2553.150, accessed 30 November 2012.
9   Scully, p. 17.
10   Maurice Scully, *A Tour of Lattice* (London: Veer, 2011).
11   Scully, p. 15.
12   C. K. Williams, *Poetry and Consciousness* (Ann Arbor: The University of Michigan Press, 1998), p. 9.
13   Scully, p. 89.
14   Ibid., p. 87.
15   Williams, p. 5.
16   Ibid.
17   Scully, p. 127.
18   Ibid., p. 51.

Chapter 35

1 Vasko Popa, *The Golden Apple*, trans. Andrew Harvey and Anne Pennington (London: Anvil Press Poetry, 1980).
2 Ibid.
3 Quoted in Elli Köngäs Maranda, 'Riddles and Riddling: An Introduction', *The Journal of American Folklore*, vol. 89, no. 352 (1976) pp. 127–37.
4 Vasko Popa, *Homage to the Lone Wolf: Vasko Popa Selected Poems* trans. and introduced by Charles Simic, Oberlin College Press, 1987).
5 Poem in a Letter to Thomas Butts, 22nd Nov 1802, William Blake.
6 Popa, *The Golden Apple*.
7 Ibid.
8 David Crystal, *Words Words Words* (Oxford: Oxford University Press, 2006).
9 Ibid.

Chapter 36

1 Muriel Ruleyser, *A Muriel Rukeyser Reader*, ed. Jan Heller Levi (New York: Norton, 1994), pp. 45–6.
2 Percy Bysshe Shelley, quoted in Wainwright, Jeffrey *PNR* 20, vol. 7, no. 6 (July–Aug 1981).
3 Muriel Ruleyser, *A Muriel Rukeyser Reader*, pp. 211–12.
4 Muriel Rukeyser, *The Life of Poetry* (Ashfield MA: Paris Press, 1996), pp. 174–5.
5 Ibid., p. 11.
6 Muriel Rukeyser, *Breaking Open* (New York: Random House, 1973), p. 50.
7 Ibid., p. 51.
8 Ruykeyser, *The Life of Poetry*, p. 122.
9 Ibid., p. 143.
10 Ibid., p. 145.

Index